Study Guide and Practice Masters

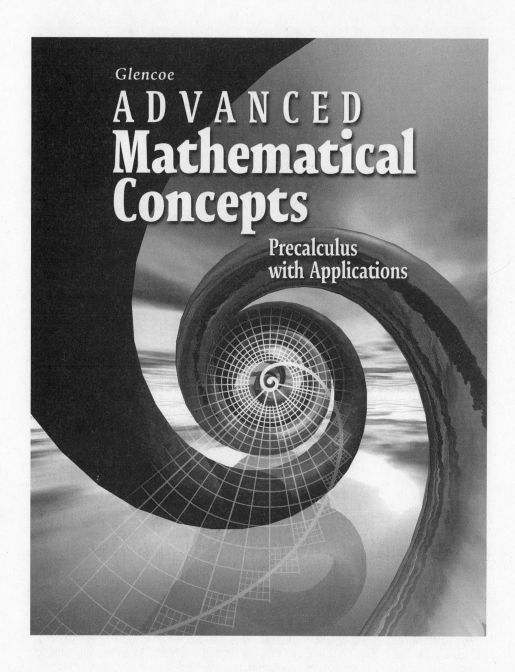

Glencoe
ADVANCED
Mathematical
Concepts
Precalculus
with Applications

Glencoe
McGraw-Hill

New York, New York   Columbus, Ohio   Woodland Hills, California   Peoria, Illinois

Glencoe/McGraw-Hill

A Division of The McGraw·Hill Companies

Send all inquiries to:
Glencoe/McGraw-Hill
8787 Orion Place
Columbus, OH 43240-4027

ISBN: 0-02-834178-3   *AMC Study Guide and Practice Masters*

1 2 3 4 5 6 7 8 9 10 024 08 07 06 05 04 03 02 01 00

Contents

1-1

Study Guide

Relations and Functions

A **relation** is a set of ordered pairs. The set of first elements in the ordered pairs is the **domain**, while the set of second elements is the **range**.

Example 1   State the domain and range of the following relation.
{(5, 2), (30, 8), (15, 3), (17, 6), (14, 9)}
Domain: {5, 14, 15, 17, 30}
Range: {2, 3, 6, 8, 9}
You can also use a table, a graph, or a rule to represent a relation.

Example 2   **The domain of a relation is all odd positive integers less than 9. The range y of the relation is 3 more than x, where x is a member of the domain. Write the relation as a table of values and as an equation. Then graph the relation.**

Table:

x	y
1	4
3	6
5	8
7	10

Equation:
$y = x + 3$

Graph:

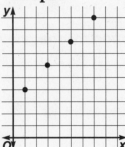

A **function** is a relation in which each element of the domain is paired with exactly one element in the range.

Example 3   **State the domain and range of each relation. Then state whether the relation is a function.**
a. {(−2, 1), (3, −1), (2, 0)}
   The domain is {−2, 2, 3} and the range is {−1, 0, 1}.
   Each element of the domain is paired with exactly one element of the range, so this relation is a function.
b. {(3, −1), (3, −2), (9, 1)}
   The domain is {3, 9}, and the range is {−2, −1, 1}. In the domain, 3 is paired with two elements in the range, −1 and −2. Therefore, this relation is not a function.

Example 4   **Evaluate each function for the given value.**
a. $f(-1)$ if $f(x) = 2x^3 + 4x^2 - 5x$
   $f(-1) = 2(-1)^3 + 4(-1)^2 - 5(-1)$ $x = -1$
   $\quad\quad = -2 + 4 + 5$ or 7
b. $g(4)$ if $g(x) = x^4 - 3x^2 + 4$
   $g(4) = (4)^4 - 3(4)^2 + 4$ $x = 4$
   $\quad\quad = 256 - 48 + 4$ or 212

1-1

Practice

Relations and Functions

State the domain and range of each relation. Then state whether the relation is a function. Write yes or no.

1. $\{(-1, 2), (3, 10), (-2, 20), (3, 11)\}$

2. $\{(0, 2), (13, 6), (2, 2), (3, 1)\}$

3. $\{(1, 4), (2, 8), (3, 24)\}$

4. $\{(-1, -2), (3, 54), (-2, -16), (3, 81)\}$

5. The domain of a relation is all even negative integers greater than -9. The range y of the relation is the set formed by adding 4 to the numbers in the domain. Write the relation as a table of values and as an equation. Then graph the relation.

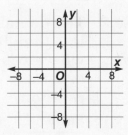

Evaluate each function for the given value.

6. $f(-2)$ if $f(x) = 4x^3 + 6x^2 + 3x$

7. $f(3)$ if $f(x) = 5x^2 - 4x - 6$

8. $h(t)$ if $h(x) = 9x^9 - 4x^4 + 3x - 2$

9. $f(g + 1)$ if $f(x) = x^2 - 2x + 1$

10. *Climate* The table shows record high and low temperatures for selected states.

  a. State the relation of the data as a set of ordered pairs.

  b. State the domain and range of the relation.

  c. Determine whether the relation is a function.

Record High and Low Temperatures (°F)		
State	High	Low
Alabama	112	−27
Delaware	110	−17
Idaho	118	−60
Michigan	112	−51
New Mexico	122	−50
Wisconsin	114	−54

Source: National Climatic Data Center

1-2

Study Guide

Composition of Functions

Operations of Functions	Two functions can be added together, subtracted, multiplied, or divided to form a new function.

Example 1 Given $f(x) = x^2 - x - 6$ and $g(x) = x + 2$, find each function.

a. $(f + g)(x)$

$\quad (f + g)(x) = f(x) + g(x)$
$\quad\quad\quad\quad\quad = x^2 - x - 6 + x + 2$
$\quad\quad\quad\quad\quad = x^2 - 4$

b. $(f - g)(x)$

$\quad (f - g)(x) = f(x) - g(x)$
$\quad\quad\quad\quad\quad = x^2 - x - 6 - (x + 2)$
$\quad\quad\quad\quad\quad = x^2 - 2x - 8$

c. $(f \cdot g)(x)$

$\quad (f \cdot g)(x) = f(x) \cdot g(x)$
$\quad\quad\quad\quad\quad = (x^2 - x - 6)(x + 2)$
$\quad\quad\quad\quad\quad = x^3 + x^2 - 8x - 12$

d. $\left(\dfrac{f}{g}\right)(x)$

$\quad \left(\dfrac{f}{g}\right)(x) = \dfrac{f(x)}{g(x)}$
$\quad\quad\quad\quad = \dfrac{x^2 - x - 6}{x + 2}$
$\quad\quad\quad\quad = \dfrac{(x - 3)(x + 2)}{x + 2}$
$\quad\quad\quad\quad = x - 3, x \neq -2$

Functions can also be combined by using **composition**. The function formed by composing two functions f and g is called the **composite** of f and g, and is denoted by $f \circ g$. $[f \circ g](x)$ is found by substituting $g(x)$ for x in $f(x)$.

Example 2 Given $f(x) = 3x^2 + 2x - 1$ and $g(x) = 4x + 2$, find $[f \circ g](x)$ and $[g \circ f](x)$.

$[f \circ g](x) = f(g(x))$
$\quad\quad\quad\quad = f(4x + 2)$ $\quad\quad\quad\quad\quad$ *Substitute $4x + 2$ for $g(x)$.*
$\quad\quad\quad\quad = 3(4x + 2)^2 + 2(4x + 2) - 1$ $\quad$ *Substitute $4x + 2$ for x in $f(x)$.*
$\quad\quad\quad\quad = 3(16x^2 + 16x + 4) + 8x + 4 - 1$
$\quad\quad\quad\quad = 48x^2 + 56x + 15$

$[g \circ f](x) = g(f(x))$
$\quad\quad\quad\quad = g(3x^2 + 2x - 1)$ $\quad\quad$ *Substitute $3x^2 + 2x - 1$ for $f(x)$.*
$\quad\quad\quad\quad = 4(3x^2 + 2x - 1) + 2$ $\quad$ *Substitute $3x^2 + 2x - 1$ for x in $g(x)$.*
$\quad\quad\quad\quad = 12x^2 + 8x - 2$

 Advanced Mathematical Concepts

1-2

Practice

Composition of Functions

Given $f(x) = 2x^2 + 8$ and $g(x) = 5x - 6$, find each function.

1. $(f + g)(x)$

2. $(f - g)(x)$

3. $(f \cdot g)(x)$

4. $\left(\dfrac{f}{g}\right)(x)$

Find $[f \circ g](x)$ and $[g \circ f](x)$ for each $f(x)$ and $g(x)$.

5. $f(x) = x + 5$
    $g(x) = x - 3$

6. $f(x) = 2x^3 - 3x^2 + 1$
    $g(x) = 3x$

7. $f(x) = 2x^2 - 5x + 1$
    $g(x) = 2x - 3$

8. $f(x) = 3x^2 - 2x + 5$
    $g(x) = 2x - 1$

9. State the domain of $[f \circ g](x)$ for $f(x) = \sqrt{x - 2}$ and $g(x) = 3x$.

Find the first three iterates of each function using the given initial value.

10. $f(x) = 2x - 6; x_0 = 1$

11. $f(x) = x^2 - 1; x_0 = 2$

12. *Fitness*   Tara has decided to start a walking program. Her initial walking time is 5 minutes. She plans to double her walking time and add 1 minute every 5 days. Provided that Tara achieves her goal, how many minutes will she be walking on days 21 through 25?

1-3

Study Guide

Graphing Linear Equations

You can graph a **linear equation** $Ax + By + C = 0$, where A and B are not both zero, by using the x- and y-intercepts. To find the x-intercept, let $y = 0$. To find the y-intercept, let $x = 0$.

Example 1   **Graph $4x + y - 3 = 0$ using the x- and y-intercepts.**
Substitute 0 for y to find the x-intercept. Then substitute 0 for x to find the y-intercept.

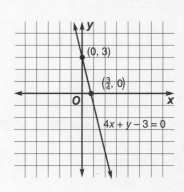

x-intercept
$$4x + y - 3 = 0$$
$$4x + 0 - 3 = 0$$
$$4x - 3 = 0$$
$$4x = 3$$
$$x = \frac{3}{4}$$

y-intercept
$$4x + y - 3 = 0$$
$$4(0) + y - 3 = 0$$
$$y - 3 = 0$$
$$y = 3$$

The line crosses the x-axis at $\left(\frac{3}{4}, 0\right)$ and the y-axis at $(0, 3)$.

Graph the intercepts and draw the line that passes through them.

The **slope** of a nonvertical line is the ratio of the change in the y-coordinates of two points to the corresponding change in the x-coordinates of the same points. The slope of a line can be interpreted as the ratio of change in the y-coordinates to the change in the x-coordinates.

Slope	The slope m of a line through two points (x_1, y_1) and (x_2, y_2) is given by $m = \dfrac{y_2 - y_1}{x_2 - x_1}$.

Example 2   **Find the slope of the line passing through $A(-3, 5)$ and $B(6, 2)$.**

$$m = \frac{y_2 - y_1}{x_2 - x_1}$$

$$= \frac{2 - 5}{6 - (-3)} \quad \textit{Let } x_1 = -3, \, y_1 = 5, \, x_2 = 6, \textit{ and } y_2 = 2.$$

$$= \frac{-3}{9} \text{ or } -\frac{1}{3}$$

1-3

Practice

Graphing Linear Equations

Graph each equation using the x- and y-intercepts.

1. $2x - y - 6 = 0$

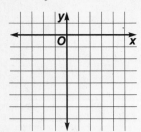

2. $4x + 2y + 8 = 0$

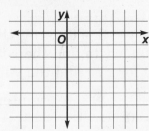

Graph each equation using the y-intercept and the slope.

3. $y = 5x - \frac{1}{2}$

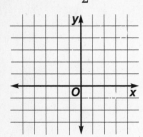

4. $y = \frac{1}{2}x$

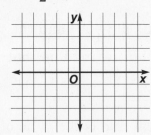

Find the zero of each function. Then graph the function.

5. $f(x) = 4x - 3$

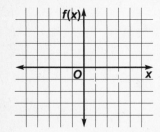

6. $f(x) = 2x + 4$

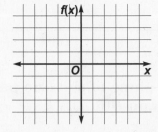

7. Business In 1990, a two-bedroom apartment at Remington Square Apartments rented for $575 per month. In 1999, the same two-bedroom apartment rented for $850 per month. Assuming a constant rate of increase, what will a tenant pay for a two-bedroom apartment at Remington Square in the year 2000?

1-4

Study Guide

Writing Linear Equations

The form in which you write an equation of a line depends on the information you are given. Given the slope and y-intercept, or given the slope and one point on the line, the **slope-intercept** form can be used to write the equation.

Example 1   Write an equation in slope-intercept form for each line described.

a. a slope of $\frac{2}{3}$ and a y-intercept of -5

Substitute $\frac{2}{3}$ for m and -5 for b in the general slope-intercept form.

$y = mx + b \quad \rightarrow \quad y = \frac{2}{3}x - 5$.

The slope-intercept form of the equation of the line is $y = \frac{2}{3}x - 5$.

b. a slope of 4 and passes through the point at $(-2, 3)$

Substitute the slope and coordinates of the point in the general slope-intercept form of a linear equation. Then solve for b.

$\quad y = mx + b$
$\quad 3 = 4(-2) + b \quad$ *Substitute -2 for x, 3 for y, and 4 for m.*
$\quad 11 = b \quad\quad\quad\quad$ *Add 8 to both sides of the equation.*

The y-intercept is 11. Thus, the equation for the line is $y = 4x + 11$.

When you know the coordinates of two points on a line, you can find the slope of the line. Then the equation of the line can be written using either the slope-intercept or the **point-slope** form, which is $y - y_1 = m(x - x_1)$.

Example 2   *Sales*   **In 1998, the average weekly first-quarter sales at Vic's Hardware store were $9250. In 1999, the average weekly first-quarter sales were $10,100. Assuming a linear relationship, find the average quarterly rate of increase.**

$(1, 9250)$ and $(5, 10,100)$ *Since there are two data points, identify the two coordinates to find the slope of the line.*

$m = \dfrac{y_2 - y_1}{x_2 - x_1}$ *Coordinate 1 represents the first quarter of 1998 and coordinate 5 represents the first quarter of 1999.*

$\quad = \dfrac{10,100 - 9250}{5 - 1}$

$\quad = \dfrac{850}{4}$ or 212.5

Thus, for each quarter, the average sales increase was $212.50.

1-4

Practice

Writing Linear Equations

Write an equation in slope-intercept form for each line described.

1. slope $= -4$, y-intercept $= 3$

2. slope $= 5$, passes through $A(-3, 2)$

3. slope $= -4$, passes through $B(3, 8)$

4. slope $= \frac{4}{3}$, passes through $C(-9, 4)$

5. slope $= 1$, passes through $D(-6, 6)$

6. slope $= -1$, passes through $E(3, -3)$

7. slope $= 3$, y-intercept $= \frac{3}{4}$

8. slope $= -2$, y-intercept $= -7$

9. slope $= -1$, passes through $F(-1, 7)$

10. slope $= 0$, passes through $G(3, 2)$

11. *Aviation*   The number of active certified commercial pilots has been declining since 1980, as shown in the table.
   a. Find a linear equation that can be used as a model to predict the number of active certified commercial pilots for any year. Assume a steady rate of decline.

Number of Active Certified Pilots	
Year	Total
1980	182,097
1985	155,929
1990	149,666
1993	143,014
1994	138,728
1995	133,980
1996	129,187

Source: U. S. Dept. of Transportation

   b. Use the model to predict the number of pilots in the year 2003.

1-5

Study Guide

Writing Equations of Parallel and Perpendicular Lines

- Two nonvertical lines in a plane are **parallel** if and only if their slopes are equal and they have no points in common.

- Graphs of two equations that represent the same line are said to **coincide**.

- Two nonvertical lines in a plane are **perpendicular** if and only if their slopes are negative reciprocals.

Example 1 **Determine whether the graphs of each pair of equations are *parallel, coinciding,* or *neither.***

    a. $2x - 3y = 5$
        $6x - 9y = 21$
                          b. $12x + 6y = 18$
                                         $4x = -2y + 6$

Write each pair of equations in slope-intercept form.

a. $2x - 3y = 5$ $6x - 9y = 21$	**b.** $12x + 6y = 18$ $4x = -2y + 6$
$y = \frac{2}{3}x - \frac{5}{3}$ $y = \frac{2}{3}x - \frac{7}{3}$	$y = -2x + 3$ $y = -2x + 3$
The lines have the same slope but different y-intercepts, so they are parallel.	The equations are identical, so the lines coincide.

Example 2 **Write the standard form of the equation of the line that passes through the point at $(3, -4)$ and is parallel to the graph of $x + 3y - 4 = 0$.**

Any line parallel to the graph of $x + 3y - 4 = 0$ will have the same slope. So, find the slope of the graph of $x + 3y - 4 = 0$.

$$m = -\frac{A}{B}$$

$$= -\frac{1}{3} \quad A = 1, B = 3$$

Use the point-slope form to write the equation of the line.

$$y - y_1 = m(x - x_1)$$

$$y - (-4) = -\frac{1}{3}(x - 3) \quad x_1 = 3, y_1 = -4, m = -\frac{1}{3}$$

$$y + 4 = -\frac{1}{3}x + 1$$

$$3y + 12 = -x + 3 \qquad \textit{Multiply each side by 3.}$$

$$x + 3y + 9 = 0 \qquad \textit{Write in standard form.}$$

1-5

Practice

Writing Equations of Parallel and Perpendicular Lines

Determine whether the graphs of each pair of equations are parallel, perpendicular, coinciding, or none of these.

1. $x + 3y = 18$
$3x + 9y = 12$

2. $2x - 4y = 8$
$x - 2y = 4$

3. $-3x + 2y = 6$
$2x + 3y = 12$

4. $x + y = 6$
$3x - y = 6$

5. $4x + 8y = 2$
$2x + 4y = 8$

6. $3x - y = 9$
$6x - 2y = 18$

Write the standard form of the equation of the line that is parallel to the graph of the given equation and that passes through the point with the given coordinates.

7. $2x + y - 5 = 0; (0, 4)$ **8.** $3x - y + 3 = 0; (-1, -2)$ **9.** $3x - 2y + 8 = 0; (2, 5)$

Write the standard form of the equation of the line that is perpendicular to the graph of the given equation and that passes through the point with the given coordinates.

10. $2x - y + 6 = 0; (0, -3)$ **11.** $2x - 5y - 6 = 0; (-4, 2)$ **12.** $3x + 4y - 13 = 0; (2, 7)$

13. Consumerism   Marillia paid $180 for 3 video games and 4 books. Three months later she purchased 8 books and 6 video games. Her brother guessed that she spent $320. Assuming that the prices of video games and books did not change, is it possible that she spent $320 for the second set of purchases? Explain.

1-6

Study Guide

Modeling Real-World Data with Linear Functions

When real-world data are collected, the data graphed usually do not form a straight line. However, the graph may approximate a linear relationship.

Example   **The table shows the amount of freight hauled by trucks in the United States. Use the data to draw a line of best fit and to predict the amount of freight that will be carried by trucks in the year 2010.**

U.S. Truck Freight Traffic

Year	Amount (billions of ton-miles)
1986	632
1987	663
1988	700
1989	716
1990	735
1991	758
1992	815
1993	861
1994	908
1995	921

Source: *Transportation in America*

Graph the data on a scatter plot. Use the year as the independent variable and the ton-miles as the dependent variable. Draw a line of best fit, with some points on the line and others close to it.

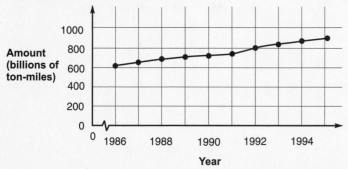

Write a prediction equation for the data. Select two points that appear to represent the data. We chose (1990, 735) and (1993, 861).

Determine the slope of the line.

$$m = \frac{y_2 - y_1}{x_2 - x_1} \rightarrow \frac{861 - 735}{1993 - 1990} = \frac{126}{3} \text{ or } 42$$

Use one of the ordered pairs, such as (1990, 735), and the slope in the point-slope form of the equation.

$$y - y_1 = m(x - x_1)$$
$$y - 735 = 42(x - 1990)$$
$$y = 42x - 82{,}845$$

A prediction equation is $y = 42x - 82{,}845$. Substitute 2010 for x to estimate the average amount of freight a truck will haul in 2010.

$$y = 42x - 82{,}845$$
$$y = 42(2010) - 82{,}845$$
$$y = 1575$$

According to this prediction equation, trucks will haul 1575 billion ton-miles in 2010.

11   *Advanced Mathematical Concepts*

1-6

Practice

Modeling Real-World Data with Linear Functions

Complete the following for each set of data.
a. Graph the data on a scatter plot.
b. Use two ordered pairs to write the equation of a best-fit line.
c. If the equation of the regression line shows a moderate or strong relationship, predict the missing value. Explain whether you think the prediction is reliable.

1.

U. S. Life Expectancy	
Birth Year	Number of Years
1990	75.4
1991	75.5
1992	75.8
1993	75.5
1994	75.7
1995	75.8
2015	?

Source: National Center for Health Statistics

a.

2.

Population Growth	
Year	Population (millions)
1991	252.1
1992	255.0
1993	257.7
1994	260.3
1995	262.8
1996	265.2
1997	267.7
1998	270.3
1999	272.9
2010	?

Source: U.S. Census Bureau

a.

1-7

Study Guide

Piecewise Functions

Piecewise functions use different equations for different intervals of the domain. When graphing piecewise functions, the partial graphs over various intervals do not necessarily connect.

Example 1 Graph $f(x) = \begin{cases} -1 & \text{if } x \le -3 \\ 1 + x & \text{if } -2 < x \le 2 \\ 2x & \text{if } x > 4 \end{cases}$

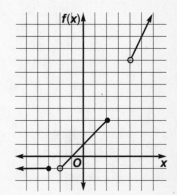

First, graph the constant function $f(x) = -1$ for $x \le -3$. This graph is a horizontal line. Because the point at $(-3, -1)$ is included in the graph, draw a closed circle at that point.

Second, graph the function $f(x) = 1 + x$ for $-2 < x \le 2$. Because $x = -2$ is not included in this region of the domain, draw an open circle at $(-2, -1)$. The value of $x = 2$ is included in the domain, so draw a closed circle at $(2, 3)$ since for $f(x) = 1 + x$, $f(2) = 3$.

Third, graph the line $f(x) = 2x$ for $x > 4$. Draw an open circle at $(4, 8)$ since for $f(x) = 2x$, $f(4) = 8$.

A piecewise function whose graph looks like a set of stairs is called a **step function**. One type of step function is the **greatest integer function**. The symbol $[\![x]\!]$ means *the greatest integer not greater than x*. The graphs of step functions are often used to model real-world problems such as fees for phone services and the cost of shipping an item of a given weight.

The **absolute value function** is another piecewise function. Consider $f(x) = |x|$. The absolute value of a number is always nonnegative.

Example 2 Graph $f(x) = 2|x| - 2$.

Use a table of values to determine points on the graph.

x	$2|x| - 2$	$(x, f(x))$
-4	$2|-4| - 2$	$(-4, 6)$
-3	$2|-3| - 2$	$(-3, 4)$
-1.5	$2|-1.5| - 2$	$(-1.5, 1)$
0	$2|0| - 2$	$(0, -2)$
1	$2|1| - 2$	$(1, 0)$
2	$2|2| - 2$	$(2, 2)$

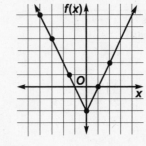

1-7

Practice

Piecewise Functions

Graph each function.

1. $f(x) = \begin{cases} 1 \text{ if } x \geq 2 \\ x \text{ if } -1 \leq x < 2 \\ -x - 3 \text{ if } x < -2 \end{cases}$

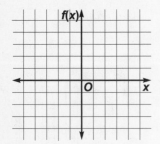

2. $f(x) = \begin{cases} -2 \text{ if } x \leq -1 \\ 1 + x \text{ if } -1 < x < 2 \\ 1 - x \text{ if } x > 2 \end{cases}$

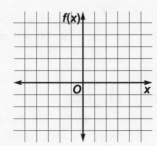

3. $f(x) = |x| - 3$

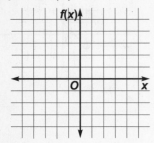

4. $f(x) = [\![x]\!] - 1$

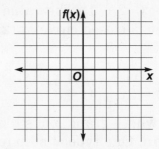

5. $f(x) = 3|x| - 2$

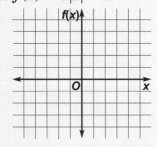

6. $f(x) = [\![2x + 1]\!]$

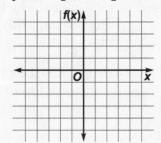

7. Graph the tax rates for the different incomes by using a step function.

Income Tax Rates for a Couple Filing Jointly	
Limits of Taxable Income	**Tax Rate**
$0 to $41,200	15%
$41,201 to $99,600	28%
$99,601 to $151,750	31%
$151,751 to $271,050	36%
$271,051 and up	39.6%

Source: Information Please Almanac

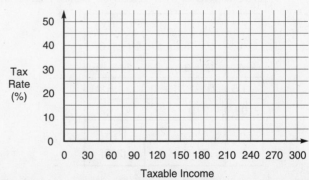

1-8

Study Guide

Graphing Linear Inequalities

The graph of $y = -\frac{1}{3}x + 2$ is a line that

separates the coordinate plane into two regions, called **half planes**. The line

described by $y = -\frac{1}{3}x + 2$ is called the

boundary of each region. If the boundary is part of a graph, it is drawn as a solid line. A boundary that is not part of the graph is drawn as a dashed line.

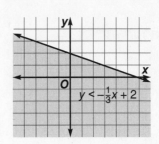

The graph of $y > -\frac{1}{3}x + 2$ is the region above

the line. The graph of $y < -\frac{1}{3}x + 2$ is the region

below the line.

You can determine which half plane to shade by testing a point on either side of the boundary in the original inequality. If it is not on the boundary, (0, 0) is often an easy point to test. If the inequality is true for your test point, then shade the half plane that contains the test point. If the inequality is false for your test point, then shade the half plane that does not contain the test point.

Example **Graph each inequality.**

a. $x - y + 2 \le 0$

$$x - y + 2 \le 0$$
$$-y \le -x - 2$$
$$y \ge x + 2$$

Reverse the inequality when you divide or multiply by a negative.

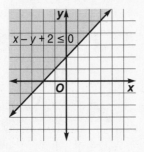

The graph does include the boundary, so the line is solid. Testing (0, 0) in the inequality yields a false inequality, $0 \ge 2$. Shade the half plane that does not include (0, 0).

b. $y > |x - 1|$

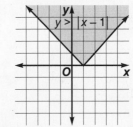

Graph the equation with a dashed boundary. Then test a point to determine which region is shaded. The test point (0, 0) yields the false inequality $0 > 1$, so shade the region that does not include (0, 0).

Practice

Graphing Linear Inequalities

Graph each inequality.

1. $x \geq -2$

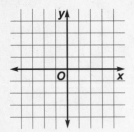

2. $y < -2x - 4$

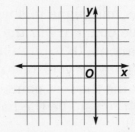

3. $y \geq 3x + 2$

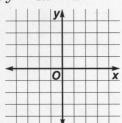

4. $y < |x + 3|$

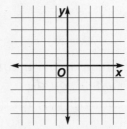

5. $y > |x - 2|$

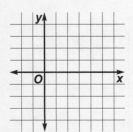

6. $y \leq -\frac{1}{2}x + 4$

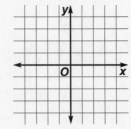

7. $\frac{3}{4}x - 3 \leq y \leq \frac{4}{5}x + 4$

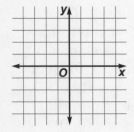

8. $-4 \leq x - 2y < 6$

Answers (Lessons 1-1 and 1-2)

1-1 Practice

Relations and Functions

State the domain and range of each relation. Then state whether the relation is a function. Write yes or no.

1. $\{(-1, 2), (3, 10), (-2, 20), (3, 11)\}$
$D = \{-2, -1, 3\}$, $R = \{2, 10, 11, 20\}$; no

2. $\{(0, 2), (13, 6), (2, 2), (3, 1)\}$
$D = \{0, 2, 3, 13\}$, $R = \{1, 2, 6\}$; yes

3. $\{(1, 4), (2, 8), (3, 24)\}$
$D = \{1, 2, 3\}$, $R = \{4, 8, 24\}$; yes

4. $\{(-1, -2), (3, 54), (-2, -16), (3, 81)\}$
$D = \{-2, -1, 3\}$; $R = \{-16, -2, 54, 81\}$; no

5. The domain of a relation is all even negative integers greater than -9. The range y of the relation is the set formed by adding 4 to the numbers in the domain. Write the relation as a table of values and as an equation. Then graph the relation.

$y = x + 4$

x	y
-2	2
-4	0
-6	-2
-8	-4

Evaluate each function for the given value.

6. $f(-2)$ if $f(x) = 4x^3 + 6x^2 + 3x$
-14

7. $f(3)$ if $f(x) = 5x^2 - 4x - 6$
27

8. $h(t)$ if $h(x) = 9x^9 - 4x^4 + 3x - 2$
$9t^9 - 4t^4 + 3t - 2$

9. $f(g + 1)$ if $f(x) = x^2 - 2x + 1$
g^2

10. **Climate** The table shows record high and low temperatures for selected states.

Record High and Low Temperatures (°F)		
State	High	Low
Alabama	112	−27
Delaware	110	−17
Idaho	118	−60
Michigan	112	−51
New Mexico	122	−50
Wisconsin	114	−54

Source: National Climatic Data Center

a. State the relation of the data as a set of ordered pairs.
$\{(112, -27), (110, -17), (118, -60),$
$(112, -51), (122, -50), (114, -54)\}$

b. State the domain and range of the relation.
$D = \{110, 112, 114, 118, 122\}$
$R = \{-60, -54, -51, -50, -27, -17\}$

c. Determine whether the relation is a function.
no

1-2 Practice

Composition of Functions

Given $f(x) = 2x^2 + 8$ and $g(x) = 5x - 6$, find each function.

1. $(f + g)(x)$
$2x^2 + 5x + 2$

2. $(f - g)(x)$
$2x^2 - 5x + 14$

3. $(f \cdot g)(x)$
$10x^3 - 12x^2 + 40x - 48$

4. $\left(\dfrac{f}{g}\right)(x)$
$\dfrac{2x^2 + 8}{5x - 6}$, $x \neq \dfrac{6}{5}$

Find $[f \circ g](x)$ and $[g \circ f](x)$ for each $f(x)$ and $g(x)$.

5. $f(x) = x + 5$
$g(x) = x - 3$
$x + 2, x + 2$

6. $f(x) = 2x^3 - 3x^2 + 1$
$g(x) = 3x$
$54x^3 - 27x^2 + 1, 6x^3 - 9x^2 + 3$

7. $f(x) = 2x^2 - 5x + 1$
$g(x) = 2x - 3$
$8x^2 - 34x + 34, 4x^2 - 10x - 1$

8. $f(x) = 3x^2 - 2x + 5$
$g(x) = 2x - 1$
$12x^2 - 16x + 10, 6x^2 - 4x + 9$

9. State the domain of $[f \circ g](x)$ for $f(x) = \sqrt{x - 2}$ and $g(x) = 3x$.
$x \geq \dfrac{2}{3}$

Find the first three iterates of each function using the given initial value.

10. $f(x) = 2x - 6; x_0 = 1$
$-4, -14, -34$

11. $f(x) = x^2 - 1; x_0 = 2$
$3, 8, 63$

12. **Fitness** Tara has decided to start a walking program. Her initial walking time is 5 minutes. She plans to double her walking time and add 1 minute every 5 days. Provided that Tara achieves her goal, how many minutes will she be walking on days 21 through 25? 95 minutes or 1 hour 35 minutes

© Glencoe/McGraw-Hill   2   Advanced Mathematical Concepts

© Glencoe/McGraw-Hill   4   Advanced Mathematical Concepts

1-3 Practice

NAME _____ DATE _____ PERIOD _____

Graphing Linear Equations

Graph each equation using the x- and y-intercepts.

1. $2x - y - 6 = 0$

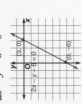

2. $4x + 2y + 8 = 0$

Graph each equation using the y-intercept and the slope.

3. $y = 5x - \frac{1}{2}$

4. $y = \frac{1}{2}x$

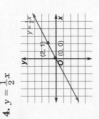

Find the zero of each function. Then graph the function.

5. $f(x) = 4x - 3$ $\frac{3}{4}$

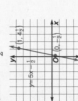

6. $f(x) = 2x + 4$ -2

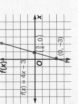

7. **Business** In 1990, a two-bedroom apartment at Remington Square Apartments rented for $575 per month. In 1999, the same two-bedroom apartment rented for $850 per month. Assuming a constant rate of increase, what will a tenant pay for a two-bedroom apartment at Remington Square in the year 2000? **about $881**

1-4 Practice

NAME _____ DATE _____ PERIOD _____

Writing Linear Equations

Write an equation in slope-intercept form for each line described.

1. slope $= -4$, y-intercept $= 3$
$y = -4x + 3$

2. slope $= 5$, passes through $A(-3, 2)$
$y = 5x + 17$

3. slope $= -4$, passes through $B(3, 8)$
$y = -4x + 20$

4. slope $= \frac{4}{3}$, passes through $C(-9, 4)$
$y = \frac{4}{3}x + 16$

5. slope $= 1$, passes through $D(-6, 6)$
$y = x + 12$

6. slope $= -1$, passes through $E(3, -3)$
$y = -x$

7. slope $= 3$, y-intercept $= \frac{3}{4}$
$y = 3x + \frac{3}{4}$

8. slope $= -2$, y-intercept $= -7$
$y = -2x - 7$

9. slope $= -1$, passes through $F(-1, 7)$
$y = -x + 6$

10. slope $= 0$, passes through $G(3, 2)$
$y = 2$

11. **Aviation** The number of active certified commercial pilots has been declining since 1980, as shown in the table.

a. Find a linear equation that can be used as a model to predict the number of active certified commercial pilots for any year. Assume a steady rate of decline. **Sample answer using (1985, 155,929) and (1995, 133,980): $y = -2195x + 4,513,004$**

b. Use the model to predict the number of pilots in the year 2003. **Sample prediction: 116,419**

Number of Active Certified Pilots	
Year	**Total**
1980	182,097
1985	155,929
1990	149,666
1993	143,014
1994	138,728
1995	133,980
1996	129,187

Source: U. S. Dept. of Transportation

Answers (Lessons 1-5 and 1-6)

1-5 Practice

Writing Equations of Parallel and Perpendicular Lines

Determine whether the graphs of each pair of equations are parallel, perpendicular, coinciding, or none of these.

1. $x + 3y = 18$ **parallel**
   $3x + 9y = 12$

2. $2x - 4y = 8$ **coinciding**
   $x - 2y = 4$

3. $-3x + 2y = 6$ **perpendicular**
   $2x + 3y = 12$

4. $x + y = 6$ **none of these**
   $3x - y = 6$

5. $4x + 8y = 2$ **parallel**
   $2x + 4y = 8$

6. $3x - y = 9$ **coinciding**
   $6x - 2y = 18$

Write the standard form of the equation of the line that is parallel to the graph of the given equation and that passes through the point with the given coordinates.

7. $2x + y - 5 = 0$; (0, 4)   8. $3x - y + 3 = 0$; (−1, −2)   9. $3x - 2y + 8 = 0$; (2, 5)
   $2x + y - 4 = 0$ $3x - y + 1 = 0$ $3x - 2y + 4 = 0$

Write the standard form of the equation of the line that is perpendicular to the graph of the given equation and that passes through the point with the given coordinates.

10. $2x - y + 6 = 0$; (0, −3)   11. $2x - 5y - 6 = 0$; (−4, 2)   12. $3x + 4y - 13 = 0$; (2, 7)
    $x + 2y + 6 = 0$ $5x + 2y + 16 = 0$ $4x - 3y + 13 = 0$

13. *Consumerism* Marillia paid $180 for 3 video games and 4 books. Three months later she purchased 8 books and 6 video games. Her brother guessed that she spent $320. Assuming that the prices of video games and books did not change, is it possible that she spent $320 for the second set of purchases? Explain.
No; the lines that represent the situation are parallel.

1-6 Practice

Modeling Real-World Data with Linear Functions

Complete the following for each set of data.
a. *Graph the data on a scatter plot.*
b. *Use two ordered pairs to write the equation of a best-fit line.*
c. *If the equation of the regression line shows a moderate or strong relationship, predict the missing value. Explain whether you think the prediction is reliable.*

1. **U. S. Life Expectancy**

Birth Year	Number of Years
1990	75.4
1991	75.5
1992	75.8
1993	75.5
1994	75.7
1995	75.8
2015	?

Source: National Center for Health Statistics

a.

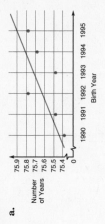

b. Sample answer using (1991, 75.5) and (1994, 75.7):
$y = 0.07x - 63.9$

c. Prediction: 77.2; the prediction is not very reliable because many points are off the line.

2. **Population Growth**

Year	Population (millions)
1991	252.1
1992	255.0
1993	257.7
1994	260.3
1995	262.8
1996	265.2
1997	267.7
1998	270.3
1999	272.9
2010	?

Source: U.S. Census Bureau

a.

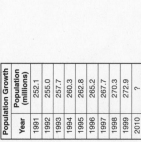

b. Sample answer using (1993, 257.7) and (1997, 267.7):
$y = 2.5x - 4724.8$

c. Prediction: 300.2; the prediction is reliable because the line passes through most of the points.

NAME _____ DATE _____ PERIOD _____

1-7 Practice

Piecewise Functions

Graph each function.

1. $f(x) = \begin{cases} 1 \text{ if } x \geq 2 \\ x \text{ if } -1 \leq x < 2 \\ -x - 3 \text{ if } x < -2 \end{cases}$

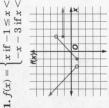

2. $f(x) = \begin{cases} -2 \text{ if } x \leq -1 \\ 1 + x \text{ if } -1 < x < 2 \\ 1 - x \text{ if } x > 2 \end{cases}$

3. $f(x) = |x| - 3$

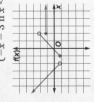

4. $f(x) = |[x]| - 1$

5. $f(x) = 3|x| - 2$

6. $f(x) = [[2x + 1]]$

7. Graph the tax rates for the different incomes by using a step function.

Income Tax Rates for a Couple Filing Jointly	
Limits of Taxable Income	Tax Rate
$0 to $41,200	15%
$41,201 to $99,600	28%
$99,601 to $151,750	31%
$151,751 to $271,050	36%
$271,051 and up	39.6%

Source: Information Please Almanac

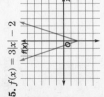

Tax Rate (%) / Taxable Income (in thousands)

NAME _____ DATE _____ PERIOD _____

1-8 Practice

Graphing Linear Inequalities

Graph each inequality.

1. $x \geq -2$

2. $y < -2x - 4$

3. $y \geq 3x + 2$

4. $y < |x + 3|$

5. $y > |x - 2|$

6. $y \leq -\frac{1}{2}x + 4$

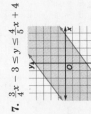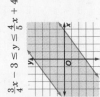

7. $\frac{3}{4}x - 3 \leq y \leq \frac{4}{5}x + 4$

8. $-4 \leq x - 2y < 6$

2-1

Study Guide

Solving Systems of Equations in Two Variables

One way to solve a system of equations in two variables is by graphing. The intersection of the graphs is called the solution to the **system of equations.**

Example 1   **Solve the system of equations by graphing.**
$$3x - y = 10$$
$$x + 4y = 12$$

First rewrite each equation of the system in slope-intercept form by solving for y.

$$3x - y = 10 \qquad \boxed{becomes} \implies \qquad y = 3x - 10$$
$$x + 4y = 12 \qquad\qquad\qquad\qquad y = -\tfrac{1}{4}x + 3$$

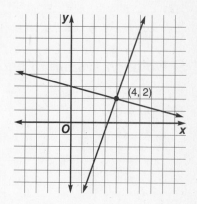

The solution to the system is $(4, 2)$.

A **consistent** system has at least one solution.
A system having exactly one solution is **independent**.
If a system has infinitely many solutions, the system is **dependent**.
Systems that have no solution are **inconsistent**.

Systems of linear equations can also be solved algebraically using the **elimination method** or the **substitution method.**

Example 2

Use the elimination method to solve the system of equations.
$$2x - 3v = -21$$
$$5x + 6v = 15$$

To solve this system, multiply each side of the first equation by 2, and add the two equations to eliminate y. Then solve the resulting equation.

$$2(2x - 3y) = 2(-21) \rightarrow 4x - 6y = -42$$

$$
\begin{array}{rl}
4x - 6y = & -42 \\
5x + 6y = & 15 \\
\hline
9x = & -27 \\
x = & -3
\end{array}
$$

Now substitute -3 for x in either of the *original* equations.
$$5x + 6y = 15$$
$$5(-3) + 6y = 15 \qquad x = -3$$
$$6y = 30$$
$$y = 5$$
The solution is $(-3, 5)$.

Example 3

Use the substitution method to solve the system of equations.
$$x = 7y + 3$$
$$2x - y = -7$$

The first equation is stated in terms of x, so substitute $7y + 3$ for x in the second equation.
$$2x - y = -7$$
$$2(7y + 3) - y = -7$$
$$13y = -13$$
$$y = -1$$

Now solve for x by substituting -1 for y in either of the *original* equations.
$$x = 7y + 3$$
$$x = 7(-1) + 3 \qquad y = -1$$
$$x = -4$$
The solution is $(-4, -1)$.

2-1

Practice

Solving Systems of Equations in Two Variables

State whether each system is consistent and independent, consistent and dependent, or inconsistent.

1. $-x + y = -4$
$3x - 3y = 12$

2. $2x - 5y = 8$
$15y - 6x = -24$

Solve each system of equations by graphing.

3. $x + y = 6$
$2x + 3y = 12$

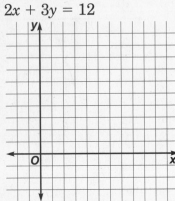

4. $x + y = 6$
$3x - y = 6$

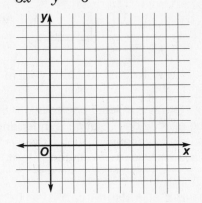

Solve each system of equations algebraically.

5. $x + y = 4$
$3x - 2y = 7$

6. $3x - 4y = 10$
$-3x + 4y = 8$

7. $4x - 3y = 15$
$2x + y = 5$

8. $4x + 5y = 11$
$3x - 2y = -9$

9. $2x + 3y = 19$
$7x - y = 9$

10. $2x - y = 6$
$x + y = 6$

11. *Real Estate* AMC Homes, Inc. is planning to build three- and four-bedroom homes in a housing development called Chestnut Hills. Consumer demand indicates a need for three times as many four-bedroom homes as for three-bedroom homes. The net profit from each three-bedroom home is $16,000 and from each four-bedroom home, $17,000. If AMC Homes must net a total profit of $13.4 million from this development, how many homes of each type should they build?

2-2

Study Guide

Solving Systems of Equations in Three Variables

You can solve systems of three equations in three variables using the same algebraic techniques you used to solve systems of two equations.

Example   **Solve the system of equations by elimination.**

$$4x + y + 2z = -8$$
$$2x - 3y - 4z = 4$$
$$-7x + 2y + 3z = 2$$

Choose a pair of equations and then eliminate one of the variables. Because the coefficient of y is 1 in the first equation, eliminate y from the second and third equations.

To eliminate y using the first and second equations, multiply both sides of the first equation by 3.

$$3(4x + y + 2z) = 3(-8)$$
$$12x + 3y + 6z = -24$$

Then add the second equation to that result.

$$\begin{array}{r} 12x + 3y + 6z = -24 \\ 2x - 3y - 4z = 4 \\ \hline 14x + 2z = -20 \end{array}$$

To eliminate y using the first and third equations, multiply both sides of the first equation by -2.

$$-2(4x + y + 2z) = -2(-8)$$
$$-8x - 2y - 4z = 16$$

Then add the second equation to that result.

$$\begin{array}{r} -8x - 2y - 4z = 16 \\ -7x + 2y + 3z = 2 \\ \hline -15x - z = 18 \end{array}$$

Now you have two linear equations in two variables. Solve this system. Eliminate z by multiplying both sides of the second equation by 2. Then add the two equations.

$$\begin{array}{ll} 2(-15x - z) = 2(18) & \quad 14x + 2z = -20 \\ -30x - 2z = 36 & \quad \underline{-30x - 2z = 36} \\ & \quad -16x = 16 \\ & \quad x = -1 \end{array} \qquad$$ The value of x is -1.

By substituting the value of x into one of the equations in two variables, we can solve for the value of z.

$$14x + 2z = -20$$
$$14(-1) + 2z = -20 \qquad x = -1$$
$$z = -3$$

The value of z is -3.

Finally, use one of the original equations to find the value of y.

$$4x + y + 2z = -8$$
$$4(-1) + y + 2(-3) = -8 \qquad x = -1, z = -3$$
$$y = 2$$

The value of y is 2.

The solution is $x = -1$, $y = 2$, $z = -3$. This can be written as the **ordered triple** $(-1, 2, -3)$.

2-2

Practice

Solving Systems of Equations in Three Variables

Solve each system of equations.

1. $x + y - z = -1$
$x + y + z = 3$
$3x - 2y - z = -4$

2. $x + y = 5$
$3x + z = 2$
$4y - z = 8$

3. $3x - 5y + z = 8$
$4y - z = 10$
$7x + y = 4$

4. $2x + 3y + 3z = 2$
$10x - 6y + 3z = 0$
$4x - 3y - 6z = 2$

5. $2x - y + z = -1$
$x - y + z = 1$
$x - 2y + z = 2$

6. $4x + 4y - 2z = 3$
$-6x - 6y + 6z = 5$
$2x - 3y - 4z = 2$

7. $x - z = 5$
$y + 3z = 12$
$2x + y = 7$

8. $2x + 4y - 2z = 9$
$4x - 6y + 2z = -9$
$x - y + 3z = -4$

9. *Business* The president of Speedy Airlines has discovered that her competitor, Zip Airlines, has purchased 13 new airplaines from Commuter Aviation for a total of $15.9 million. She knows that Commuter Aviation produces three types of planes and that type A sells for $1.1 million, type B sells for $1.2 million, and type C sells for $1.7 million. The president of Speedy Airlines also managed to find out that Zip Airlines purchased 5 more type A planes than type C planes. How many planes of each type did Zip Airlines purchase?

2-3

Study Guide

Modeling Real-World Data with Matrices

A **matrix** is a rectangular array of terms called **elements**.
A matrix with m rows and n columns is an $m \times n$ **matrix**.
The dimensions of the matrix are m and n.

Example 1 **Find the values of x and y for which**
$$\begin{bmatrix} 3x + 5 \\ y \end{bmatrix} = \begin{bmatrix} y - 9 \\ -4x \end{bmatrix} \text{ is true.}$$

Since the corresponding elements must
be equal, we can express the equal
matrices as two equations.

$3x + 5 = y - 9$
$\quad y = -4x$

Solve the system of equations by using
substitution.

$3x + 5 = y - 9$
$3x + 5 = (-4x) - 9$ *Substitute $-4x$ for y.*
$\quad\quad x = -2$

$y = -4x$
$y = -4(-2)$ *Substitute -2 for x.*
$y = 8$

The matrices are equal if $x = -2$ and $y = 8$.

To add or subtract matrices, the dimensions of the matrices
must be the same.

Example 2 **Find $C - D$ if $C = \begin{bmatrix} 3 & 6 \\ -2 & 4 \end{bmatrix}$ and $D = \begin{bmatrix} 1 & 5 \\ -7 & 8 \end{bmatrix}$.**

$$C - D = C + (-D)$$
$$= \begin{bmatrix} 3 & 6 \\ -2 & 4 \end{bmatrix} + \begin{bmatrix} -1 & -5 \\ 7 & -8 \end{bmatrix}$$
$$= \begin{bmatrix} 3 + (-1) & 6 + (-5) \\ -2 + 7 & 4 + (-8) \end{bmatrix}$$
$$= \begin{bmatrix} 2 & 1 \\ 5 & -4 \end{bmatrix}$$

To multiply two matrices, the number of columns in the first matrix
must be equal to the number of rows in the second matrix. The
product of two matrices is found by multiplying columns and rows.

Example 3 **Find each product if $Z = \begin{bmatrix} 4 & 3 \\ 5 & 2 \end{bmatrix}$ and $Y = \begin{bmatrix} 8 & 0 \\ 9 & -6 \end{bmatrix}$.**

a. XY

$$XY = \begin{bmatrix} 4(8) + 3(9) & 4(0) + 3(-6) \\ 5(8) + 2(9) & 5(0) + 2(-6) \end{bmatrix} \text{ or } \begin{bmatrix} 59 & -18 \\ 58 & -12 \end{bmatrix}$$

b. YX

$$YX = \begin{bmatrix} 8(4) + 0(5) & 8(3) + 0(2) \\ 9(4) + (-6)(5) & 9(3) + (-6)(2) \end{bmatrix} \text{ or } \begin{bmatrix} 32 & 24 \\ 6 & 15 \end{bmatrix}$$

2-3

Practice

Modeling Real-World Data with Matrices

Find the values of x and for which each matrix equation is true.

1. $\begin{bmatrix} x \\ y \end{bmatrix} = \begin{bmatrix} 2y - 4 \\ 2x \end{bmatrix}$

2. $\begin{bmatrix} 2x - 3 \\ 4y \end{bmatrix} = \begin{bmatrix} y \\ 3x \end{bmatrix}$

Use matrices A, B, and C to find each sum, difference, or product.

$$A = \begin{bmatrix} -1 & 5 & 6 \\ 2 & -7 & -2 \\ 4 & 4 & 2 \end{bmatrix} \quad B = \begin{bmatrix} 2 & 3 & 1 \\ -1 & 1 & 4 \\ 5 & -2 & 3 \end{bmatrix} \quad C = \begin{bmatrix} 8 & 10 & -9 \\ -6 & 12 & 14 \end{bmatrix}$$

3. $A + B$

4. $A - B$

5. $B - A$

6. $-2A$

7. CA

8. AB

9. AA

10. CB

11. $(CA)B$

12. $C(AB)$

13. *Entertainment* On one weekend, the Goxfield Theater reported the following ticket sales for three first-run movies, as shown in the matrix at the right. If the ticket prices were $6 for each adult and $4 for each child, what were the weekend sales for each movie.

$$\begin{array}{c} \\ \text{Movie 1} \\ \text{Movie 2} \\ \text{Movie 3} \end{array} \begin{array}{cc} \textbf{Adults} & \textbf{Children} \end{array} \\ \begin{bmatrix} 1021 & 523 \\ 2547 & 785 \\ 3652 & 2456 \end{bmatrix}$$

2-4

Study Guide

Modeling Motion with Matrices

You can use matrices to perform many **transformations**, such as **translations** (slides), **reflections** (flips), **rotations** (turns), and **dilations** (enlargements or reductions).

Example 1 Suppose quadrilateral *EFGH* with vertices $E(-1, 5)$, $F(3, 4)$, $G(4, 0)$, and $H(-2, 1)$ is translated 2 units left and 3 units down.

The **vertex matrix** for the quadrilateral is $\begin{bmatrix} -1 & 3 & 4 & -2 \\ 5 & 4 & 0 & 1 \end{bmatrix}$.

The **translation matrix** is $\begin{bmatrix} -2 & -2 & -2 & -2 \\ -3 & -3 & -3 & -3 \end{bmatrix}$.

Adding the two matrices gives the coordinates of the vertices of the translated quadrilateral.

$$\begin{bmatrix} -1 & 3 & 4 & -2 \\ 5 & 4 & 0 & 1 \end{bmatrix} + \begin{bmatrix} -2 & -2 & -2 & -2 \\ -3 & -3 & -3 & -3 \end{bmatrix} = \begin{bmatrix} -3 & 1 & 2 & -4 \\ 2 & 1 & -3 & -2 \end{bmatrix}$$

Graphing the **pre-image** and the **image** of the translated quadrilateral on the same axes, we can see the effect of the translation.

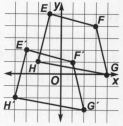

The chart below summarizes the matrices needed to produce specific reflections or rotations. All rotations are counterclockwise about the origin.

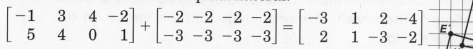

Reflections	$R_{x\text{-axis}} = \begin{bmatrix} 1 & 0 \\ 0 & -1 \end{bmatrix}$	$R_{y\text{-axis}} = \begin{bmatrix} -1 & 0 \\ 0 & 1 \end{bmatrix}$	$R_{y=x} = \begin{bmatrix} 0 & 1 \\ 1 & 0 \end{bmatrix}$
Rotations	$Rot_{90} = \begin{bmatrix} 0 & -1 \\ 1 & 0 \end{bmatrix}$	$Rot_{180} = \begin{bmatrix} -1 & 0 \\ 0 & -1 \end{bmatrix}$	$Rot_{270} = \begin{bmatrix} 0 & 1 \\ -1 & 0 \end{bmatrix}$

Example 2 A triangle has vertices $A(-1, 2)$, $B(4, 4)$, and $C(3, -2)$. Find the coordinates of the image of the triangle after a rotation of 90° counterclockwise about the origin.

The vertex matrix is $\begin{bmatrix} -1 & 4 & 3 \\ 2 & 4 & -2 \end{bmatrix}$.

Multiply it by the 90° **rotation matrix**.

$$\begin{bmatrix} 0 & -1 \\ 1 & 0 \end{bmatrix} \cdot \begin{bmatrix} -1 & 4 & 3 \\ 2 & 4 & -2 \end{bmatrix} = \begin{bmatrix} -2 & -4 & 2 \\ -1 & 4 & 3 \end{bmatrix}$$

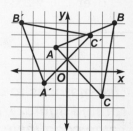

Example 3 Trapezoid *WXYZ* has vertices $W(2, 1)$, $X(1, -2)$, $Y(-1, -2)$, and $Z(-2, 1)$. Find the coordinates of dilated trapezoid *W'X'Y'Z'* for a scale factor of 2.5.

Perform scalar multiplication on the vertex matrix for the trapezoid.

$$2.5\begin{bmatrix} 2 & 1 & -1 & -2 \\ 1 & -2 & -2 & 1 \end{bmatrix} = \begin{bmatrix} 5 & 2.5 & -2.5 & -5 \\ 2.5 & -5 & -5 & 2.5 \end{bmatrix}$$

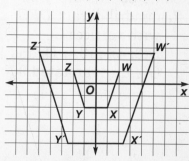

2-4

Practice

Modeling Motion with Matrices

Use scalar multiplication to determine the coordinates of the vertices of each dilated figure. Then graph the pre-image and the image on the same coordinate grid.

1. triangle with vertices A(1, 2), B(2, −1), and C(−2, 0); scale factor 2

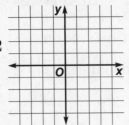

2. quadrilateral with vertices E(−2, −7), F(4, −3), G(0, 1), and H(−4, −2); scale factor 0.5

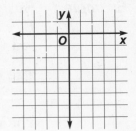

Use matrices to determine the coordinates of the vertices of each translated figure. Then graph the pre-image and the image on the same coordinate grid.

3. square with vertices W(1, −3), X(−4, −2), Y(−3, 3), and Z(2, 2) translated 2 units right and 3 units down

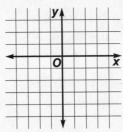

4. triangle with vertices J(3, 1), K(2, −4), and L(0, −2) translated 4 units left and 2 units up

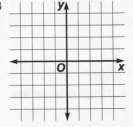

Use matrices to determine the coordinates of the vertices of each reflected figure. Then graph the pre-image and the image on the same coordinate grid.

5. △MNP with vertices M(−3, 4), N(3, 1), and P(−4, −3) reflected over the y-axis

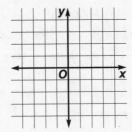

6. a rhombus with vertices Q(2, 3), R(4, −1), S(−1, −2), and T(−3, 2) reflected over the line y = x

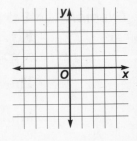

Use matrices to determine the coordinates of the vertices of each rotated figure. Then graph the pre-image and the image on the same coordinate grid.

7. quadrilateral CDFG with vertices C(−2, 3), D(3, 4), F(3, −1), and G(−3, −4) rotated 90°

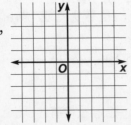

8. Pentagon VWXYZ with vertices V(1, 3), W(4, 2), X(3, −2), Y(−1, −4), Z(−2, 1) rotated 180°

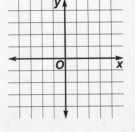

Advanced Mathematical Concepts

2-5

Study Guide

Determinants and Multiplicative Inverses of Matrices

Each square matrix has a **determinant**. The determinant of a 2×2 matrix is a number denoted by $\begin{vmatrix} a_1 & b_1 \\ a_2 & b_2 \end{vmatrix}$ or $\det \begin{bmatrix} a_1 & b_1 \\ a_2 & b_2 \end{bmatrix}$. Its value is $a_1b_2 - a_2b_1$.

Example 1 Find the value of $\begin{vmatrix} 5 & -2 \\ 3 & 1 \end{vmatrix}$.

$$\begin{vmatrix} 5 & -2 \\ 3 & 1 \end{vmatrix} = 5(1) - 3(-2) \text{ or } 11$$

The **minor** of an element can be found by deleting the row and column containing the element.

$$\begin{vmatrix} a_1 & b_1 & c_1 \\ a_2 & b_2 & c_2 \\ a_3 & b_3 & c_3 \end{vmatrix}$$

The minor of a_1 is $\begin{vmatrix} b_2 & c_2 \\ b_3 & c_3 \end{vmatrix}$.

Example 2 Find the value of $\begin{vmatrix} 8 & 9 & 3 \\ 3 & 5 & 7 \\ -1 & 2 & 4 \end{vmatrix}$.

$$\begin{vmatrix} 8 & 9 & 3 \\ 3 & 5 & 7 \\ -1 & 2 & 4 \end{vmatrix} = 8\begin{vmatrix} 5 & 7 \\ 2 & 4 \end{vmatrix} - 9\begin{vmatrix} 3 & 7 \\ -1 & 4 \end{vmatrix} + 3\begin{vmatrix} 3 & 5 \\ -1 & 2 \end{vmatrix}$$
$$= 8(6) - 9(19) + 3(11) \text{ or } -90$$

The multiplicative inverse of a matrix is defined as follows.

If $A = \begin{bmatrix} a_1 & b_1 \\ a_2 & b_2 \end{bmatrix}$ and $\begin{vmatrix} a_1 & b_1 \\ a_2 & b_2 \end{vmatrix} \neq 0$, then $A^{-1} = \dfrac{1}{\begin{vmatrix} a_1 & b_1 \\ a_2 & b_2 \end{vmatrix}} \begin{bmatrix} b_2 & -b_1 \\ -a_2 & a_1 \end{bmatrix}$.

Example 3 Solve the system of equations by using matrix equations.
$5x + 4y = -3$
$3x - 5y = -24$

Write the system as a matrix equation.

$$\begin{bmatrix} 5 & 4 \\ 3 & -5 \end{bmatrix} \cdot \begin{bmatrix} x \\ y \end{bmatrix} = \begin{bmatrix} -3 \\ -24 \end{bmatrix}$$

To solve the matrix equation, first find the inverse of the coefficient matrix.

$$\dfrac{1}{\begin{vmatrix} 5 & 4 \\ 3 & -5 \end{vmatrix}} \begin{bmatrix} -5 & -4 \\ -3 & 5 \end{bmatrix} = \dfrac{1}{37} \begin{bmatrix} -5 & -4 \\ -3 & 5 \end{bmatrix}$$

Now multiply each side of the matrix equation by the inverse and solve.

$$-\dfrac{1}{37} \begin{bmatrix} -5 & -4 \\ -3 & 5 \end{bmatrix} \cdot$$

$$\begin{bmatrix} 5 & 4 \\ 3 & -5 \end{bmatrix} \cdot \begin{bmatrix} x \\ y \end{bmatrix} = \dfrac{1}{37}\begin{bmatrix} -5 & -4 \\ -3 & 5 \end{bmatrix} \cdot \begin{bmatrix} -3 \\ -24 \end{bmatrix}$$

$$\begin{bmatrix} x \\ y \end{bmatrix} = \begin{bmatrix} -3 \\ -3 \end{bmatrix}$$

The solution is $(-3, 3)$.

2-5

Practice

Determinants and Multiplicative Inverses of Matrices

Find the value of each determinant.

1. $\begin{vmatrix} -2 & 3 \\ 8 & -12 \end{vmatrix}$

2. $\begin{vmatrix} 3 & -5 \\ 7 & 9 \end{vmatrix}$

3. $\begin{vmatrix} 1 & -1 & 0 \\ 2 & 1 & 4 \\ 5 & -3 & 5 \end{vmatrix}$

4. $\begin{vmatrix} 2 & 3 & 1 \\ -3 & -1 & 5 \\ 1 & -4 & 2 \end{vmatrix}$

Find the inverse of each matrix, if it exists.

5. $\begin{vmatrix} 3 & 8 \\ -1 & 5 \end{vmatrix}$

6. $\begin{vmatrix} 5 & 2 \\ 10 & 4 \end{vmatrix}$

Solve each system by using matrix equations.

7. $2x - 3y = 17$
   $3x + y = 9$

8. $4x - 3y = -16$
   $2x + 5y = 18$

Solve each matrix equation.

9. $\begin{bmatrix} 2 & -1 & 3 \\ 1 & 2 & 1 \\ -1 & -3 & -2 \end{bmatrix} \cdot \begin{bmatrix} x \\ y \\ z \end{bmatrix} = \begin{bmatrix} -8 \\ 3 \\ -7 \end{bmatrix}$, if the inverse is $-\dfrac{1}{6}\begin{bmatrix} -1 & -11 & -7 \\ 1 & -1 & 1 \\ -1 & 7 & 5 \end{bmatrix}$

10. $\begin{bmatrix} 5 & -2 & 4 \\ 3 & -4 & 2 \\ 1 & -3 & 1 \end{bmatrix} \cdot \begin{bmatrix} x \\ y \\ z \end{bmatrix} = \begin{bmatrix} -2 \\ 0 \\ 1 \end{bmatrix}$, if the inverse is $-\dfrac{1}{8}\begin{bmatrix} 2 & -10 & 12 \\ -1 & 1 & 2 \\ -5 & 13 & -14 \end{bmatrix}$

11. **Landscaping** Two dump truck have capacities of 10 tons and 12 tons. They make a total of 20 round trips to haul 226 tons of topsoil for a landscaping project. How many round trips does each truck make?

2-6

Study Guide

Solving Systems of Linear Inequalities

To solve a **system of linear inequalities**, you must find the ordered pairs that satisfy all inequalities. One way to do this is to graph the inequalities on the same coordinate plane. The intersection of the graphs contains points with ordered pairs in the solution set. If the graphs of the inequalities do not intersect, then the system has no solution.

Example 1   **Solve the system of inequalities** $-x + 2y \le 2$
by graphing. $x \le 4$

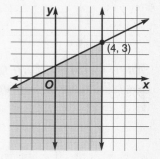

The shaded region represents the solution to the system of inequalities.

A system of more than two linear inequalities can have a solution that is a bounded set of points called a **polygonal convex set.**

Example 2   **Solve the system of inequalities** $x \ge 0$
by graphing and name the $y \ge 0$
coordinates of the vertices of $5x + 8y \le 40$
the polygonal convex set.

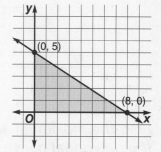

The region shows points that satisfy all three inequalities. The region is a triangle whose vertices are the points at $(0, 0)$, $(0, 5)$, and $(8, 0)$.

Example 3   **Find the maximum and minimum values of**
$f(x, y) = x + 2y + 1$ **for the polygonal convex**
set determined by the following inequalities.
$x \ge 0$ $y \ge 0$ $2x + y \le 4$ $x + y \le 3$

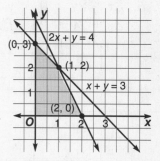

First, graph the inequalities and find the coordinates of the vertices of the resulting polygon.

The coordinates of the vertices are $(0, 0)$, $(2, 0)$, $(1, 2)$, and $(0, 3)$.

Then, evaluate the function $f(x, y) = x + 2y + 1$ at each vertex.

$f(0, 0) = 0 + 2(0) + 1 = 1$ $f(1, 2) = 1 + 2(2) + 1 = 6$
$f(2, 0) = 2 + 2(0) + 1 = 3$ $f(0, 3) = 0 + 2(3) + 1 = 7$

Thus, the maximum value of the function is 7, and the minimum value is 1.

2-6

Practice

Solving Systems of Linear Inequalities

Solve each system of inequalities by graphing.

1. $-4x + 7y \geq -21$; $3x + 7y \leq 28$

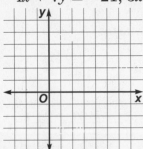

2. $x \leq 3$; $y \leq 5$; $x + y \geq 1$

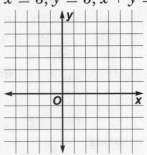

Solve each system of inequalities by graphing. Name the coordinates of the vertices of the polygonal convex set.

3. $x \geq 0$; $y \geq 0$; $y \geq x - 4$; $7x + 6y \leq 54$

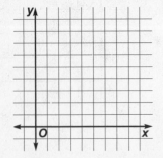

4. $x \geq 0$; $y + 2 \geq 0$; $5x + 6y \leq 18$

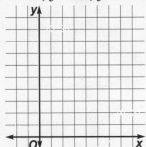

Find the maximum and minimum values of each function for the polygonal convex set determined by the given system of inequalities.

5. $3x - 2y \geq 0$ $y \geq 0$
    $3x + 2y \leq 24$ $f(x, y) = 7y - 3x$

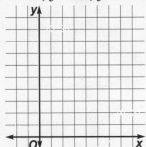

6. $y \leq -x + 8$ $4x - 3y \geq -3$
    $x + 8y \geq 8$ $f(x, y) = 4x - 5y$

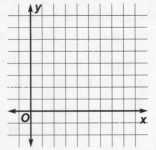

7. *Business* Henry Jackson, a recent college graduate, plans to start his own business manufacturing bicycle tires. Henry knows that his start-up costs are going to be $3000 and that each tire will cost him at least $2 to manufacture. In order to remain competitive, Henry cannot charge more than $5 per tire. Draw a graph to show when Henry will make a profit.

2-7 Study Guide

Linear Programming

The following example outlines the procedure used to solve **linear programming** problems.

Example **The B & W Leather Company wants to add handmade belts and wallets to its product line. Each belt nets the company $18 in profit, and each wallet nets $12. Both belts and wallets require cutting and sewing. Belts require 2 hours of cutting time and 6 hours of sewing time. Wallets require 3 hours of cutting time and 3 hours of sewing time. If the cutting machine is available 12 hours a week and the sewing machine is available 18 hours per week, what mix of belts and wallets will produce the most profit within the constraints?**

Define variables.	Let b = the number of belts. Let w = the number of wallets.
Write inequalities.	$b \geq 0$ $w \geq 0$ $2b + 3w \leq 12$ cutting $6b + 3w \leq 18$ sewing
Graph the system.	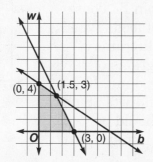
Write an equation.	Since the profit on belts is $18 and the profit on wallets is $12, the profit function is $B(b, w) = 18b + 12w$.
Substitute values.	$B(0, 0) = 18(0) + 12(0) = 0$ $B(0, 4) = 18(0) + 12(4) = 48$ $B(1.5, 3) = 18(1.5) + 12(3) = 63$ $B(3, 0) = 18(3) + 12(0) = 54$
Answer the problem.	The B & W Company will maximize profit if it makes and sells 1.5 belts for every 3 wallets.

When constraints of a linear programming problem cannot be satisfied simultaneously, then **infeasibility** is said to occur.

The solution of a linear programming problem is **unbounded** if the region defined by the constraints is infinitely large.

2-7

Practice

Linear Programming

Graph each system of inequalities. In a problem asking you to find the maximum value of f(x, y), state whether the situation is infeasible, has alternate optimal solutions, or is unbounded. In each system, assume that x ≥ 0 and y ≥ 0 unless stated otherwise.

1. $-2y \le 2x - 36$
$x + y \ge 30$
$f(x, y) = 3x + 3y$

2. $2x + 2y \ge 10$
$2x + y \ge 8$
$f(x, y) = x + y$

Solve each problem, if possible. If not possible, state whether the problem is infeasible, has alternate optimal solutions, or is unbounded.

3. *Nutrition*   A diet is to include at least 140 milligrams of Vitamin A and at least 145 milligrams of Vitamin B. These requirements can be obtained from two types of food. Type X contains 10 milligrams of Vitamin A and 20 milligrams of Vitamin B per pound. Type Y contains 30 milligrams of Vitamin A and 15 milligrams of Vitamin B per pound. If type X food costs $12 per pound and type Y food costs $8 per pound how many pounds of each type of food should be purchased to satisfy the requirements at the minimum cost?

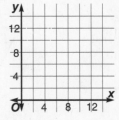

4. *Manufacturing*   The Cruiser Bicycle Company makes two styles of bicycles: the Traveler, which sells for $200, and the Tourester, which sells $600. Each bicycle has the same frame and tires, but the assembly and painting time required for the Traveler is only 1 hour, while it is 3 hours for the Tourister. There are 300 frames and 360 hours of labor available for production. How many bicycles of each model should be produced to maximize revenue?

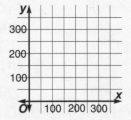

2-1

Practice

Solving Systems of Equations in Two Variables

State whether each system is consistent and independent, consistent and dependent, or inconsistent.

1. $-x + y = -4$
$3x - 3y = 12$ **consistent and dependent**

2. $2x - 5y = 8$
$15y - 6x = -24$ **consistent and independent**

Solve each system of equations by graphing.

3. $x + y = 6$
$2x + 3y = 12$

4. $x + y = 6$
$3x - y = 6$

Solve each system of equations algebraically.

5. $x + y = 4$
$3x - 2y = 7$
(3, 1)

6. $3x - 4y = 10$
$-3x + 4y = 8$
no solution

7. $4x - 3y = 15$
$2x + y = 5$
(3, -1)

8. $4x + 5y = 11$
$3x - 2y = -9$
(-1, 3)

9. $2x + 3y = 19$
$7x - y = 9$
(2, 5)

10. $2x - y = 6$
$x + y = 6$
(4, 2)

11. Real Estate AMC Homes, Inc. is planning to build three- and four-bedroom homes in a housing development called Chestnut Hills. Consumer demand indicates a need for three times as many four-bedroom homes as for three-bedroom homes. The net profit from each three-bedroom home is $16,000 and from each four-bedroom home, $17,000. If AMC Homes must net a total profit of $13.4 million from this development, how many homes of each type should they build?
200 three-bedroom, 600 four-bedroom

2-2

Practice

Solving Systems of Equations in Three Variables

Solve each system of equations.

1. $x + y - z = -1$
$x + y + z = 3$
$3x - 2y - z = -4$
(0, 1, 2)

2. $x + y = 5$
$3x + z = 2$
$4y - z = 8$
(10, -5, -28)

3. $3x - 5y + z = 8$
$4y - z = 10$
$7x + y = 4$
(2.2, -11.4, -55.6)

4. $2x + 3y + 3z = 2$
$10x - 6y + 3z = 0$
$4x - 3y - 6z = 2$
$\left(\frac{1}{2}, \frac{2}{3}, -\frac{1}{3}\right)$

5. $2x - y + z = -1$
$x - y + z = 1$
$x - 2y + z = 2$
(-2, -1, 2)

6. $4x + 4y - 2z = 3$
$-6x - 6y + 6z = 5$
$2x - 3y - 4z = 2$
$\left(\frac{13}{3}, -2, \frac{19}{6}\right)$

7. $x - z = 5$
$y + 3z = 12$
$2x + y = 7$
(20, -33, 15)

8. $2x + 4y - 2z = 9$
$4x - 6y + 2z = -9$
$x - y + 3z = -4$
$\left(\frac{1}{2}, \frac{3}{2}, -1\right)$

9. Business The president of Speedy Airlines has discovered that her competitor, Zip Airlines, has purchased 13 new airplanes from Commuter Aviation for a total of $15.9 million. She knows that Commuter Aviation produces three types of planes and that type A sells for $1.1 million, type B sells for $1.2 million, and type C sells for $1.7 million. The president of Speedy Airlines also managed to find out that Zip Airlines purchased 5 more type A planes than type C planes. How many planes of each type did Zip Airlines purchase?
7 type A planes, 4 type B planes, and 2 type C planes

Answers (Lessons 2-3 and 2-4)

2-3 Practice

Modeling Real-World Data with Matrices

Find the values of x and y for which each matrix equation is true.

1. $\begin{bmatrix} x \\ y \end{bmatrix} = \begin{bmatrix} 2y-4 \\ 2x \end{bmatrix}$ $\left(\dfrac{4}{3}, \dfrac{8}{3}\right)$

2. $\begin{bmatrix} 2x-3 \\ 4y \end{bmatrix} = \begin{bmatrix} y \\ 3x \end{bmatrix}$ $\left(\dfrac{12}{5}, \dfrac{9}{5}\right)$

Use matrices A, B, and C to find each sum, difference, or product.

$A = \begin{bmatrix} -1 & 5 & 6 \\ 2 & -7 & -2 \\ 4 & 4 & 2 \end{bmatrix}$ $B = \begin{bmatrix} 2 & 3 & 1 \\ -1 & 1 & 4 \\ 5 & -2 & 3 \end{bmatrix}$ $C = \begin{bmatrix} 8 & 10 & -9 \\ -6 & 12 & 14 \end{bmatrix}$

3. $A + B$ $\begin{bmatrix} 1 & 8 & 7 \\ 1 & -6 & 2 \\ 9 & 2 & 5 \end{bmatrix}$

4. $A - B$ $\begin{bmatrix} -3 & 2 & 5 \\ 3 & -8 & -6 \\ -1 & 6 & -1 \end{bmatrix}$

5. $B - A$ $\begin{bmatrix} 3 & -2 & -5 \\ -3 & 8 & 6 \\ 1 & -6 & 1 \end{bmatrix}$

6. $-2A$ $\begin{bmatrix} 2 & -10 & -12 \\ -4 & 14 & 4 \\ -8 & -8 & -4 \end{bmatrix}$

7. CA $\begin{bmatrix} -24 & -66 & 10 \\ 86 & -58 & -32 \end{bmatrix}$

8. AB $\begin{bmatrix} 23 & -10 & 37 \\ 1 & 3 & -32 \\ 14 & 12 & 26 \end{bmatrix}$

9. AA $\begin{bmatrix} 35 & -16 & -4 \\ -24 & 51 & 22 \\ -12 & 0 & 20 \end{bmatrix}$

10. CB $\begin{bmatrix} -39 & 52 & 21 \\ 46 & -34 & 84 \end{bmatrix}$

11. $(CA)B$ $\begin{bmatrix} 68 & -158 & -258 \\ 70 & 264 & -242 \end{bmatrix}$

12. $C(AB)$ $\begin{bmatrix} 68 & -158 & -258 \\ 70 & 264 & -242 \end{bmatrix}$

13. **Entertainment** On one weekend, the Goxfield Theater reported the following ticket sales for three first-run movies, as shown in the matrix at the right. If the ticket prices were \$6 for each adult and \$4 for each child, what were the weekend sales for each movie.
M1: \$8218; M2: \$18,422; M3: \$31,736

	Adults	Children
Movie 1	1021	523
Movie 2	2547	785
Movie 3	3652	2456

2-4 Practice

Modeling Motion with Matrices

Use scalar multiplication to determine the coordinates of the vertices of each dilated figure. Then graph the pre-image and the image on the same coordinate grid.

1. triangle with vertices A(1, 2), B(2, −1), and C(−2, 0); scale factor 2
A'(2, 4), B'(4, −2), C'(−4, 0)

2. quadrilateral with vertices E(−2, −7), F(4, −3), G(0, 1), and H(−4, −2); scale factor 0.5
E'(−1, −3.5), F'(2, −1.5), G'(0, 0.5), H'(−2, −1)

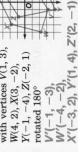

Use matrices to determine the coordinates of the vertices of each translated figure. Then graph the pre-image and the image on the same coordinate grid.

3. square with vertices W(1, −3), X(−4, −2), Y(−3, 3), and Z(2, 2) translated 2 units right and 3 units down W'(3, −6), X'(−2, −5), Y'(−1, 0), Z'(4, −1)

4. triangle with vertices J(3, 1), K(2, −4), and L(0, −2) translated 4 units left and 2 units up J'(−1, 3), K'(−2, −2), L'(−4, 0)

Use matrices to determine the coordinates of the vertices of each reflected figure. Then graph the pre-image and the image on the same coordinate grid.

5. △MNP with vertices M(−3, 4), N(3, 1), and P(−4, −3) reflected over the y-axis M'(3, 4), N'(−3, 1), P'(4, −3)

6. a rhombus with vertices Q(2, 3), R(4, −1), S(−1, −2), and T(−3, 2) reflected over the line y = x Q'(3, 2), R'(−1, 4), S'(−2, −1), T'(2, −3)

Use matrices to determine the coordinates of the vertices of each rotated figure. Then graph the pre-image and the image on the same coordinate grid.

7. quadrilateral CDFG with vertices C(−2, 3), D(3, 4), F(3, −1), and G(−3, −4) rotated 90°
C'(−3, −2), D'(−4, 3), F'(1, 3), G'(4, −3)

8. Pentagon VWXYZ with vertices V(1, 3), W(4, 2), X(3, −2), Y(−1, −4), Z(−2, 1) rotated 180°
V'(−1, −3), W'(−4, −2), X'(−3, 2), Y'(1, 4), Z'(2, −1)

2-5

NAME _____ DATE _____ PERIOD _____

Practice

Determinants and Multiplicative Inverses of Matrices

Find the value of each determinant.

1. $\begin{vmatrix} -2 & 3 \\ 8 & -12 \end{vmatrix}$

   0

2. $\begin{vmatrix} 3 & -5 \\ 7 & 9 \end{vmatrix}$

   62

3. $\begin{vmatrix} 1 & -1 & 0 \\ 3 & 2 & 4 \\ 5 & -3 & 5 \end{vmatrix}$

   7

4. $\begin{vmatrix} 2 & 3 & 1 \\ -3 & -1 & 5 \\ 1 & -4 & 2 \end{vmatrix}$

   82

Find the inverse of each matrix, if it exists.

5. $\begin{vmatrix} 3 & 8 \\ -1 & 5 \end{vmatrix}$

   $\frac{1}{23}\begin{vmatrix} 5 & -8 \\ 1 & 3 \end{vmatrix}$

6. $\begin{vmatrix} 5 & 2 \\ 10 & 4 \end{vmatrix}$

   does not exist

Solve each system by using matrix equations.

7. $2x - 3y = 17$
   $3x + y = 9$
   $(4, -3)$

8. $4x - 3y = -16$
   $2x + 5y = 18$
   $(-1, 4)$

Solve each matrix equation.

9. $\begin{vmatrix} 2 & -1 & 3 \\ 1 & 2 & 1 \\ -1 & -3 & -2 \end{vmatrix} \cdot \begin{vmatrix} x \\ y \\ z \end{vmatrix} = \begin{vmatrix} -8 \\ 3 \\ -7 \end{vmatrix}$, if the inverse is $-\frac{1}{6}\begin{vmatrix} -1 & -11 & -7 \\ 1 & -1 & 1 \\ -1 & 7 & 5 \end{vmatrix}$

   $(-4, 3, 1)$

10. $\begin{vmatrix} 5 & -2 & 4 \\ 3 & -4 & 2 \\ 1 & -3 & 1 \end{vmatrix} \cdot \begin{vmatrix} x \\ y \\ z \end{vmatrix} = \begin{vmatrix} -2 \\ 0 \\ 1 \end{vmatrix}$, if the inverse is $-\frac{1}{8}\begin{vmatrix} 2 & -10 & 12 \\ -1 & 1 & 2 \\ -5 & 13 & -14 \end{vmatrix}$

    $\left(-1, -\frac{1}{2}, \frac{1}{2}\right)$

11. **Landscaping** Two dump truck have capacities of 10 tons and 12 tons. They make a total of 20 round trips to haul 226 tons of topsoil for a landscaping project. How many round trips does each truck make?
    7 trips by the 10-ton truck, 13 trips by the 12-ton truck

30 *Advanced Mathematical Concepts*

2-6

NAME _____ DATE _____ PERIOD _____

Practice

Solving Systems of Linear Inequalities

Solve each system of inequalities by graphing.

1. $-4x + 7y \geq -21; \ 3x + 7y \leq 28$

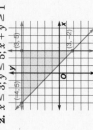

2. $x \leq 3; \ y \leq 5; \ x + y \geq 1$

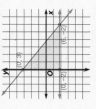

Solve each system of inequalities by graphing. Name the coordinates of the vertices of the polygonal convex set.

3. $x \geq 0; \ y \geq 0; \ y \geq x - 4; \ 7x + 6y \leq 54$

   vertices: $(0, 0), (0, 9), (6, 2), (4, 0)$

4. $x \geq 0; \ y \geq 0; \ y + 2 \geq 0; \ 5x + 6y \leq 18$

   vertices: $(0, 3), (0, -2), (6, -2)$

Find the maximum and minimum values of each function for the polygonal convex set determined by the given system of inequalities.

5. $3x - 2y \geq 0 \quad y \geq 0 \quad f(x, y) = 7y - 3x$
   $3x + 2y \leq 24$
   max $= 30$
   min $= -24$

6. $y \leq -x + 8 \quad 4x - 3y \geq -3 \quad f(x, y) = 4x - 5y$
   $x + 8y \geq 8$
   max $= 32$
   min $= -13$

7. **Business** Henry Jackson, a recent college graduate, plans to start his own business manufacturing bicycle tires. Henry knows that his start-up costs are going to be $3000 and that each tire will cost him at least $2 to manufacture. In order to remain competitive, Henry cannot charge more than $5 per tire. Draw a graph to show when Henry will make a profit.

32 *Advanced Mathematical Concepts*

NAME _____ DATE _____ PERIOD _____

2-7

Practice

Linear Programing

Graph each system of inequalities. In a problem asking you to find the maximum value of f(x, y), state whether the situation is infeasible, has alternate optimal solutions, or is unbounded. In each system, assume that $x \geq 0$ and $y \geq 0$ unless stated otherwise.

1. $-2y \leq 2x - 36$ **infeasible**

$x + y \geq 30$

$f(x, y) = 3x + 3y$

2. $2x + 2y \geq 10$ **unbounded**

$2x + y \geq 8$

$f(x, y) = x + y$

Solve each problem, if possible. If not possible, state whether the problem is infeasible, has alternate optimal solutions, or is unbounded.

3. *Nutrition* A diet is to include at least 140 milligrams of Vitamin A and at least 145 milligrams of Vitamin B. These requirements can be obtained from two types of food. Type X contains 10 milligrams of Vitamin A and 20 milligrams of Vitamin B per pound. Type Y contains 30 milligrams of Vitamin A and 15 milligrams of Vitamin B per pound. If type X food costs $12 per pound and type Y food costs $8 per pound how many pounds of each type of food should be purchased to satisfy the requirements at the minimum cost?

$9\frac{2}{3}$ **pounds of Y and 0 pounds of X**

4. *Manufacturing* The Cruiser Bicycle Company makes two styles of bicycles: the Traveler, which sells for $200, and the Tourester, which sells $600. Each bicycle has the same frame and tires, but the assembly and painting time required for the Traveler is only 1 hour, while it is 3 hours for the Tourister. There are 300 frames and 360 hours of labor available for production. How many bicycles of each model should be produced to maximize revenue?

alternate optimal

Advanced Mathematical Concepts

© Glencoe/McGraw-Hill

3-1

Study Guide

Symmetry and Coordinate Graphs

One type of symmetry a graph may have is **point symmetry.** A
common point of symmetry is the origin. Another type is **line
symmetry.** Some common lines of symmetry are the x-axis, the
y-axis, and the lines $y = x$ and $y = -x$.

point	x-axis	y-axis	$y = x$	$y = -x$

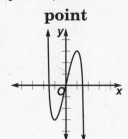 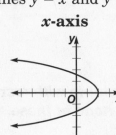 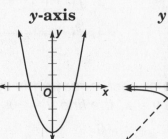 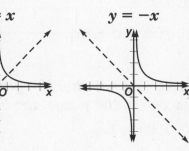

Example 1 **Determine whether $f(x) = x^3$ is symmetric with
respect to the origin.**

If $f(-x) = -f(x)$, the graph has point symmetry.

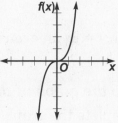

Find $f(-x)$.
$f(-x) = (-x)^3$
$f(-x) = -x^3$

Find $-f(x)$.
$-f(x) = -x^3$

The graph of $f(x) = x^3$ is symmetric with respect
to the origin because $f(-x) = -f(x)$.

Example 2 **Determine whether the graph of $x^2 + 2 = y^2$ is
symmetric with respect to the x-axis, the y-axis,
the line $y = x$, the line $y = -x$, or none of these.**

Substituting (a, b) into the equation yields
$a^2 + 2 = b^2$. Check to see if each test produces
an equation equivalent to $a^2 + 2 = b^2$.

x-axis
$a^2 + 2 = (-b)^2$ *Substitute $(a, -b)$ into the equation.*
$a^2 + 2 = b^2$ *Equivalent to $a^2 + 2 = b^2$*

y-axis
$(-a)^2 + 2 = b^2$ *Substitute $(-a, b)$ into the equation.*
$a^2 + 2 = b^2$ *Equivalent to $a^2 + 2 = b^2$*

$y = x$
$(b)^2 + 2 = (a)^2$ *Substitute (b, a) into the equation.*
$a^2 - 2 = b^2$ *Not equivalent to $a^2 + 2 = b^2$*

$y = -x$
$(-b)^2 + 2 = (-a)^2$ *Substitute $(-b, -a)$ into the equation.*
$b^2 + 2 = a^2$ *Simplify.*
$a^2 - 2 = b^2$ *Not equivalent to $a^2 + 2 = b^2$*

Therefore, the graph of $x^2 + 2 = y^2$ is symmetric with respect to
the x-axis and the y-axis.

Advanced Mathematical Concepts

3-1

Practice

Symmetry and Coordinate Graphs

Determine whether the graph of each function is symmetric with respect to the origin.

1. $f(x) = \dfrac{-12}{x}$

2. $f(x) = x^5 - 2$

3. $f(x) = x^3 - 4x$

4. $f(x) = \dfrac{x^2}{3 - x}$

Determine whether the graph of each equation is symmetric with respect to the x-axis, the y-axis, the line y = x, the line y = −x, or none of these.

5. $x + y = 6$

6. $x^2 + y = 2$

7. $xy = 3$

8. $x^3 + y^2 = 4$

9. $y = 4x$

10. $y = x^2 - 1$

11. Is $f(x) = |x|$ an even function, an odd function, or neither?

Refer to the graph at the right for Exercises 12 and 13.

12. Complete the graph so that it is the graph of an odd function.

13. Complete the graph so that it is the graph of an even function.

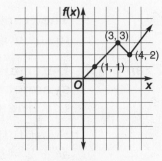

14. *Geometry*   Cameron told her friend Juanita that the graph of $|y| = 6 - |3x|$ has the shape of a geometric figure. Determine whether the graph of $|y| = 6 - |3x|$ is symmetric with respect to the *x*-axis, the *y*-axis, both, or neither. Then make a sketch of the graph. Is Cameron correct?

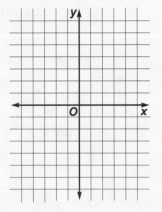

3-2

Study Guide

Families of Graphs

A **parent graph** is a basic graph that is transformed to create other members in a family of graphs. The transformed graph may appear in a different location, but it will resemble the parent graph.

A **reflection** flips a graph over a line called the *axis of symmetry*.
A **translation** moves a graph vertically or horizontally.
A **dilation** expands or compresses a graph vertically or horizontally.

Example 1 **Describe how the graphs of $f(x) = \sqrt{x}$ and $g(x) = \sqrt{-x} - 1$ are related.**

The graph of $g(x)$ is a reflection of the graph of $f(x)$ over the y-axis and then translated down 1 unit.

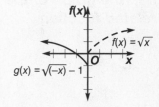

Example 2 **Use the graph of the given parent function to sketch the graph of each related function.**

a. $f(x) = x^3;\ y = x^3 + 2$

When 2 is added to the parent function, the graph of the parent function moves up 2 units.

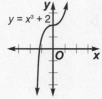
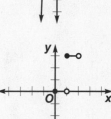

b. $f(x) = [\![x]\!];\ y = 3[\![x]\!]$

The parent function is expanded vertically by a factor of 3, so the vertical distance between the steps is 3 units.

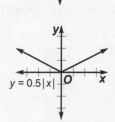

c. $f(x) = |x|;\ y = 0.5|x|$

When $|x|$ is multiplied by a constant greater than 0 but less than 1, the graph compresses vertically, in this case, by a factor of 0.5.

d. $f(x) = x^2;\ y = |x^2 - 4|$

The parent function is translated down 4 units and then any portion of the graph below the x-axis is reflected so that it is above the x-axis.

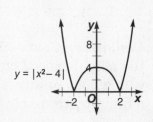

41

3-2

Practice

Families of Graphs

Describe how the graphs of *f(x)* and *g(x)* are related.

1. $f(x) = x^2$ and $g(x) = (x + 3)^2 - 1$

2. $f(x) = |x|$ and $g(x) = -|2x|$

Use the graph of the given parent function to describe the graph of each related function.

3. $f(x) = x^3$

    a. $y = 2x^3$

    b. $y = -0.5(x - 2)^3$

    c. $y = |(x + 1)^3|$

4. $f(x) = \sqrt{x}$

    a. $y = \sqrt{x + 3} + 1$

    b. $y = \sqrt{-x} - 2$

    c. $y = \sqrt{0.25x} - 4$

Sketch the graph of each function.

5. $f(x) = -(x - 1)^2 + 1$

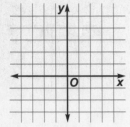

6. $f(x) = 2|x + 2| - 3$

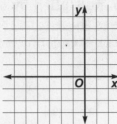

7. Consumer Costs During her free time, Jill baby-sits the neighborhood children. She charges $4.50 for each whole hour or any fraction of an hour. Write and graph a function that shows the cost of *x* hours of baby-sitting.

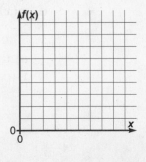

3-3

Study Guide

Graphs of Nonlinear Inequalities

Graphing an inequality in two variables identifies all ordered pairs that satisfy the inequality. The first step in graphing nonlinear inequalities is graphing the boundary.

Example 1   **Graph $y < \sqrt{x - 3} + 2$.**

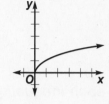

The boundary of the inequality is the graph of $y = \sqrt{x - 3} + 2$. To graph the boundary curve, start with the parent graph $y = \sqrt{x}$. Analyze the boundary equation to determine how the boundary relates to the parent graph.

$$y = \sqrt{x - 3} + 2$$
$$\qquad \uparrow \qquad \uparrow$$
move 3 units right   move 2 units up

Since the boundary is not included in the inequality, the graph is drawn as a dashed curve.

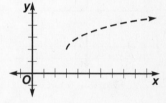

The inequality states that the y−values of the solution are less than the y−values on the graph of $y = \sqrt{x - 3} + 2$. Therefore, for a particular value of x, all of the points in the plane lie below the curve. This portion of the graph should be shaded.

To verify numerically, test a point not on the boundary.

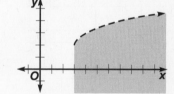

$$y < \sqrt{x - 3} + 2$$
$$0 \overset{?}{<} \sqrt{4 - 3} + 2 \quad \textit{Replace (x, y) with (4, 0).}$$
$$0 < 3 \quad \checkmark \qquad\qquad \textit{True}$$

Since (4, 0) satisfies the inequality, the correct region is shaded.

Example 2   **Solve $|x - 3| - 2 > 7$.**

Two cases must be solved. In one case, $x - 3$ is negative, and in the other, $x - 3$ is positive.

Case 1   If $a < 0$, then $|a| = -a$.   **Case 2**   If $a > 0$, then $|a| = a$.
$$\qquad -(x - 3) - 2 > 7 \qquad\qquad\qquad\qquad x - 3 - 2 > 7$$
$$\qquad\quad -x + 3 - 2 > 7 \qquad\qquad\qquad\qquad\quad x - 5 > 7$$
$$\qquad\qquad\qquad -x > 6 \qquad\qquad\qquad\qquad\qquad\qquad x > 12$$
$$\qquad\qquad\qquad\quad x < -6$$

The solution set is $\{x \mid x < -6 \text{ or } x > 12\}$.

3-3

Practice

Graphs of Nonlinear Inequalities

Determine whether the ordered pair is a solution for the given inequality.
Write yes or no.

1. $y > (x + 2)^2 + 3, (-2, 6)$ **2.** $y < (x - 3)^3 + 2, (4, 5)$ **3.** $y \leq |2x - 4| - 1, (-4, 1)$

Graph each inequality.

4. $y \leq 2|x - 1|$

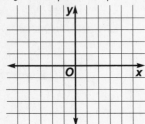

5. $y > 2(x - 1)^2$

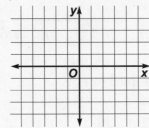

6. $y < \sqrt{x - 2} + 1$

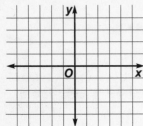

7. $y \geq (x + 3)^3$

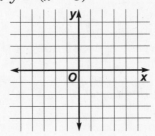

Solve each inequality.

8. $|4x - 10| \leq 6$

9. $|x + 5| + 2 > 6$

10. $|2x - 2| - 1 < 7$

11. *Measurement* Instructions for building a birdhouse warn that the platform, which ideally measures 14.75 cm², should not vary in size by more than 0.30 cm². If it does, the preconstructed roof for the birdhouse will not fit properly.

   a. Write an absolute value inequality that represents the range of possible sizes for the platform. Then solve for x to find the range.

   b. Dena cut a board 14.42 cm². Does the platform that Dena cut fit within the acceptable range?

 Advanced Mathematical Concepts

3-4

Study Guide

Inverse Functions and Relations

Two relations are inverse relations if and only if one relation contains the element (b, a) whenever the other relation contains the element (a, b). If $f(x)$ denotes a function, then $f^{-1}(x)$ denotes the inverse of $f(x)$.

Example 1   **Graph $f(x) = \frac{1}{4}x^3 - 3$ and its inverse.**

To graph the function, let $y = f(x)$. To graph $f^{-1}(x)$, interchange the x- and y-coordinates of the ordered pairs of the function.

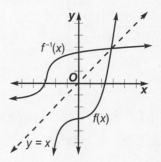

$f(x) = \frac{1}{4}x^3 - 3$	
x	y
−3	−9.75
−2	−5
−1	−3.25
0	−3
1	−2.75
2	−1
3	3.75

$f^{-1}(x)$	
x	y
−9.75	−3
−5	−2
−3.25	−1
−3	0
−2.75	1
−1	2
3.75	3

You can use the **horizontal line test** to determine if the inverse of a relation will be a function. If every horizontal line intersects the graph of the relation in at most one point, then the inverse of the relation is a function.

You can find the inverse of a relation algebraically. First, let $y = f(x)$. Then interchange x and y. Finally, solve the resulting equation for y.

Example 2   **Find the inverse of $f(x) = (x - 1)^2 + 2$. Determine if the inverse is a function.**

$y = (x - 1)^2 + 2$	*Let $y = f(x)$.*
$x = (y - 1)^2 + 2$	*Interchange x and y.*
$x - 2 = (y - 1)^2$	*Isolate the expression containing y.*
$\pm\sqrt{x - 2} = y - 1$	*Take the square root of each side.*
$y = 1 \pm \sqrt{x - 2}$	*Solve for y.*
$f^{-1}(x) = 1 \pm \sqrt{x - 2}$	*Replace y with $f^{-1}(x)$.*

Since the line $y = 4$ intersects the graph of $f(x)$ at more than one point, the function fails the horizontal line test. Thus, the inverse of $f(x)$ is not a function.

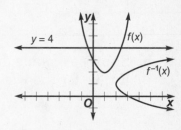

3-4

Practice

Inverse Functions and Relations

Graph each function and its inverse.

1. $f(x) = (x - 1)^3 + 1$

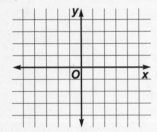

2. $f(x) = 3|x| + 2$

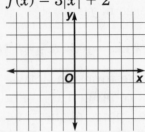

Find $f^{-1}(x)$. Then state whether $f^{-1}(x)$ is a function.

3. $f(x) = -4x^2 + 1$

4. $f(x) = \sqrt[3]{x - 1}$

5. $f(x) = \dfrac{4}{(x - 3)^2}$

Graph each equation using the graph of the given parent function.

6. $y = -\sqrt{x + 3} - 1, \; p(x) = x^2$

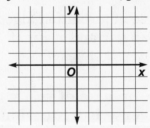

7. $y = 2 + \sqrt[5]{x + 2}, \; p(x) = x^5$

8. *Fire Fighting* Airplanes are often used to drop water on forest fires in an effort to stop the spread of the fire. The time t it takes the water to travel from height h to the ground can be derived from the equation $h = \frac{1}{2}gt^2$ where g is the acceleration due to gravity (32 feet/second^2).

a. Write an equation that will give time as a function of height.

b. Suppose a plane drops water from a height of 1024 feet. How many seconds will it take for the water to hit the ground?

3-5

Study Guide

Continuity and End Behavior

> A function is **continuous** at $x = c$ if it satisfies the following three conditions.
>
> (1) the function is defined at c; in other words, $f(c)$ exists;
>
> (2) the function approaches the same y-value to the left and right of $x = c$; and
>
> (3) the y-value that the function approaches from each side is $f(c)$.

Functions can be continuous or **discontinuous**. Graphs that are discontinuous can exhibit **infinite discontinuity**, **jump discontinuity**, or **point discontinuity**.

Example 1 **Determine whether each function is continuous at the given x-value. Justify your answer using the continuity test.**

a. $f(x) = 2|x| + 3; x = 2$

    (1) The function is defined at $x = 2$; $f(2) = 7$.

    (2) The tables below show that y approaches 7 as x approaches 2 from the left and that y approaches 7 as x approaches 2 from the right.

x	$y = f(x)$
1.9	6.8
1.99	6.98
1.999	6.998

x	$y = f(x)$
2.1	7.2
2.01	7.02
2.001	7.002

    (3) Since the y-values approach 7 as x approaches 2 from both sides and $f(2) = 7$, the function is continuous at $x = 2$.

b. $f(x) = \frac{2x}{x^2 - 1}; x = 1$

Start with the first condition in the continuity test. The function is not defined at $x = 1$ because substituting 1 for x results in a denominator of zero. So the function is discontinuous at $x = 1$.

c. $f(x) = \begin{cases} 2x + 1 & \text{if} \quad x > 2 \\ x - 1 & \text{if} \end{cases}; x = 2$

This function fails the second part of the continuity test because the values of $f(x)$ approach 1 as x approaches 2 from the left, but the values of $f(x)$ approach 5 as x approaches 2 from the right.

The **end behavior** of a function describes what the y-values do as $|x|$ becomes greater and greater. In general, the end behavior of any polynomial function can be modeled by the function made up solely of the term with the highest power of x and its coefficient.

Example 2 **Describe the end behavior of $p(x) = -x^5 + 2x^3 - 4$.**

Determine $f(x) = a_n x^n$ where x^n is the term in $p(x)$ with the highest power of x and a_n is its coefficient.

$f(x) = -x^5 \quad x^n = x^5 \quad a_n = -1$

Thus, by using the table on page 163 of your text, you can see that when a^n is negative and n is odd, the end behavior can be stated as $p(x) \to -\infty$ as $x \to \infty$ and $p(x) \to \infty$ as $x \to -\infty$.

3-5

Practice

Continuity and End Behavior

Determine whether each function is continuous at the given x-value. Justify your answer using the continuity test.

1. $y = \frac{2}{3x^2}; x = -1$

2. $y = \frac{x^2 + x + 4}{2}; x = 1$

3. $y = x^3 - 2x + 2; x = 1$

4. $y = \frac{x - 2}{x + 4}; x = -4$

Describe the end behavior of each function.

5. $y = 2x^5 - 4x$

6. $y = -2x^6 + 4x^4 - 2x + 1$

7. $y = x^4 - 2x^3 + x$

8. $y = -4x^3 + 5$

Given the graph of the function, determine the interval(s) for which the function is increasing and the interval(s) for which the function is decreasing.

9.

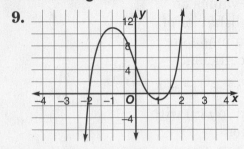

10. *Electronics*   Ohm's Law gives the relationship between resistance R, voltage E, and current I in a circuit as $R = \frac{E}{I}$. If the voltage remains constant but the current keeps increasing in the circuit, what happens to the resistance?

3-6

Study Guide

Critical Points and Extrema

Critical points are points on a graph at which a line drawn tangent to the curve is horizontal or vertical. A critical point may be a **maximum**, a **minimum**, or a **point of inflection.** A point of inflection is a point where the graph changes its curvature. Graphs can have an **absolute maximum**, an **absolute minimum**, a **relative maximum**, or a **relative minimum.** The general term for maximum or minimum is **extremum** (plural, *extrema*).

Example 1 **Locate the extrema for the graph of $y = f(x)$. Name and classify the extrema of the function.**

a.

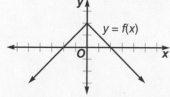

The function has an absolute maximum at $(0, 2)$. The absolute maximum is the greatest value that a function assumes over its domain.

b.

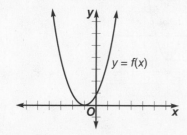

The function has an absolute minimum at $(-1, 0)$. The absolute minimum is the least value that a function assumes over its domain.

c.

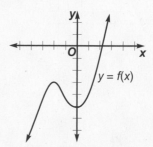

The relative maximum and minimum may not be the greatest and the least y-value for the domain, respectively, but they are the greatest and least y-value on some interval of the domain. The function has a relative maximum at $(-2, -3)$ and a relative minimum at $(0, -5)$. Because the graph indicates that the function increases or decreases without bound as x increases or decreases, there is neither an absolute maximum nor an absolute minimum.

By testing points on both sides of a critical point, you can determine whether the critical point is a relative maximum, a relative minimum, or a point of inflection.

Example 2 **The function $f(x) = 2x^6 + 2x^4 - 9x^2$ has a critical point at $x = 0$. Determine whether the critical point is the location of a maximum, a minimum, or a point of inflection.**

x	$x - 0.1$	$x + 0.1$	$f(x - 0.1)$	$f(x)$	$f(x + 0.1)$	Type of Critical Point
0	−0.1	0.1	−0.0899	0	−0.0899	maximum

Because 0 is greater than both $f(x - 0.1)$ and $f(x + 0.1)$, $x = 0$ is the location of a relative maximum.

NAME _____ DATE _____ PERIOD _____

3-6

Practice

Critical Points and Extrema

Locate the extrema for the graph of y = f(x). Name and classify the extrema of the function.

1.
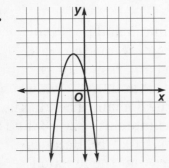

2.
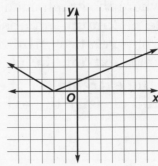

3.
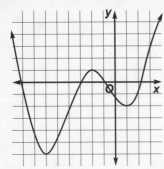

4.
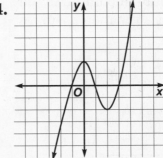

Determine whether the given critical point is the location of a maximum, a minimum, or a point of inflection.

5. $y = x^2 - 6x + 1, x = 3$ **6.** $y = x^2 - 2x - 6, x = 1$ **7.** $y = x^4 + 3x^2 - 5, x = 0$

8. $y = x^5 - 2x^3 - 2x^2, x = 0$ **9.** $y = x^3 + x^2 - x, x = -1$ **10.** $y = 2x^3 + 4, x = 0$

11. *Physics* Suppose that during an experiment you launch a toy rocket straight upward from a height of 6 inches with an initial velocity of 32 feet per second. The height at any time t can be modeled by the function $s(t) = -16t^2 + 32t + 0.5$ where $s(t)$ is measured in feet and t is measured in seconds. Graph the function to find the maximum height obtained by the rocket before it begins to fall.

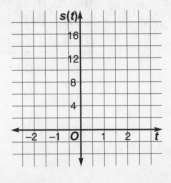

3-7

Study Guide

Graphs of Rational Functions

A **rational function** is a quotient of two polynomial functions.

The line $x = a$ is a **vertical asymptote** for a function $f(x)$ if $f(x) \to \infty$ or $f(x) \to -\infty$ as $x \to a$ from either the left or the right.

The line $y = b$ is a **horizontal asymptote** for a function $f(x)$ if $f(x) \to b$ as $x \to \infty$ or as $x \to -\infty$.

A **slant asymptote** occurs when the degree of the numerator of a rational function is exactly one greater than that of the denominator.

Example 1 Determine the asymptotes for the graph of $f(x) = \frac{2x - 1}{x + 3}$.

Since $f(-3)$ is undefined, there may be a vertical asymptote at $x = -3$. To verify that $x = -3$ is a vertical asymptote, check to see that $f(x) \to \infty$ or $f(x) \to -\infty$ as $x \to -3$ from either the left or the right.

x	$f(x)$
-2.9	-68
-2.99	-698
-2.999	-6998
-2.9999	-69998

The values in the table confirm that $f(x) \to -\infty$ as $x \to -3$ from the right, so there is a vertical asymptote at $x = -3$.

One way to find the horizontal asymptote is to let $f(x) = y$ and solve for x in terms of y. Then find where the function is undefined for values of y.

$$y = \frac{2x - 1}{x + 3}$$
$$y(x + 3) = 2x - 1$$
$$xy + 3y = 2x - 1$$
$$xy - 2x = -3y - 1$$
$$x(y - 2) = -3y - 1$$
$$x = \frac{-3y - 1}{y - 2}$$

The rational expression $\frac{-3y - 1}{y - 2}$ is undefined for $y = 2$. Thus, the horizontal asymptote is the line $y = 2$.

Example 2 Determine the slant asymptote for $f(x) = \frac{3x^2 - 2x + 2}{x - 1}$.

First use division to rewrite the function.

$$
\begin{array}{r}
3x + 1 \\
x - 1 \overline{) 3x^2 - 2x + 2} \\
\underline{3x^2 - 3x} \\
x + 2 \\
\underline{x - 1} \\
3
\end{array}
\quad \to \quad f(x) = 3x + 1 + \frac{3}{x - 1}
$$

As $x \to \infty$, $\frac{3}{x - 1} \to 0$. Therefore, the graph of $f(x)$ will approach that of $y = 3x + 1$. This means that the line $y = 3x + 1$ is a slant asymptote for the graph of $f(x)$.

3-7

Practice

Graphs of Rational Functions

Determine the equations of the vertical and horizontal asymptotes, if any, of each function.

1. $f(x) = \dfrac{4}{x^2 + 1}$

2. $f(x) = \dfrac{2x + 1}{x + 1}$

3. $g(x) = \dfrac{x + 3}{(x + 1)(x - 2)}$

Use the parent graph $f(x) = \dfrac{1}{x}$ to graph each equation. Describe the transformation(s) that have taken place. Identify the new locations of the asymptotes.

4. $y = \dfrac{3}{x + 1} - 2$

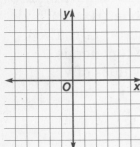

5. $y = -\dfrac{4}{x - 3} + 3$

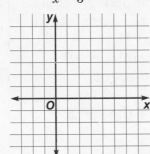

Determine the slant asymptotes of each equation.

6. $y = \dfrac{5x^2 - 10x + 1}{x - 2}$

7. $y = \dfrac{x^2 - x}{x + 1}$

8. Graph the function $y = \dfrac{x^2 + x - 6}{x + 1}$.

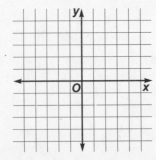

9. *Physics* The illumination I from a light source is given by the formula $I = \dfrac{k}{d^2}$, where k is a constant and d is distance. As the distance from the light source doubles, how does the illumination change?

3-8

Study Guide

Direct, Inverse, and Joint Variation

A **direct variation** can be described by the equation $y = kx^n$. The k in this equation is called the **constant of variation.** To express a direct variation, we say that y varies directly as x^n. An inverse variation can be described by the equation $y = \frac{k}{x^n}$ or $x^n y = k$. When quantities are **inversely proportional,** we say they *vary inversely* with each other. **Joint variation** occurs when one quantity varies directly as the product of two or more other quantities and can be described by the equation $y = kx^n z^n$.

Example 1 Suppose y varies directly as x and $y = 14$ when $x = 8$.
  a. Find the constant of variation and write an equation of the form $y = kx^n$.
  b. Use the equation to find the value of y when $x = 4$.

  a. The power of x is 1, so the direct variation equation is $y = kx$.

  $y = kx$
  $14 = k(8)$ $y = 14, x = 8$
  $1.75 = k$ *Divide each side by 8.*
  The constant of variation is 1.75. The equation relating x and y is $y = 1.75x$.

  b. $y = 1.75x$
  $y = 1.75(4)$ $x = 4$
  $y = 7$
  When $x = 4$, the value of y is 8.

Example 2 If y varies inversely as x and $y = 102$ when $x = 7$, find x when $y = 12$.

  Use a proportion that relates the values.
  $$\frac{x_1{}^n}{y_2} = \frac{x_2{}^n}{y_1}$$
  $\frac{7}{12} = \frac{x}{102}$ *Substitute the known values.*
  $12x = 714$ *Cross multiply.*
  $x = \frac{714}{12}$ or 59.5   *Divide each side by 12.*

  When $y = 12$, the value of x is 59.5.

3-8

Practice

Direct, Inverse, and Joint Variation

Write a statement of variation relating the variables of each equation.
Then name the constant of variation.

1. $-\dfrac{x^2}{y} = 3$

2. $E = IR$

3. $y = 2x$

4. $d = 6t^2$

Find the constant of variation for each relation and use it to write an
equation for each statement. Then solve the equation.

5. Suppose y varies directly as x and $y = 35$ when $x = 5$. Find y when $x = 7$.

6. If y varies directly as the cube of x and $y = 3$ when $x = 2$, find x when $y = 24$.

7. If y varies inversely as x and $y = 3$ when $x = 25$, find x when $y = 10$.

8. Suppose y varies jointly as x and z, and $y = 64$ when $x = 4$ and $z = 8$.
   Find y when $x = 7$ and $z = 11$.

9. Suppose V varies jointly as h and the square of r, and $V = 45\pi$ when $r = 3$ and
   $h = 5$. Find r when $V = 175\pi$ and $h = 7$.

10. If y varies directly as x and inversely as the square of z, and $y = -5$ when $x = 10$ and
    $z = 2$, find y when $x = 5$ and $z = 5$.

11. **Finances**   Enrique deposited $200.00 into a savings account. The simple
    interest I on his account varies jointly as the time t in years and the principal P.
    After one quarter (three months), the interest on Enrique's account is $2.75.
    Write an equation relating interest, principal, and time. Find the constant of
    variation. Then find the interest after three quarters.

3-1

NAME _____ DATE _____ PERIOD _____

Practice

Symmetry and Coordinate Graphs

Determine whether the graph of each function is symmetric with respect to the origin.

1. $f(x) = \dfrac{-12}{x}$ yes

2. $f(x) = x^5 - 2$ no

3. $f(x) = x^3 - 4x$ yes

4. $f(x) = \dfrac{x^2}{3} - x$ no

Determine whether the graph of each equation is symmetric with respect to the x-axis, the y-axis, the line y = x, the line y = -x, or none of these.

5. $x + y = 6$ $y = x$

6. $x^2 + y = 2$ y-axis

7. $xy = 3$ $y = x$ and $y = -x$

8. $x^3 + y^2 = 4$ x-axis

9. $y = 4x$ none of these

10. $y = x^2 - 1$ y-axis

11. Is $f(x) = |x|$ an even function, an odd function, or neither?   even

Refer to the graph at the right for Exercises 12 and 13.

12. Complete the graph so that it is the graph of an odd function.

13. Complete the graph so that it is the graph of an even function.

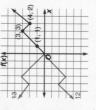

14. **Geometry** Cameron told her friend Juanita that the graph of $|y| = 6 - |3x|$ has the shape of a geometric figure. Determine whether the graph of $|y| = 6 - |3x|$ is symmetric with respect to the x-axis, the y-axis, both, or neither. Then make a sketch of the graph. Is Cameron correct? **x-axis and y-axis; yes, the graph is that of a diamond or parallelogram.**

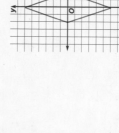

40   *Advanced Mathematical Concepts*

3-2

NAME _____ DATE _____ PERIOD _____

Practice

Families of Graphs

Describe how the graphs of f(x) and g(x) are related.

1. $f(x) = x^2$ and $g(x) = (x + 3)^2 - 1$
   g(x) is the graph of f(x) translated left 3 units and down 1 unit.

2. $f(x) = |x|$ and $g(x) = -|2x|$
   g(x) is the graph of f(x) reflected over the x-axis and compressed horizontally by a factor of 0.5.

Use the graph of the given parent function to describe the graph of each related function.

3. $f(x) = x^3$
   a. $y = 2x^3$
   expanded vertically by a factor of 2

4. $f(x) = \sqrt{x}$
   a. $y = \sqrt{x + 3} + 1$
   translated left 3 units and up 1 unit

   b. $y = -0.5(x - 2)^3$
   reflected over the x-axis, translated right 2 units, compressed vertically by a factor of 0.5

   b. $y = \sqrt{-x} - 2$
   reflected over the y-axis, translated down 2 units

   c. $y = |(x + 1)^3|$
   translated left 1 unit, portion below the x-axis reflected so that it is above the x-axis

   c. $y = \sqrt{0.25x} - 4$
   expanded horizontally by a factor of 4, translated down 4 units

Sketch the graph of each function.

5. $f(x) = -(x - 1)^2 + 1$

6. $f(x) = 2|x + 2| - 3$

7. **Consumer Costs** During her free time, Jill baby-sits the neighborhood children. She charges $4.50 for each whole hour or any fraction of an hour. Write and graph a function that shows the cost of x hours of baby-sitting.

$$f(x) = \begin{cases} 4.5 \text{ if } [\![x]\!] = x \\ 4.5[\![x + 1]\!] \text{ if } [\![x]\!] < x \end{cases}$$

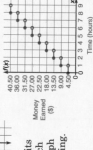

Money Earned ($)

Time (hours)

42   *Advanced Mathematical Concepts*

3-3 Practice

Graphs of Nonlinear Inequalities

Determine whether the ordered pair is a solution for the given inequality. Write yes or no.

1. $y > (x + 2)^2 + 3$, $(-2, 6)$
yes

2. $y < (x - 3)^3 + 2$, $(4, 5)$
no

3. $y \leq |2x - 4| - 1$, $(-4, 1)$
yes

Graph each inequality.

4. $y \leq 2|x - 1|$

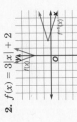

5. $y > 2(x - 1)^2$

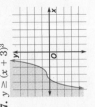

6. $y < \sqrt{x - 2} + 1$

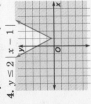

7. $y \geq (x + 3)^3$

Solve each inequality.

8. $|4x - 10| \leq 6$
$\{x \mid 1 \leq x \leq 4\}$

9. $|x + 5| + 2 > 6$
$\{x \mid x < -9 \text{ or } x > -1\}$

10. $|2x - 2| - 1 < 7$
$\{x \mid -3 < x < 5\}$

11. **Measurement** Instructions for building a birdhouse warn that the platform, which ideally measures 14.75 cm², should not vary in size by more than 0.30 cm². If it does, the preconstructed roof for the birdhouse will not fit properly.

a. Write an absolute value inequality that represents the range of possible sizes for the platform. Then solve for x to find the range.
$|x - 14.75| \leq 0.30$; $\{x \mid 14.45 \leq x \leq 15.05\}$

b. Dena cut a board 14.42 cm². Does the platform that Dena cut fit within the acceptable range? **no**

3-4 Practice

Inverse Functions and Relations

Graph each function and its inverse.

1. $f(x) = (x - 1)^3 + 1$

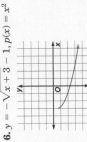

2. $f(x) = 3|x| + 2$

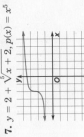

Find $f^{-1}(x)$. Then state whether $f^{-1}(x)$ is a function.

3. $f(x) = -4x^2 + 1$
$f^{-1}(x) = \pm\frac{1}{2}\sqrt{1 - x}$
no

4. $f(x) = \sqrt[3]{x - 1}$
$f^{-1}(x) = x^3 + 1$
yes

5. $f(x) = \frac{4}{(x - 3)^2}$
$f^{-1}(x) = 3 \pm \frac{2\sqrt{x}}{x}$
no

Graph each equation using the graph of the given parent function.

6. $y = -\sqrt{x + 3} - 1$, $p(x) = x^2$

7. $y = 2 + \sqrt[5]{x + 2}$, $p(x) = x^5$

8. **Fire Fighting** Airplanes are often used to drop water on forest fires in an effort to stop the spread of the fire. The time t it takes the water to travel from height h to the ground can be derived from the equation $h = \frac{1}{2}gt^2$ where g is the acceleration due to gravity (32 feet/second²).

a. Write an equation that will give time as a function of height.
$t = \sqrt{\frac{h}{16}}$

b. Suppose a plane drops water from a height of 1024 feet. How many seconds will it take for the water to hit the ground? **8 seconds**

3-5 Practice

Continuity and End Behavior

Determine whether each function is continuous at the given x-value. Justify your answer using the continuity test.

1. $y = \dfrac{2}{3x^2}; x = -1$
   Yes; the function is defined at $x = -1$; y approaches $\frac{2}{3}$ as x approaches -1 from both sides; $f(-1) = \frac{2}{3}$.

2. $y = \dfrac{x^2 + x + 4}{2}; x = 1$
   Yes; the function is defined at $x = 1$; y approaches 3 as x approaches 1 from both sides; $f(1) = 3$.

3. $y = x^3 - 2x + 2; x = 1$
   Yes; the function is defined at $x = 1$; y approaches 1 as x approaches 1 from both sides; $f(1) = 1$.

4. $y = \dfrac{x - 2}{x + 4}; x = -4$
   No; the function is undefined at $x = -4$.

Describe the end behavior of each function.

5. $y = 2x^5 - 4x$
   $y \to \infty$ as $x \to \infty$,
   $y \to -\infty$ as $x \to -\infty$

6. $y = -2x^6 + 4x^4 - 2x + 1$
   $y \to -\infty$ as $x \to \infty$,
   $y \to -\infty$ as $x \to -\infty$

7. $y = x^4 - 2x^3 + x$
   $y \to \infty$ as $x \to \infty$,
   $y \to \infty$ as $x \to -\infty$

8. $y = -4x^3 + 5$
   $y \to -\infty$ as $x \to \infty$,
   $y \to \infty$ as $x \to -\infty$

Given the graph of the function, determine the interval(s) for which the function is increasing and the interval(s) for which the function is decreasing.

9.

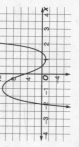

increasing for $x < -1$ and $x > 1$; decreasing for $-1 < x < 1$

10. **Electronics** Ohm's Law gives the relationship between resistance R, voltage E, and current I in a circuit as $R = \dfrac{E}{I}$. If the voltage remains constant but the current keeps increasing in the circuit, what happens to the resistance? Resistance decreases and approaches zero.

48 *Advanced Mathematical Concepts*

3-6 Practice

Critical Points and Extrema

Locate the extrema for the graph of $y = f(x)$. Name and classify the extrema of the function.

1.

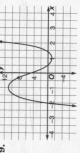

relative maximum: $(-2, 1)$
relative minimum: $(1, -2)$
absolute minimum: $(-6, -6)$

2.

absolute minimum: $(-2, 0)$

3.

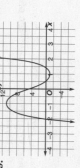

absolute maximum: $(-1, 3)$

4.

relative maximum: $(0, 2)$
relative minimum: $(2, -2)$

Determine whether the given critical point is the location of a maximum, a minimum, or a point of inflection.

5. $y = x^2 - 6x + 1, x = 3$
   minimum

6. $y = x^2 - 2x - 6, x = 1$
   minimum

7. $y = x^4 + 3x^2 - 5, x = 0$
   minimum

8. $y = x^5 - 2x^3 - 2x^2, x = 0$
   maximum

9. $y = x^3 + x^2 - x, x = -1$
   maximum

10. $y = 2x^3 + 4, x = 0$
    point of inflection

11. **Physics** Suppose that during an experiment you launch a toy rocket straight upward from a height of 6 inches with an initial velocity of 32 feet per second. The height at any time t can be modeled by the function $s(t) = -16t^2 + 32t + 0.5$ where $s(t)$ is measured in feet and t is measured in seconds. Graph the function to find the maximum height obtained by the rocket before it begins to fall. **16.5 ft**

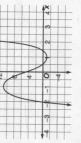

50 *Advanced Mathematical Concepts*

3-7

NAME _____ DATE _____ PERIOD _____

Practice

Graphs of Rational Functions

Determine the equations of the vertical and horizontal asymptotes, if any, of each function.

1. $f(x) = \dfrac{4}{x^2 + 1}$
$y = 0$

2. $f(x) = \dfrac{2x+1}{x+1}$
$x = -1, y = 2$

3. $g(x) = \dfrac{x+3}{(x+1)(x-2)}$
$x = -1, x = 2, y = 0$

Use the parent graph $f(x) = \dfrac{1}{x}$ to graph each equation. Describe the transformation(s) that have taken place. Identify the new locations of the asymptotes.

4. $y = \dfrac{3}{x+1} - 2$

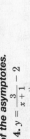

expanded vertically by a factor of 3; translated left 1 unit and down 2 units;
$x = -1, y = -2$

5. $y = -\dfrac{4}{x-3} + 3$

reflected over x-axis; expanded vertically by a factor of 4; translated right 3 units and up 3 units; $x = 3, y = 3$

Determine the slant asymptotes of each equation.

6. $y = \dfrac{5x^2 - 10x + 1}{x - 2}$
$y = 5x$

7. $y = \dfrac{x^2 - x}{x + 1}$
$y = x - 2$

8. Graph the function $y = \dfrac{x^2 + x - 6}{x + 1}$.

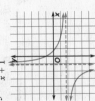

9. **Physics** The illumination I from a light source is given by the formula $I = \dfrac{k}{d^2}$, where k is a constant and d is distance. As the distance from the light source doubles, how does the illumination change? It decreases by one fourth.

3-8

NAME _____ DATE _____ PERIOD _____

Practice

Direct, Inverse, and Joint Variation

Write a statement of variation relating the variables of each equation. Then name the constant of variation.

1. $-\dfrac{x^2}{y} = 3$
y varies directly as the square of x; $-\dfrac{1}{3}$

2. $E = IR$
E varies jointly as I and R; 1

3. $y = 2x$
y varies directly as x; 2

4. $d = 6t^2$
d varies directly as the square of t; 6

Find the constant of variation for each relation and use it to write an equation for each statement. Then solve the equation.

5. Suppose y varies directly as x and $y = 35$ when $x = 5$. Find y when $x = 7$.
$7; y = 7x; 49$

6. If y varies directly as the cube of x and $y = 3$ when $x = 2$, find x when $y = 24$.
$\dfrac{3}{8}; y = \dfrac{3}{8}x^3; 4$

7. If y varies inversely as x and $y = 3$ when $x = 25$, find x when $y = 10$.
$75; y = \dfrac{75}{x}; 7.5$

8. Suppose y varies jointly as x and z, and $y = 64$ when $x = 4$ and $z = 8$. Find y when $x = 7$ and $z = 11$.
$2; y = 2xz; 154$

9. Suppose V varies jointly as h and the square of r, and $V = 45\pi$ when $r = 3$ and $h = 5$. Find r when $V = 175\pi$ and $h = 7$.
$\pi; V = \pi r^2 h; 5$

10. If y varies directly as x and inversely as the square of z, and $y = -5$ when $x = 10$ and $z = 2$, find y when $x = 5$ and $z = 5$.
$-2; y = -2\dfrac{x}{z^2}; -0.4$

11. **Finances** Enrique deposited $200.00 into a savings account. The simple interest I on his account varies jointly as the time t in years and the principal P. After one quarter (three months), the interest on Enrique's account is $2.75. Write an equation relating interest, principal, and time. Find the constant of variation. Then find the interest after three quarters.
$I = kPt; 0.055; 8.25

4-1

Study Guide

Polynomial Functions

The **degree** of a polynomial in one variable is the greatest exponent of its variable. The coefficient of the variable with the greatest exponent is called the **leading coefficient.** If a function $f(x)$ is defined by a polynomial in one variable, then it is a polynomial function. The values of x for which $f(x) = 0$ are called the **zeros** of the function. Zeros of the function are **roots** of the **polynomial equation** when $f(x) = 0$. A polynomial equation of degree n has exactly n roots in the set of complex numbers.

Example 1 **State the degree and leading coefficient of the polynomial function $f(x) = 6x^5 + 8x^3 - 8x$. Then determine whether $\sqrt{\frac{2}{3}}$ is a zero of $f(x)$.**

$6x^5 + 8x^3 - 8x$ has a degree of 5 and a leading coefficient of 6.

Evaluate the function for $x = \sqrt{\frac{2}{3}}$. That is, find $f\left(\sqrt{\frac{2}{3}}\right)$.

$$f\left(\sqrt{\frac{2}{3}}\right) = 6\left(\sqrt{\frac{2}{3}}\right)^5 + 8\left(\sqrt{\frac{2}{3}}\right)^3 - 8\left(\sqrt{\frac{2}{3}}\right) \qquad x = \sqrt{\frac{2}{3}}$$

$$= \frac{24}{9}\sqrt{\frac{2}{3}} + \frac{16}{3}\sqrt{\frac{2}{3}} - 8\sqrt{\frac{2}{3}}$$

$$= 0$$

Since $f\left(\sqrt{\frac{2}{3}}\right) = 0$, $\sqrt{\frac{2}{3}}$ is a zero of $f(x) = 6x^5 + 8x^3 - 8x$.

Example 2 **Write a polynomial equation of least degree with roots 0, $\sqrt{2}i$, and $-\sqrt{2}i$.**

The linear factors for the polynomial are $x - 0$, $x - \sqrt{2}i$, and $x + \sqrt{2}i$. Find the products of these factors.

$$(x - 0)(x - \sqrt{2}i)(x + \sqrt{2}i) = 0$$
$$x(x^2 - 2i^2) = 0$$
$$x(x^2 + 2) = 0 \quad -2i^2 = -2(-1) \text{ or } 2$$
$$x^3 + 2x = 0$$

Example 3 **State the number of complex roots of the equation $3x^2 + 11x - 4 = 0$. Then find the roots.**

The polynomial has a degree of 2, so there are two complex roots. Factor the equation to find the roots.

$$3x^2 + 11x - 4 = 0$$
$$(3x - 1)(x + 4) = 0$$

To find each root, set each factor equal to zero.

$$3x - 1 = 0 \qquad \qquad x + 4 = 0$$
$$3x = 1 \qquad \qquad x = -4$$
$$x = \frac{1}{3}$$

The roots are -4 and $\frac{1}{3}$.

4-1

Practice

Polynomial Functions

State the degree and leading coefficient of each polynomial.

1. $6a^4 + a^3 - 2a$

2. $3p^2 - 7p^5 - 2p^3 + 5$

Write a polynomial equation of least degree for each set of roots.

3. $3, -0.5, 1$

4. $3, 3, 1, 1, -2$

5. $\pm 2i, 3, -3$

6. $-1, 3 \pm i, 2 \pm 3i$

State the number of complex roots of each equation. Then find the roots and graph the related function.

7. $3x - 5 = 0$

8. $x^2 + 4 = 0$

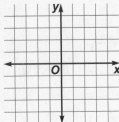

9. $c^2 + 2c + 1 = 0$

10. $x^3 + 2x^2 - 15x = 0$

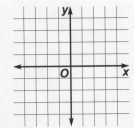

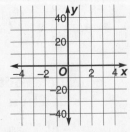

11. *Real Estate* A developer wants to build homes on a rectangular plot of land 3 kilometers long and 4 kilometers wide. In this part of the city, regulations require a greenbelt of uniform width along two adjacent sides. The greenbelt must be 10 times the area of the development. Find the width of the greenbelt.

4-2

Study Guide

Quadratic Equations

A quadratic equation is a polynomial equation with a degree of 2. Solving quadratic equations by graphing usually does not yield exact answers. Also, some quadratic expressions are not factorable. However, solutions can always be obtained by **completing the square.**

Example 1 **Solve $x^2 - 12x + 7 = 0$ by completing the square.**

$$x^2 - 12x + 7 = 0$$

$$x^2 - 12x = -7 \qquad \text{\textit{Subtract 7 from each side.}}$$

$$x^2 - 12x + 36 = -7 + 36 \qquad \begin{array}{l}\textit{Complete the square by adding } \left[\tfrac{1}{2}(-12)\right]^2, \\ \textit{or 36, to each side.}\end{array}$$

$$(x - 6)^2 = 29 \qquad \textit{Factor the perfect square trinomial.}$$

$$x - 6 = \pm\sqrt{29} \qquad \textit{Take the square root of each side.}$$

$$x = 6 \pm \sqrt{29} \qquad \textit{Add 6 to each side.}$$

The roots of the equation are $6 \pm \sqrt{29}$.

Completing the square can be used to develop a general formula for solving any quadratic equation of the form $ax^2 + bx + c = 0$. This formula is called the **Quadratic Formula** and can be used to find the roots of any quadratic equation.

Quadratic Formula	If $ax^2 + bx + c = 0$ with $a \neq 0$, $x = \dfrac{-b \pm \sqrt{b^2 - 4ac}}{2a}$.

In the Quadratic Formula, the radicand $b^2 - 4ac$ is called the **discriminant** of the equation. The discriminant tells the nature of the roots of a quadratic equation or the zeros of the related quadratic function.

Example 2 **Find the discriminant of $2x^2 - 3x = 7$ and describe the nature of the roots of the equation. Then solve the equation by using the Quadratic Formula.**

Rewrite the equation using the standard form $ax^2 + bx + c = 0$.

$2x^2 - 3x - 7 = 0 \qquad a = 2,\ b = -3,\ and\ c = -7$

The value of the discriminant $b^2 - 4ac$ is $(-3)^2 - 4(2)(-7)$, or 65.

Since the value of the discriminant is greater than zero, there are two distinct real roots.

Now substitute the coefficients into the quadratic formula and solve.

$$x = \frac{-(-3) \pm \sqrt{(-3)^2 - 4(2)(-7)}}{2(2)} \qquad x = \frac{-b \pm \sqrt{b^2 - 4ac}}{2a}$$

$$x = \frac{3 \pm \sqrt{65}}{4}$$

The roots are $\dfrac{3 + \sqrt{65}}{4}$ and $\dfrac{3 - \sqrt{65}}{4}$.

4-2

Practice

Quadratic Equations

Solve each equation by completing the square.

1. $x^2 - 5x - \frac{11}{4} = 0$

2. $-4x^2 - 11x = 7$

Find the discriminant of each equation and describe the nature of the roots of the equation. Then solve the equation by using the Quadratic Formula.

3. $x^2 + x - 6 = 0$

4. $4x^2 - 4x - 15 = 0$

5. $9x^2 - 12x + 4 = 0$

6. $3x^2 + 2x + 5 = 0$

Solve each equation.

7. $2x^2 + 5x - 12 = 0$

8. $5x^2 - 14x + 11 = 0$

9. *Architecture* The ancient Greek mathematicians thought that the most pleasing geometric forms, such as the ratio of the height to the width of a doorway, were created using the *golden section*. However, they were surprised to learn that the golden section is not a rational number. One way of expressing the golden section is by using a line segment. In the line segment shown, $\frac{AB}{AC} = \frac{AC}{CB}$. If $AC = 1$ unit, find the ratio $\frac{AB}{AC}$.

A   C   B

4-3

Study Guide

The Remainder and Factor Theorems

The Remainder Theorem	If a polynomial $P(x)$ is divided by $x - r$, the remainder is a constant $P(r)$, and $P(x) = (x - r) \cdot Q(x) + P(r)$ where $Q(x)$ is a polynomial with degree one less than the degree of $P(x)$.

Example 1 **Divide $x^4 - 5x^2 - 17x - 12$ by $x + 3$.**

$$
\begin{array}{r}
x^3 - 3x^2 + 4x - 29 \\
x + 3\overline{)x^4 + 0x^3 - 5x^2 - 17x - 12} \\
\underline{x^4 + 3x^3} \\
-3x^3 - 5x^2 \\
\underline{-3x^3 - 9x^2} \\
4x^2 - 17x \\
\underline{4x^2 + 12x} \\
-29x - 12 \\
\underline{-29x - 87} \\
75 \leftarrow remainder
\end{array}
$$

Find the value of r in this division.

$x - r = x + 3$

$-r = 3$

$r = -3$

According to the Remainder Theorem, $P(r)$ or $P(-3)$ should equal 75.

Use the Remainder Theorem to check the remainder found by long division.

$$P(x) = x^4 - 5x^2 - 17x - 12$$
$$P(-3) = (-3)^4 - 5(-3)^2 - 17(-3) - 12$$
$$= 81 - 45 + 51 - 12 \text{ or } 75$$

The Factor Theorem is a special case of the Remainder Theorem and can be used to quickly test for factors of a polynomial.

The Factor Theorem	The binomial $x - r$ is a factor of the polynomial $P(x)$ if and only if $P(r) = 0$.

Example 2 **Use the Remainder Theorem to find the remainder when $2x^3 + 5x^2 - 14x - 8$ is divided by $x - 2$. State whether the binomial is a factor of the polynomial. Explain.**

Find $f(2)$ to see if $x - 2$ is a factor.

$$f(x) = 2x^3 + 5x^2 - 14x - 8$$
$$f(2) = 2(2)^3 + 5(2)^2 - 14(2) - 8$$
$$= 16 + 20 - 28 - 8$$
$$= 0$$

Since $f(2) = 0$, the remainder is 0. So the binomial $x - 2$ is a factor of the polynomial by the Factor Theorem.

4-3

Practice

The Remainder and Factor Theorems

Divide using synthetic division.

1. $(3x^2 + 4x - 12) \div (x + 5)$ **2.** $(x^2 - 5x - 12) \div (x - 3)$

3. $(x^4 - 3x^2 + 12) \div (x + 1)$ **4.** $(2x^3 + 3x^2 - 8x + 3) \div (x + 3)$

Use the Remainder Theorem to find the remainder for each division. State whether the binomial is a factor of the polynomial.

5. $(2x^4 + 4x^3 - x^2 + 9) \div (x + 1)$ **6.** $(2x^3 - 3x^2 - 10x + 3) \div (x - 3)$

7. $(3t^3 - 10t^2 + t - 5) \div (t - 4)$ **8.** $(10x^3 - 11x^2 - 47x + 30) \div (x + 2)$

9. $(x^4 + 5x^3 - 14x^2) \div (x - 2)$ **10.** $(2x^4 + 14x^3 - 2x^2 - 14x) \div (x + 7)$

11. $(y^3 + y^2 - 10) \div (y + 3)$ **12.** $(n^4 - n^3 - 10n^2 + 4n + 24) \div (n + 2)$

13. Use synthetic division to find all the factors of $x^3 + 6x^2 - 9x - 54$ if one of the factors is $x - 3$.

14. *Manufacturing*   A cylindrical chemical storage tank must have a height 4 meters greater than the radius of the top of the tank. Determine the radius of the top and the height of the tank if the tank must have a volume of 15.71 cubic meters.

Study Guide

The Rational Root Theorem

The **Rational Root Theorem** provides a means of determining possible rational roots of an equation. **Descartes' Rule of Signs** can be used to determine the possible number of positive real zeros and the possible number of negative real zeros.

Rational Root Theorem	Let $a_0x^n + a_1x^{n-1} + \cdots + a_{n-1}x + a_n = 0$ represent a polynomial equation of degree n with integral coefficients. If a rational number $\frac{p}{q}$, where p and q have no common factors, is a root of the equation, then p is a factor of a_n and q is a factor of a_0.

Example 1 **List the possible rational roots of $x^3 - 5x^2 - 17x - 6 = 0$. Then determine the rational roots.**

p is a factor of 6 and q is a factor of 1

possible values of p: $\pm 1, \pm 2, \pm 3, \pm 6$

possible values of q: ± 1

possible rational roots, $\frac{p}{q}$: $\pm 1, \pm 2, \pm 3, \pm 6$

Test the possible roots using synthetic division.

r	1	−5	−17	−6
1	1	−4	−21	−27
−1	1	−6	−11	5
2	1	−3	−23	−52
−2	1	−7	−3	0
3	1	−2	−23	−75
−3	1	−8	7	−27
6	1	1	−11	−72
−6	1	−11	49	−300

$\leftarrow$ *There is a root at $x = -2$. The depressed polynomial is $x^2 - 7x - 3$. You can use the Quadratic Formula to find the two irrational roots.*

Example 2 **Find the number of possible positive real zeros and the number of possible negative real zeros for $f(x) = 4x^4 - 13x^3 - 21x^2 + 38x - 8$.**

According to Descartes' Rule of Signs, the number of positive real zeros is the same as the number of sign changes of the coefficients of the terms in descending order or is less than this by an even number. Count the sign changes.

$$f(x) = 4x^4 - 13x^3 - 21x^2 + 38x - 8$$
$$4 \quad -13 \quad -21 \quad 38 \quad -8$$

There are three changes. So, there are 3 or 1 positive real zeros.

The number of negative real zeros is the same as the number of sign changes of the coefficients of the terms of $f(-x)$, or less than this number by an even number.

$$f(-x) = 4(-x)^4 - 13(-x)^3 - 21(-x)^2 + 38(-x) - 8$$
$$4 \quad 13 \quad -21 \quad -38 \quad -8$$

There is one change. So, there is 1 negative real zero.

4-4

Practice

The Rational Root Theorem

List the possible rational roots of each equation. Then determine the rational roots.

1. $x^3 - x^2 - 8x + 12 = 0$

2. $2x^3 - 3x^2 - 2x + 3 = 0$

3. $36x^4 - 13x^2 + 1 = 0$

4. $x^3 + 3x^2 - 6x - 8 = 0$

5. $x^4 - 3x^3 - 11x^2 + 3x + 10 = 0$

6. $x^4 + x^2 - 2 = 0$

7. $3x^3 + x^2 - 8x + 6 = 0$

8. $x^3 + 4x^2 - 2x + 15 = 0$

Find the number of possible positive real zeros and the number of possible negative real zeros. Then determine the rational zeros.

9. $f(x) = x^3 - 2x^2 - 19x + 20$ **10.** $f(x) = x^4 + x^3 - 7x^2 - x + 6$

11. *Driving* An automobile moving at 12 meters per second on level ground begins to slow down with an acceleration of -1.6 meters per second squared. The formula for the distance an object has traveled is $d(t) = v_0 t + \frac{1}{2}at^2$, where v_0 is the initial velocity and a is the acceleration. For what value(s) of t does $d(t) = 40$ meters?

4-5

Study Guide

Locating Zeros of a Polynomial Function

A polynomial function may have real zeros that are not rational numbers. The **Location Principle** provides a means of locating and approximating real zeros. For the polynomial function $y = f(x)$, if a and b are two numbers with $f(a)$ positive and $f(b)$ negative, then there must be at least one real zero between a and b. For example, if $f(x) = x^2 - 2$, $f(0) = -2$ and $f(2) = 2$. Thus, a zero exists somewhere between 0 and 2.

The **Upper Bound Theorem** and the **Lower Bound Theorem** are also useful in locating the zeros of a function and in determining whether all the zeros have been found. If a polynomial function $P(x)$ is divided by $x - c$, and the quotient and the remainder have no change in sign, c is an **upper bound** of the zeros of $P(x)$. If c is an upper bound of the zeros of $P(-x)$, then $-c$ is a **lower bound** of the zeros of $P(x)$.

Example 1 Determine between which consecutive integers the real zeros of $f(x) = x^3 - 2x^2 - 4x + 5$ are located.

According to Descartes' Rule of Signs, there are two or zero positive real roots and one negative real root. Use synthetic division to evaluate $f(x)$ for consecutive integral values of x.

r	1	−2	−4	5
−4	1	−6	20	−75
−3	1	−5	11	−28
−2	1	−4	4	−3
−1	1	−3	−1	6
0	1	−2	−4	5
1	1	−1	−5	0
2	1	0	−4	−3
3	1	1	−1	2

There is a zero at 1. The changes in sign indicate that there are also zeros between −2 and −1 and between 2 and 3. This result is consistent with Descartes' Rule of Signs.

Example 2 Use the Upper Bound Theorem to show that 3 is an upper bound and the Lower Bound Theorem to show that −2 is a lower bound of the zeros of $f(x) = x^3 - 3x^2 + x - 1$.

Synthetic division is the most efficient way to test potential upper and lower bounds. First, test for the upper bound.

r	1	−3	1	−1
3	1	0	1	2

Since there is no change in the signs in the quotient and remainder, 3 is an upper bound.
Now, test for the lower bound of $f(x)$ by showing that 2 is an upper bound of $f(-x)$.

$$f(-x) = (-x)^3 - 3(-x)^2 + (-x) - 1 = -x^3 - 3x^2 - x - 1$$

r	−1	−3	−1	−1
2	−1	−5	−11	−23

Since there is no change in the signs, −2 is a lower bound of $f(x)$.

4-5

Practice

Locating Zeros of a Polynomial Function

Determine between which consecutive integers the real zeros of each function are located.

1. $f(x) = 3x^3 - 10x^2 + 22x - 4$ **2.** $f(x) = 2x^3 + 5x^2 - 7x - 3$

3. $f(x) = 2x^3 - 13x^2 + 14x - 4$ **4.** $f(x) = x^3 - 12x^2 + 17x - 9$

5. $f(x) = 4x^4 - 16x^3 - 25x^2 + 196x - 146$

6. $f(x) = x^3 - 9$

Approximate the real zeros of each function to the nearest tenth.

7. $f(x) = 3x^4 + 4x^2 - 1$ **8.** $f(x) = 3x^3 - x + 2$

9. $f(x) = 4x^4 - 6x^2 + 1$ **10.** $f(x) = 2x^3 + x^2 - 1$

11. $f(x) = x^3 - 2x^2 - 2x + 3$ **12.** $f(x) = x^3 - 5x^2 + 4$

Use the Upper Bound Theorem to find an integral upper bound and the Lower Bound Theorem to find an integral lower bound of the zeros of each function.

13. $f(x) = 3x^4 - x^3 - 8x^2 - 3x - 20$ **14.** $f(x) = 2x^3 - x^2 + x - 6$

15. For $f(x) = x^3 - 3x^2$, determine the number and type of possible complex zeros. Use the Location Principle to determine the zeros to the nearest tenth. The graph has a relative maximum at $(0, 0)$ and a relative minimum at $(2, -4)$. Sketch the graph.

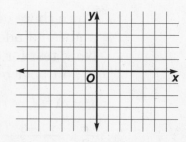

4-6

Study Guide

Rational Equations and Partial Fractions

A **rational equation** consists of one or more rational expressions. One way to solve a rational equation is to multiply each side of the equation by the least common denominator (LCD). Any possible solution that results in a zero in the denominator must be excluded from your list of solutions. In order to find the LCD, it is sometimes necessary to factor the denominators. If a denominator can be factored, the expression can be rewritten as the sum of **partial fractions.**

Example 1   Solve $\frac{x+1}{3(x-2)} = \frac{5x}{6} + \frac{1}{x-2}$.

$$6(x-2)\left[\frac{x+1}{3(x-2)}\right] = 6(x-2)\left(\frac{5x}{6} + \frac{1}{x-2}\right) \quad \textit{Multiply each side by the}$$
$$\textit{LCD, } 6(x-2).$$

$$2(x+1) = (x-2)(5x) + 6(1)$$
$$2x + 2 = 5x^2 - 10x + 6 \qquad \textit{Simplify.}$$
$$5x^2 - 12x + 4 = 0 \qquad\qquad \textit{Write in standard form.}$$
$$(5x - 2)(x - 2) = 0 \qquad\qquad \textit{Factor.}$$
$$5x - 2 = 0 \qquad\qquad x - 2 = 0$$
$$x = \frac{2}{5} \qquad\qquad\qquad x = 2$$

Since x cannot equal 2 because a zero denominator results, the only solution is $\frac{2}{5}$.

Example 2   **Decompose** $\dfrac{2x-1}{x^2+2x-3}$ **into partial fractions.**

Factor the denominator and express the factored form as the sum of two fractions using A and B as numerators and the factors as denominators.

$$x^2 + 2x - 3 = (x-1)(x+3)$$
$$\frac{2x-1}{x^2+2x-3} = \frac{A}{x-1} + \frac{B}{x+3}$$
$$2x - 1 = A(x+3) + B(x-1)$$

Let $x = 1$.   Let $x = -3$.
$$2(1) - 1 = A(1+3) \quad 2(-3) - 1 = B(-3-1)$$
$$1 = 4A \qquad\qquad\qquad -7 = -4B$$
$$A = \frac{1}{4} \qquad\qquad\qquad B = \frac{7}{4}$$

$$\frac{2x-1}{x^2+2x-3} = \frac{\frac{1}{4}}{x-1} + \frac{\frac{7}{4}}{x+3} \text{ or } \frac{1}{4(x-1)} + \frac{7}{4(x+3)}$$

Example 3   Solve $\frac{1}{2t} + \frac{3}{4t} > 1$.

Rewrite the inequality as the related function $f(t) = \frac{1}{2t} + \frac{3}{4t} - 1$.

Find the zeros of this function.
$$4t\left(\frac{1}{2t}\right) + 4t\left(\frac{3}{4t}\right) - 4t(1) = 4t(0)$$
$$5 - 4t = 0$$
$$t = 1.25$$

The zero is 1.25. The excluded value is 0. On a number line, mark these values with vertical dashed lines. Testing each interval shows the solution set to be $0 < t < 1.25$.

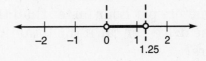

4-6

Practice

Rational Equations and Partial Fractions

Solve each equation.

1. $\frac{15}{m} - m + 8 = 10$

2. $\frac{4}{b-3} + \frac{3}{b} = \frac{-2b}{b-3}$

3. $\frac{1}{2n} + \frac{6n-9}{3n} = \frac{2}{n}$

4. $t - \frac{4}{t} = 3$

5. $\frac{3a}{2a+1} - \frac{4}{2a-1} = 1$

6. $\frac{2p}{p+1} + \frac{3}{p-1} = \frac{15-p}{p^2-1}$

Decompose each expression into partial fractions.

7. $\frac{-3x-29}{x^2-4x-21}$

8. $\frac{11x-7}{2x^2-3x-2}$

Solve each inequality.

9. $\frac{6}{t} + 3 > \frac{2}{t}$

10. $\frac{2n+1}{3n+1} \leq \frac{n-1}{3n+1}$

11. $1 + \frac{3y}{1-y} > 2$

12. $\frac{2x}{4} - \frac{5x+1}{3} > 3$

13. **Commuting** Rosea drives her car 30 kilometers to the train station, where she boards a train to complete her trip. The total trip is 120 kilometers. The average speed of the train is 20 kilometers per hour faster than that of the car. At what speed must she drive her car if the total time for the trip is less than 2.5 hours?

4-7

Study Guide

Radical Equations and Inequalities

Equations in which radical expressions include variables are known as **radical equations.** To solve radical equations, first isolate the radical on one side of the equation. Then raise each side of the equation to the proper power to eliminate the radical expression. This process of raising each side of an equation to a power often introduces **extraneous solutions.** Therefore, it is important to check all possible solutions in the original equation to determine if any of them should be eliminated from the solution set. **Radical inequalities** are solved using the same techniques used for solving radical equations.

Example 1 **Solve $3 = \sqrt[3]{x^2 - 2x + 1} - 1$.**

$$3 = \sqrt[3]{x^2 - 2x + 1} - 1$$
$$4 = \sqrt[3]{x^2 - 2x + 1} \qquad \textit{Isolate the cube root.}$$
$$64 = x^2 - 2x + 1 \qquad \textit{Cube each side.}$$
$$0 = x^2 - 2x - 63$$
$$0 = (x - 9)(x + 7) \qquad \textit{Factor.}$$
$$x - 9 = 0 \qquad\qquad x + 7 = 0$$
$$x = 9 \qquad\qquad\quad x = -7$$

Check both solutions to make sure they are not extraneous.

$x = 9$: $3 = \sqrt[3]{x^2 - 2x + 1} - 1$ $\qquad$ $x = -7$: $3 = \sqrt[3]{x^2 - 2x + 1} - 1$

$\qquad 3 \stackrel{?}{=} \sqrt[3]{(9)^2 - 2(9) + 1} - 1 \qquad\qquad 3 \stackrel{?}{=} \sqrt[3]{(-7)^2 - 2(-7) + 1} - 1$

$\qquad 3 \stackrel{?}{=} \sqrt[3]{64} - 1 \qquad\qquad\qquad\qquad 3 \stackrel{?}{=} \sqrt[3]{64} - 1$

$\qquad 3 \stackrel{?}{=} 4 - 1 \qquad\qquad\qquad\qquad\quad 3 \stackrel{?}{=} 4 - 1$

$\qquad 3 = 3 \;\; ✔ \qquad\qquad\qquad\qquad\quad 3 = 3 \;\; ✔$

Example 2 **Solve $2\sqrt{3x + 5} > 2$.**

$$2\sqrt{3x + 5} > 2$$
$$4(3x + 5) > 4 \qquad \textit{Square each side.}$$
$$3x + 5 > 1 \qquad \textit{Divide each side by 4.}$$
$$3x > -4$$
$$x > -1.33$$

In order for $\sqrt{3x + 5}$ to be a real number, $3x + 5$ must be greater than or equal to zero.

$$3x + 5 \geq 0$$
$$3x \geq -5$$
$$x \geq -1.67$$

Since -1.33 is greater than -1.67, the solution is $x > -1.33$. Check this solution by testing values in the intervals defined by the solution. Then graph the solution on a number line.

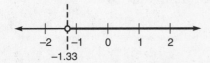

71

4-7

Practice

Radical Equations and Inequalities

Solve each equation.

1. $\sqrt{x-2} = 6$

2. $\sqrt[3]{x^2-1} = 3$

3. $\sqrt[3]{7r+5} = -3$

4. $\sqrt{6x+12} - \sqrt{4x+9} = 1$

5. $\sqrt{x-3} - 3\sqrt{x+12} = -11$

6. $\sqrt{6n-3} = \sqrt{4+7n}$

7. $5 + 2x = \sqrt{x^2-2x+1}$

8. $3 - \sqrt{r+1} = \sqrt{4-r}$

Solve each inequality.

9. $\sqrt{3r+5} > 1$

10. $\sqrt{2t-3} < 5$

11. $\sqrt{2m+3} > 5$

12. $\sqrt{3x+5} < 9$

13. **Engineering**   A team of engineers must design a fuel tank in the shape of a cone. The surface area of a cone (excluding the base) is given by the formula $S = \pi\sqrt{r^2+h^2}$. Find the radius of a cone with a height of 21 meters and a surface area of 155 meters squared.

Study Guide

Modeling Real-World Data with Polynomial Functions

In order to model real-world data using polynomial functions, you must be able to identify the general shape of the graph of each type of polynomial function.

Example 1 **Determine the type of polynomial function that could be used to represent the data in each scatter plot.**

a.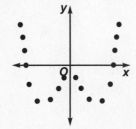

The scatter plot seems to change direction three times, so a quartic function would best fit the scatter plot.

b.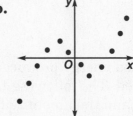

The scatter plot seems to change direction two times, so a cubic function would best fit the scatter plot.

Example 2 **An oil tanker collides with another ship and starts leaking oil. The Coast Guard measures the rate of flow of oil from the tanker and obtains the data shown in the table. Use a graphing calculator to write a polynomial function to model the set of data.**

Time (hours)	Flow rate (100s of liters per hour)
1	18.0
2	20.5
3	21.3
4	21.1
5	19.9
6	17.8
7	15.9
8	11.3
9	7.6
10	3.7

Clear the statistical memory and input the data. Adjust the window to an appropriate setting and graph the statistical data. The data appear to change direction one time, so a quadratic function will fit the scatter plot. Press [STAT], highlight **CALC**, and choose **5:QuadReg**. Then enter [2nd] [L1] [,] [2nd] [L2] [ENTER]. Rounding the coefficients to the nearest tenth, $f(x) = -0.4x^2 + 2.8x + 16.3$ models the data. Since the value of the coefficient of determination r^2 is very close to 1, the polynomial is an excellent fit.

L1	L2	L3	1
1	18	------	
2	20.5		
3	21.3		
4	21.1		
5	19.9		
6	17.8		
7	15.9		

L1(1)=1

L1	L2	L3	1
1	18	------	
2	20.5		
3	21.3		
4	21.1		
5	19.9		
6	17.8		
7	15.9		

L1(1)=1

[0, 10] scl: 1 by [0.25] scl: 5

```
QuadReg
y=ax²+bx+c
a=-.4090909091
b=2.762424242
c=16.26666667
R²=.9927513576
■
```

4-8

Practice

Modeling Real-World Data with Polynomial Functions

Write a polynomial function to model each set of data.

1. The farther a planet is from the Sun, the longer it takes to complete an orbit.

Distance (AU)	0.39	0.72	1.00	1.49	5.19	9.51	19.1	30.0	39.3
Period (days)	88	225	365	687	4344	10,775	30,681	60,267	90,582

Source: *Astronomy: Fundamentals and Frontiers, by Jastrow, Robert, and Malcolm H. Thompson.*

2. The amount of food energy produced by farms increases as more energy is expended. The following table shows the amount of energy produced and the amount of energy expended to produce the food.

Energy Input (Calories)	606	970	1121	1227	1318	1455	1636	2030	2182	2242
Energy Output (Calories)	133	144	148	157	171	175	187	193	198	198

Source: *NSTA Energy-Environment Source Book.*

3. The temperature of Earth's atmosphere varies with altitude.

Altitude (km)	0	10	20	30	40	50	60	70	80	90
Temperature (K)	293	228	217	235	254	269	244	207	178	178

Source: *Living in the Environment, by Miller G. Tyler.*

4. Water quality varies with the season. This table shows the average hardness (amount of dissolved minerals) of water in the Missouri River measured at Kansas City, Missouri.

Month	Jan.	Feb.	Mar.	April	May	June	July	Aug.	Sept.	Oct.	Nov.	Dec.
Hardness ($CaCO_3$ ppm)	310	250	180	175	230	175	170	180	210	230	295	300

Source: *The Encyclopedia of Environmental Science, 1974.*

Advanced Mathematical Concepts

4-1 Practice

Polynomial Functions

State the degree and leading coefficient of each polynomial.

1. $6a^4 + a^3 - 2a$
   4; 6

2. $3p^2 - 7p^5 - 2p^3 + 5$
   5; -7

Write a polynomial equation of least degree for each set of roots.

3. 3, -0.5, 1
   $2x^3 - 7x^2 + 2x + 3 = 0$

4. 3, 3, 1, 1, -2
   $x^5 - 6x^4 + 6x^3 + 20x^2 - 39x + 18 = 0$

5. ±2i, 3, -3
   $x^4 - 5x^2 - 36 = 0$

6. -1, 3 ± i, 2 ± 3i
   $x^5 - 9x^4 + 37x^3 - 71x^2 + 12x + 130 = 0$

State the number of complex roots of each equation. Then find the roots and graph the related function.

7. 3x - 5 = 0
   1; $\frac{5}{3}$

8. $x^2 + 4 = 0$
   2; ±2i

9. $c^2 + 2c + 1 = 0$
   2; -1, -1

10. $x^3 + 2x^2 - 15x = 0$
    3; -5, 0, 3

11. **Real Estate** A developer wants to build homes on a rectangular plot of land 3 kilometers long and 4 kilometers wide. In this part of the city, regulations require a greenbelt of uniform width along two adjacent sides. The greenbelt must be 10 times the area of the development. Find the width of the greenbelt.
    8 km

4-2 Practice

Quadratic Equations

Solve each equation by completing the square.

1. $x^2 - 5x - \frac{11}{4} = 0$
   $-\frac{1}{2}, \frac{11}{2}$

2. $-4x^2 - 11x = 7$
   $-1, -\frac{7}{4}$

Find the discriminant of each equation and describe the nature of the roots of the equation. Then solve the equation by using the Quadratic Formula.

3. $x^2 + x - 6 = 0$
   25; 2 real; -3, 2

4. $4x^2 - 4x - 15 = 0$
   256; 2 real; $\frac{5}{2}, -\frac{3}{2}$

5. $9x^2 - 12x + 4 = 0$
   0; 1 real; $\frac{2}{3}$

6. $3x^2 + 2x + 5 = 0$
   -56; 2 imaginary; $\frac{-1 \pm i\sqrt{14}}{3}$

Solve each equation.

7. $2x^2 + 5x - 12 = 0$
   $-4, \frac{3}{2}$

8. $5x^2 - 14x + 11 = 0$
   $\frac{7 \pm \sqrt{6}i}{5}$

9. **Architecture** The ancient Greek mathematicians thought that the most pleasing geometric forms, such as the ratio of the height to the width of a doorway, were created using the *golden section*. However, they were surprised to learn that the golden section is not a rational number. One way of expressing the golden section is by using a line segment. In the line segment shown, $\frac{AB}{AC} = \frac{AC}{CB}$. If AC = 1 unit, find the ratio $\frac{AB}{AC}$.

   $\frac{AB}{AC} = \frac{1+\sqrt{5}}{2}$

NAME _____ DATE _____ PERIOD _____

4-3 Practice

The Remainder and Factor Theorems

Divide using synthetic division.

1. $(3x^2 + 4x - 12) \div (x + 5)$
$3x - 11$, R43

2. $(x^2 - 5x - 12) \div (x - 3)$
$x - 2$, R-18

3. $(x^4 - 3x^2 + 12) \div (x + 1)$
$x^3 - x^2 - 2x + 2$, R10

4. $(2x^3 + 3x^2 - 8x + 3) \div (x + 3)$
$2x^2 - 3x + 1$

Use the Remainder Theorem to find the remainder for each division. State whether the binomial is a factor of the polynomial.

5. $(2x^4 + 4x^3 - x^2 + 9) \div (x + 1)$
6; no

6. $(2x^3 - 3x^2 - 10x + 3) \div (x - 3)$
0; yes

7. $(3t^3 - 10t^2 + t - 5) \div (t - 4)$
31; no

8. $(10x^3 - 11x^2 - 47x + 30) \div (x + 2)$
0; yes

9. $(x^4 + 5x^3 - 14x^2) \div (x - 2)$
0; yes

10. $(2x^4 + 14x^3 - 2x^2 - 14x) \div (x + 7)$
0; yes

11. $(y^3 + y^2 - 10) \div (y + 3)$
-28; no

12. $(n^4 - n^3 - 10n^2 + 4n + 24) \div (n + 2)$
0; yes

13. Use synthetic division to find all the factors of $x^3 + 6x^2 - 9x - 54$ if one of the factors is $x - 3$.
$(x - 3)(x + 3)(x + 6)$

14. *Manufacturing* A cylindrical chemical storage tank must have a height 4 meters greater than the radius of the top of the tank. Determine the radius of the top and the height of the tank if the tank must have a volume of 15.71 cubic meters.
$r \approx 1$ m, $h \approx 5$ m

NAME _____ DATE _____ PERIOD _____

4-4 Practice

The Rational Root Theorem

List the possible rational roots of each equation. Then determine the rational roots.

1. $x^3 - x^2 - 8x + 12 = 0$
$\pm 1, \pm 2, \pm 3, \pm 4, \pm 6, \pm 12; -3, 2$

2. $2x^3 - 3x^2 - 2x + 3 = 0$
$\pm 1, \pm 3, \pm \frac{1}{2}, \pm \frac{3}{2}; \pm 1, \frac{3}{2}$

3. $36x^4 - 13x^2 + 1 = 0$
$\pm \frac{1}{36}, \pm \frac{1}{18}, \pm \frac{1}{12}, \pm \frac{1}{9}, \pm \frac{1}{6}, \pm \frac{1}{4}, \pm \frac{1}{3}, \pm \frac{1}{2}, \pm 1; \pm \frac{1}{2}, \pm \frac{1}{3}$

4. $x^3 + 3x^2 - 6x - 8 = 0$
$\pm 1, \pm 2, \pm 4, \pm 8; -4, -1, 2$

5. $x^4 - 3x^3 - 11x^2 + 3x + 10 = 0$
$\pm 1, \pm 2, \pm 5, \pm 10; \pm 1, -2, 5$

6. $x^4 + x^2 - 2 = 0$
$\pm 1, \pm 2; \pm 1$

7. $3x^3 + x^2 - 8x + 6 = 0$
$\pm 1, \pm 2, \pm 3, \pm 6, \pm \frac{1}{3}, \pm \frac{2}{3};$ none

8. $x^3 + 4x^2 - 2x + 15 = 0$
$\pm 1, \pm 3, \pm 5, \pm 15; -5$

Find the number of possible positive real zeros and the number of possible negative real zeros. Then determine the rational zeros.

9. $f(x) = x^3 - 2x^2 - 19x + 20$
2 or 0; 1; $-4, 1, 5$

10. $f(x) = x^4 + x^3 - 7x^2 - x + 6$
2 or 0; 2 or 0; $-3, -1, 1, 2$

11. *Driving* An automobile moving at 12 meters per second on level ground begins to slow down with an acceleration of -1.6 meters per second squared. The formula for the distance an object has traveled is $d(t) = v_0 t + \frac{1}{2}at^2$, where v_0 is the initial velocity and a is the acceleration. For what value(s) of t does $d(t) = 40$ meters? 5 s and 10 s

4-5 Practice

NAME _____ DATE _____ PERIOD _____

Locating Zeros of a Polynomial Function

Determine between which consecutive integers the real zeros of each function are located.

1. $f(x) = 3x^3 - 10x^2 + 22x - 4$
   0 and 1

2. $f(x) = 2x^3 + 5x^2 - 7x - 3$
   −4 and −3, −1 and 0, 1 and 2

3. $f(x) = 2x^3 - 13x^2 + 14x - 4$
   0 and 1, 5 and 6

4. $f(x) = x^3 - 12x^2 + 17x - 9$
   10 and 11

5. $f(x) = 4x^4 - 16x^3 - 25x^2 + 196x - 146$
   −4 and −3, 0 and 1

6. $f(x) = x^3 - 9$
   2 and 3

Approximate the real zeros of each function to the nearest tenth.

7. $f(x) = 3x^4 + 4x^2 - 1$
   ±0.5

8. $f(x) = 3x^3 - x + 2$
   −1.0

9. $f(x) = 4x^4 - 6x^2 + 1$
   ±0.4, ±1.1

10. $f(x) = 2x^3 + x^2 - 1$
    0.7

11. $f(x) = x^3 - 2x^2 - 2x + 3$
    −1.3, 1.0, 2.3

12. $f(x) = x^3 - 5x^2 + 4$
    −0.8, 1.0, 4.8

Use the Upper Bound Theorem to find an integral upper bound and the Lower Bound Theorem to find an integral lower bound of the zeros of each function. Sample answers given.

13. $f(x) = 3x^4 - x^3 - 8x^2 - 3x - 20$
    3, −2

14. $f(x) = 2x^3 - x^2 + x - 6$
    2, 0

15. For $f(x) = x^3 - 3x^2$, determine the number and type of possible complex zeros. Use the Location Principle to determine the zeros to the nearest tenth. The graph has a relative maximum at (0, 0) and a relative minimum at (2, −4). Sketch the graph.
    three real roots; 3, 0, 0

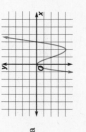

4-6 Practice

NAME _____ DATE _____ PERIOD _____

Rational Equations and Partial Fractions

Solve each equation.

1. $\dfrac{15}{m} - m + 8 = 10$
   −5, 3

2. $\dfrac{4}{b-3} + \dfrac{3}{b} = \dfrac{-2b}{b-3}$
   $-\dfrac{9}{2}$, 1

3. $\dfrac{1}{2n} + \dfrac{6n-9}{3n} = \dfrac{2}{n}$
   $\dfrac{9}{4}$

4. $t - \dfrac{4}{t} = 3$
   −1, 4

5. $\dfrac{3a}{2a+1} - \dfrac{4}{2a-1} = 1$
   $\dfrac{11 \pm \sqrt{145}}{4}$

6. $\dfrac{2p}{p+1} + \dfrac{3}{p-1} = \dfrac{15-p}{p^2-1}$
   −3, 2

Decompose each expression into partial fractions.

7. $\dfrac{-3x-29}{x^2-4x-21}$
   $-\dfrac{5}{x-7} + \dfrac{2}{x+3}$

8. $\dfrac{11x-7}{2x^2-3x-2}$
   $\dfrac{3}{x-2} + \dfrac{5}{2x+1}$

Solve each inequality.

9. $\dfrac{6}{t} + 3 > \dfrac{2}{t}$
   $t < -\dfrac{4}{3}$ or $t > 0$

10. $\dfrac{2n+1}{3n+1} \le \dfrac{n-1}{3n+1}$
    $-2 \le n < -\dfrac{1}{3}$

11. $1 + \dfrac{3y}{1-y} > 2$
    $\dfrac{1}{4} < y < 1$

12. $\dfrac{2x}{4} - \dfrac{5x+1}{3} > 3$
    $x < -\dfrac{20}{7}$

13. **Commuting** Rosea drives her car 30 kilometers to the train station, where she boards a train to complete her trip. The total trip is 120 kilometers. The average speed of the train is 20 kilometers per hour faster than that of the car. At what speed must she drive her car if the total time for the trip is less than 2.5 hours? at least 35 km/hr

4-7 Practice

Radical Equations and Inequalities

Solve each equation.

1. $\sqrt{x-2} = 6$
   38

2. $\sqrt[3]{x^2 - 1} = 3$
   $\pm 2\sqrt{7}$

3. $\sqrt[3]{7r+5} = -3$
   $-\dfrac{32}{7}$

4. $\sqrt{6x+12} - \sqrt{4x+9} = 1$
   4

5. $\sqrt{x-3} - 3\sqrt{x+12} = -11$
   $4, \dfrac{97}{16}$

6. $\sqrt{6n-3} = \sqrt{4+7n}$
   no real solution

7. $5 + 2x = \sqrt{x^2 - 2x + 1}$
   $-\dfrac{4}{3}$

8. $3 - \sqrt{r+1} = \sqrt{4-r}$
   0, 3

Solve each inequality.

9. $\sqrt{3r+5} > 1$
   $r > -\dfrac{4}{3}$

10. $\sqrt{2t-3} < 5$
    $\dfrac{3}{2} < t < 14$

11. $\sqrt{2m+3} > 5$
    $m > 11$

12. $\sqrt{3x+5} < 9$
    $-\dfrac{5}{3} < x < \dfrac{76}{3}$

13. **Engineering** A team of engineers must design a fuel tank in the shape of a cone. The surface area of a cone (excluding the base) is given by the formula $S = \pi\sqrt{r^2 + h^2}$. Find the radius of a cone with a height of 21 meters and a surface area of 155 meters squared. **about 2.34 m**

4-8 Practice

Modeling Real-World Data with Polynomial Functions

Write a polynomial function to model each set of data.

1. The farther a planet is from the Sun, the longer it takes to complete an orbit.

Distance (AU)	0.39	0.72	1.00	1.49	5.19	9.51	19.1	30.0	39.3
Period (days)	88	225	365	687	4344	10,775	30,681	60,267	90,582

Source: *Astronomy: Fundamentals and Frontiers*, by Jastrow, Robert, and Malcolm H. Thompson.

Sample answer: $f(x) = 35x^2 + 962x - 791$

2. The amount of food energy produced by farms increases as more energy is expended. The following table shows the amount of energy produced and the amount of energy expended to produce the food.

Energy Input (Calories)	606	970	1121	1227	1318	1455	1636	2030	2182	2242
Energy Output (Calories)	133	144	148	157	171	175	187	193	198	198

Source: *NSTA Energy-Environment Source Book.*

Sample answer: $f(x) = -3.9x^3 + 1.5x^2 - 0.1x + 167.0$

3. The temperature of Earth's atmosphere varies with altitude.

Altitude (km)	0	10	20	30	40	50	60	70	80	90
Temperature (K)	293	228	217	235	254	269	244	207	178	178

Source: *Living in the Environment*, by Miller G. Tyler.

Sample answer: $f(x) = -0.0008x^3 + 0.1x^2 - 3.6x + 274.7$

4. Water quality varies with the season. This table shows the average hardness (amount of dissolved minerals) of water in the Missouri River measured at Kansas City, Missouri.

Month	Jan.	Feb.	Mar.	April	May	June	July	Aug.	Sept.	Oct.	Nov.	Dec.
Hardness ($CaCO_3$ ppm)	310	250	180	175	230	175	170	180	210	230	295	300

Source: *The Encyclopedia of Environmental Science*, 1974.

Sample answer: $f(x) = 0.1x^4 - 1.6x^3 + 19.7x^2 - 110.0x + 397.7$

5-1

Study Guide

Angles and Degree Measure

Decimal degree measures can be expressed in **degrees(°)**, **minutes(′)**, and **seconds(″)**.

Example 1 **a. Change 12.520° to degrees, minutes, and seconds.**

$12.520° = 12° + (0.520 \cdot 60)′$ *Multiply the decimal portion of*
$= 12° + 31.2′$ *the degrees by 60 to find minutes.*
$= 12° + 31′ + (0.2 \cdot 60)″$ *Multiply the decimal portion of*
$= 12° + 31′ + 12″$ *the minutes by 60 to find seconds.*

12.520° can be written as 12° 31′ 12″.

b. Write 24° 15′ 33″ as a decimal rounded to the nearest thousandth.

$$24° \ 15′ \ 33″ = 24° + 15′\left(\frac{1°}{60′}\right) + 33″\left(\frac{1°}{3600″}\right)$$
$$= 24.259°$$

24° 15′ 33″ can be written as 24.259°.

An angle may be generated by the rotation of one ray multiple times about the origin.

Example 2 **Give the angle measure represented by each rotation.**

a. 2.3 rotations clockwise

$2.3 \times -360 = -828$ *Clockwise rotations have negative measures.*

The angle measure of 2.3 clockwise rotations is −828°.

b. 4.2 rotations counterclockwise

$4.2 \times 360 = 1512$ *Counterclockwise rotations have positive measures.*

The angle measure of 4.2 counterclockwise rotations is 1512°.

If α is a nonquadrantal angle in standard position, its **reference angle** is defined as the acute angle formed by the terminal side of the given angle and the x-axis.

Reference Angle Rule	For any angle α, 0° < α < 360°, its reference angle α' is defined by a. α, when the terminal side is in Quadrant I, b. 180° − α, when the terminal side is in Quadrant II, c. α − 180°, when the terminal side is in Quadrant III, and d. 360° − α, when the terminal side is in Quadrant IV.

Example 3 **Find the measure of the reference angle for 220°.**

Because 220° is between 180° and 270°, the terminal side of the angle is in Quadrant III.

$220° − 180° = 40°$

The reference angle is 40°.

    79   *Advanced Mathematical Concepts*

5-1

Practice

Angles and Degree Measure

Change each measure to degrees, minutes, and seconds.
1. 28.955°   2. −57.327°

Write each measure as a decimal degree to the nearest thousandth.
3. 32° 28′ 10″   4. −73° 14′ 35″

Give the angle measure represented by each rotation.
5. 1.5 rotations clockwise   6. 2.6 rotations counterclockwise

Identify all angles that are coterminal with each angle. Then find one positive angle and one negative angle that are coterminal with each angle.
7. 43°   8. −30°

If each angle is in standard position, determine a coterminal angle that is between 0° and 360°, and state the quadrant in which the terminal side lies.
9. 472°   10. −995°

Find the measure of the reference angle for each angle.
11. 227°   12. 640°

13. *Navigation*   For an upcoming trip, Jackie plans to sail from Santa Barbara Island, located at 33° 28′ 32″ N, 119° 2′ 7″ W, to Santa Catalina Island, located at 33.386° N, 118.430° W. Write the latitude and longitude for Santa Barbara Island as decimals to the nearest thousandth and the latitude and longitude for Santa Catalina Island as degrees, minutes, and seconds.

5-2

Study Guide

Trigonometric Ratios in Right Triangles

The ratios of the sides of right triangles can be used to define the **trigonometric** ratios known as the **sine, cosine,** and **tangent.**

Example 1 **Find the values of the sine, cosine, and tangent for $\angle A$.**

First find the length of $\overline{BC}$.

$(AC)^2 + (BC)^2 = (AB)^2$ *Pythagorean Theorem*

$10^2 + (BC)^2 = 20^2$ *Substitute 10 for AC and 20 for AB.*

$(BC)^2 = 300$

$BC = \sqrt{300}$ or $10\sqrt{3}$ *Take the square root of each side. Disregard the negative root.*

Then write each trigonometric ratio.

$\sin A = \dfrac{side\ opposite}{hypotenuse}$ $\cos A = \dfrac{side\ adjacent}{hypotenuse}$ $\tan A = \dfrac{side\ opposite}{side\ adjacent}$

$\sin A = \dfrac{10\sqrt{3}}{20}$ or $\dfrac{\sqrt{3}}{2}$ $\cos A = \dfrac{10}{20}$ or $\dfrac{1}{2}$ $\tan A = \dfrac{10\sqrt{3}}{10}$ or $\sqrt{3}$

Trigonometric ratios are often simplified but never written as mixed numbers.

Three other trigonometric ratios, called **cosecant, secant,** and **cotangent,** are reciprocals of sine, cosine, and tangent, respectively.

Example 2 **Find the values of the six trigonometric ratios for $\angle R$.**

First determine the length of the hypotenuse.

$(RT)^2 + (ST)^2 = (RS)^2$ *Pythagorean Theorem*

$15^2 + 3^2 = (RS)^2$ *RT = 15, ST = 3*

$(RS)^2 = 234$

$RS = \sqrt{234}$ or $3\sqrt{26}$ *Disregard the negative root.*

$\sin R = \dfrac{side\ opposite}{hypotenuse}$ $\cos R = \dfrac{side\ adjacent}{hypotenuse}$ $\tan R = \dfrac{side\ opposite}{side\ adjacent}$

$\sin R = \dfrac{3}{3\sqrt{26}}$ or $\dfrac{\sqrt{26}}{26}$ $\cos R = \dfrac{15}{3\sqrt{26}}$ or $\dfrac{5\sqrt{26}}{26}$ $\tan R = \dfrac{3}{15}$ or $\dfrac{1}{5}$

$\csc R = \dfrac{hypotenuse}{side\ opposite}$ $\sec R = \dfrac{hypotenuse}{side\ adjacent}$ $\cot R = \dfrac{side\ adjacent}{side\ opposite}$

$\csc R = \dfrac{3\sqrt{26}}{3}$ or $\sqrt{26}$ $\sec R = \dfrac{3\sqrt{26}}{15}$ or $\dfrac{\sqrt{26}}{5}$ $\cot R = \dfrac{15}{3}$ or 5

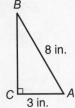

5-2   **Practice**

Trigonometric Ratios in Right Triangles

Find the values of the sine, cosine, and tangent for each ∠B.

1.

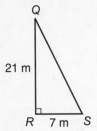

B

8 in.

C ⌐ 3 in. A

2.

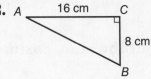

A ___16 cm___ C

8 cm

B

3. If $\tan \theta = 5$, find $\cot \theta$.

4. If $\sin \theta = \frac{3}{8}$, find $\csc \theta$.

Find the values of the six trigonometric ratios for each ∠S.

5.

Q

21 m

R 7 m S

6.

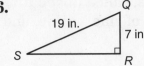

Q

19 in.

7 in.

S _____ R

7. _Physics_   Suppose you are traveling in a car when a beam of light
passes from the air to the windshield. The measure of the angle
of incidence is 55°, and the measure of the angle of refraction is
35° 15'. Use Snell's Law, $\frac{\sin \theta_i}{\sin \theta_r} = n$, to find the index of refraction n
of the windshield to the nearest thousandth.

5-3

Study Guide

Trigonometric Functions on the Unit Circle

Example 1 **Use the unit circle to find cot (−270°).**

The terminal side of a −270° angle in
standard position is the positive y-axis,
which intersects the unit circle at (0, 1).

By definition, cot (−270°) = $\frac{x}{y}$ or $\frac{0}{1}$.

Therefore, cot (−270°) = 0.

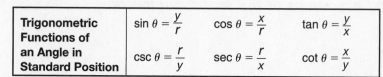

Trigonometric Functions of an Angle in Standard Position	$\sin \theta = \frac{y}{r}$	$\cos \theta = \frac{x}{r}$	$\tan \theta = \frac{y}{x}$
	$\csc \theta = \frac{r}{y}$	$\sec \theta = \frac{r}{x}$	$\cot \theta = \frac{x}{y}$

Example 2 **Find the values of the six trigonometric functions
for angle θ in standard position if a point with
coordinates (−9, 12) lies on its terminal side.**

We know that $x = -9$ and $y = 12$. We need to
find r.

$r = \sqrt{x^2 + y^2}$ *Pythagorean Theorem*

$r = \sqrt{(-9)^2 + 12^2}$ *Substitute −9 for x and 12 for y.*

$r = \sqrt{225}$ or 15   *Disregard the negative root.*

$\sin \theta = \frac{12}{15}$ or $\frac{4}{5}$ $\cos \theta = \frac{-9}{15}$ or $-\frac{3}{5}$ $\tan \theta = \frac{12}{-9}$ or $-\frac{4}{3}$

$\csc \theta = \frac{15}{12}$ or $\frac{5}{4}$ $\sec \theta = \frac{15}{-9}$ or $-\frac{5}{3}$ $\cot \theta = \frac{-9}{12}$ or $-\frac{3}{4}$

Example 3 **Suppose θ is an angle in standard position whose
terminal side lies in Quadrant I. If $\cos \theta = \frac{3}{5}$, find
the values of the remaining five trigonometric
functions of θ.**

$r^2 = x^2 + y^2$ *Pythagorean Theorem*
$5^2 = 3^2 + y^2$ *Substitute 5 for r and 3 for x.*
$16 = y^2$
$\pm 4 = y$ *Take the square root of each side.*

Since the terminal side of θ lies in Quadrant I, y must
be positive.

$\sin \theta = \frac{4}{5}$ $\tan \theta = \frac{4}{3}$

$\csc \theta = \frac{5}{4}$ $\sec \theta = \frac{5}{3}$ $\cot \theta = \frac{3}{4}$

5-3

Practice

Trigonometric Functions on the Unit Circle

Use the unit circle to find each value.

1. csc 90°

2. tan 270°

3. sin (−90°)

Use the unit circle to find the values of the six trigonometric functions for each angle.

4. 45°

5. 120°

Find the values of the six trigonometric functions for angle θ in standard position if a point with the given coordinates lies on its terminal side.

6. (−1, 5)

7. (7, 0)

8. (−3, −4)

5-4

Study Guide

Applying Trigonometric Functions

Trigonometric functions can be used to solve problems involving right triangles.

Example 1   **If $T = 45°$ and $u = 20$, find t to the nearest tenth.**

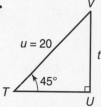

From the figure, we know the measures of an angle and the hypotenuse. We want to know the measure of the side opposite the given angle. The sine function relates the side opposite the angle and the hypotenuse.

$$\sin T = \frac{t}{u} \qquad sin = \frac{side\ opposite}{hypotenuse}$$

$$\sin 45° = \frac{t}{20} \qquad Substitute\ 45°\ for\ T\ and\ 20\ for\ u.$$

$$20 \sin 45° = t \qquad Multiply\ each\ side\ by\ 20.$$

$$14.14213562 \approx t \qquad Use\ a\ calculator.$$

Therefore, t is about 14.1.

Example 2   *Geometry* **The apothem of a regular polygon is the measure of a line segment from the center of the polygon to the midpoint of one of its sides. The apothem of a regular hexagon is 2.6 centimeters. Find the radius of the circle circumscribed about the hexagon to the nearest tenth.**

First draw a diagram. Let a be the angle measure formed by a radius and its adjacent apothem. The measure of a is $360° \div 12$ or $30°$. Now we know the measures of an angle and the side adjacent to the angle.

$$\cos 30° = \frac{2.6}{r} \qquad cos = \frac{side\ adjacent}{hypotenuse}$$

$$r \cos 30° = 2.6 \qquad Multiply\ each\ side\ by\ r.$$

$$r = \frac{2.6}{\cos 30°} \qquad Divide\ each\ side\ by\ \cos 30°.$$

$$r \approx 3.0022214 \qquad Use\ a\ calculator.$$

Therefore, the radius is about 3.0 centimeters.

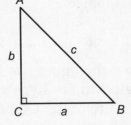

5-4

Practice

Applying Trigonometric Functions

Solve each problem. Round to the nearest tenth.

1. If $A = 55°\ 55'$ and $c = 16$, find a.

2. If $a = 9$ and $B = 49°$, find b.

3. If $B = 56°\ 48'$ and $c = 63.1$, find b.

4. If $B = 64°$ and $b = 19.2$, find a.

5. If $b = 14$ and $A = 16°$, find c.

6. **Construction** A 30-foot ladder leaning against the side of a house makes a $70°\ 5'$ angle with the ground.
   a. How far up the side of the house does the ladder reach?

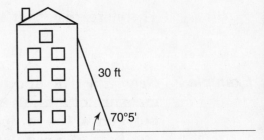

   b. What is the horizontal distance between the bottom of the ladder and the house?

7. **Geometry** A circle is circumscribed about a regular hexagon with an apothem of 4.8 centimeters.
   a. Find the radius of the circumscribed circle.

   b. What is the length of a side of the hexagon?

   c. What is the perimeter of the hexagon?

8. **Observation** A person standing 100 feet from the bottom of a cliff notices a tower on top of the cliff. The angle of elevation to the top of the cliff is $30°$. The angle of elevation to the top of the tower is $58°$. How tall is the tower?

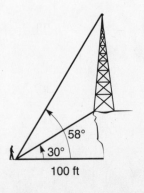

5-5

Study Guide
Solving Right Triangles

When we know a trigonometric value of an angle but not the value of the angle, we need to use the inverse of the trigonometric function.

Trigonometric Function	Inverse Trigonometric Relation
$y = \sin x$	$x = \sin^{-1} y$ or $x = \arcsin y$
$y = \cos x$	$x = \cos^{-1} y$ or $x = \arccos y$
$y = \tan x$	$x = \tan^{-1} y$ or $x = \arctan y$

Example 1 Solve $\tan x = \sqrt{3}$.

If $\tan x = \sqrt{3}$, then x is an angle whose tangent is $\sqrt{3}$.

$x = \arctan \sqrt{3}$

From a table of values, you can determine that x equals 60°, 240°, or any angle coterminal with these angles.

Example 2 If $c = 22$ and $b = 12$, find B.

In this problem, we know the side opposite the angle and the hypotenuse. The sine function relates the side opposite the angle and the hypotenuse.

$\sin B = \dfrac{b}{c}$ $\sin = \dfrac{side\ opposite}{hypotenuse}$

$\sin B = \dfrac{12}{22}$ *Substitute 12 for b and 22 for c.*

$B = \sin^{-1}\left(\dfrac{12}{22}\right)$ *Definition of inverse*

$B \approx 33.05573115$ or about 33.1°.

Example 3 Solve the triangle where $b = 20$ and $c = 35$, given the triangle above.

$a^2 + b^2 = c^2$ $\cos A = \dfrac{b}{c}$

$a^2 + 20^2 = 35^2$ $\cos A = \dfrac{20}{35}$

$\quad a = \sqrt{825}$ $A = \cos^{-1}\left(\dfrac{20}{35}\right)$

$\quad a \approx 28.72281323$ $A \approx 55.15009542$

$55.15009542 + B \approx 90$

$\quad\quad\quad B \approx 34.84990458$

Therefore, $a \approx 28.7$, $A \approx 55.2°$, and $B \approx 34.8°$.

5-5

Practice

Solving Right Triangles

Solve each equation if $0° \leq x \leq 360°$.

1. $\cos x = \dfrac{\sqrt{2}}{2}$

2. $\tan x = 1$

3. $\sin x = \dfrac{1}{2}$

Evaluate each expression. Assume that all angles are in Quadrant I.

4. $\tan\left(\tan^{-1} \dfrac{\sqrt{3}}{3}\right)$

5. $\tan\left(\cos^{-1} \dfrac{2}{3}\right)$

6. $\cos\left(\arcsin \dfrac{5}{13}\right)$

Solve each problem. Round to the nearest tenth.

7. If $q = 10$ and $s = 3$, find S.

8. If $r = 12$ and $s = 4$, find R.

9. If $q = 20$ and $r = 15$, find S.

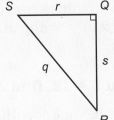

Solve each triangle described, given the triangle at the right. Round to the nearest tenth, if necessary.

10. $a = 9, B = 49°$

11. $A = 16°, c = 14$

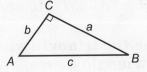

12. $a = 2, b = 7$

13. Recreation   The swimming pool at Perris Hill Plunge is 50 feet long and 25 feet wide. The bottom of the pool is slanted so that the water depth is 3 feet at the shallow end and 15 feet at the deep end. What is the angle of elevation at the bottom of the pool?

5-6

Study Guide

The Law of Sines

Given the measures of two angles and one side of a triangle, we can use the **Law of Sines** to find one unique solution for the triangle.

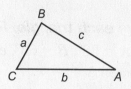

Law of Sines	$\dfrac{a}{\sin A} = \dfrac{b}{\sin B} = \dfrac{c}{\sin C}$

Example 1 Solve $\triangle ABC$ if $A = 30°$, $B = 100°$, and $a = 15$.

First find the measure of $\angle C$.
$C = 180° - (30° + 100°)$ or $50°$

Use the Law of Sines to find b and c.

$$\frac{a}{\sin A} = \frac{b}{\sin B} \qquad\qquad \frac{c}{\sin C} = \frac{a}{\sin A}$$

$$\frac{15}{\sin 30°} = \frac{b}{\sin 100°} \qquad\qquad \frac{c}{\sin 50°} = \frac{15}{\sin 30°}$$

$$\frac{15 \sin 100°}{\sin 30°} = b \qquad\qquad c = \frac{15 \sin 50°}{\sin 30°}$$

$$29.54423259 \approx b \qquad\qquad c \approx 22.98133329$$

Therefore, $C = 50°$, $b \approx 29.5$, and $c \approx 23.0$.

The area of any triangle can be expressed in terms of two sides of a triangle and the measure of the included angle.

Area (K) of a Triangle	$K = \frac{1}{2}bc \sin A$ $K = \frac{1}{2}ac \sin B$ $K = \frac{1}{2}ab \sin C$

Example 2 Find the area of $\triangle ABC$ if $a = 6.8$, $b = 9.3$, and $C = 57°$.

$$K = \frac{1}{2}ab \sin C$$

$$K = \frac{1}{2}(6.8)(9.3) \sin 57°$$

$$K \approx 26.51876336$$

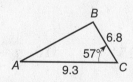

The area of $\triangle ABC$ is about 26.5 square units.

5-6

Practice

The Law of Sines

Solve each triangle. Round to the nearest tenth.

1. $A = 38°, B = 63°, c = 15$ **2.** $A = 33°, B = 29°, b = 41$

3. $A = 150°, C = 20°, a = 200$ **4.** $A = 30°, B = 45°, a = 10$

Find the area of each triangle. Round to the nearest tenth.

5. $c = 4, A = 37°, B = 69°$ **6.** $C = 85°, a = 2, B = 19°$

7. $A = 50°, b = 12, c = 14$ **8.** $b = 14, C = 110°, B = 25°$

9. $b = 15, c = 20, A = 115°$ **10.** $a = 68, c = 110, B = 42.5°$

11. *Street Lighting* A lamppost tilts toward the sun
at a 2° angle from the vertical and casts a 25-foot
shadow. The angle from the tip of the shadow to the
top of the lamppost is 45°. Find the length of the
lamppost.

2°

45°

25 ft

5-7

Study Guide

The Ambiguous Case for the Law of Sines

If we know the measures of two sides and a nonincluded angle of a triangle, three situations are possible: no triangle exists, exactly one triangle exists, or two triangles exist. A triangle with two solutions is called the **ambiguous case**.

Case 1: $A < 90°$ for a, b, and A	
$a < b \sin A$	no solution
$a = b \sin A$	one solution
$a \geq b$	one solution
$b \sin A < a < b$	two solutions
Case 2: $A \geq 90°$	
$a \leq b$	no solution
$a > b$	one solution

Example **Find all solutions for the triangle if $a = 20$, $b = 30$, and $A = 40°$. If no solutions exist, write *none*.**

Since $40° < 90°$, consider Case 1.
$b \sin A = 30 \sin 40°$
$b \sin A \approx 19.28362829$
Since $19.3 < 20 < 30$, there are two solutions for the triangle.
Use the Law of Sines to find B.

$$\frac{20}{\sin 40°} = \frac{30}{\sin B} \qquad\qquad \frac{a}{\sin A} = \frac{b}{\sin B}$$

$$\sin B = \frac{30 \sin 40°}{20}$$

$$B = \sin^{-1}\left(\frac{30 \sin 40°}{20}\right)$$

$$B \approx 74.61856831$$

So, $B \approx 74.6°$. Since we know there are two solutions, there must be another possible measurement for B. In the second case, B must be less than 180° and have the same sine value. Since we know that if $\alpha < 90$, $\sin \alpha = \sin (180 - \alpha)$, $180° - 74.6°$ or $105.4°$ is another possible measure for B. Now solve the triangle for each possible measure of B.

Solution I

$C \approx 180° - (40° + 74.6°)$ or $65.4°$

$$\frac{a}{\sin A} = \frac{c}{\sin C}$$

$$\frac{20}{\sin 40°} \approx \frac{c}{\sin 65.4°}$$

$$c \approx \frac{20 \sin 65.4°}{\sin 40°}$$

$$c \approx 28.29040558$$

One solution is $B \approx 74.6°$, $C \approx 65.4°$, and $c \approx 28.3$.

Solution II

$C \approx 180° - (40° + 105.4°)$ or $34.6°$

$$\frac{a}{\sin A} = \frac{c}{\sin C}$$

$$\frac{20}{\sin 40°} \approx \frac{c}{\sin 34.6°}$$

$$c \approx \frac{20 \sin 34.6°}{\sin 40°}$$

$$c \approx 17.66816088$$

Another solution is $B \approx 105.4°$, $C \approx 34.6°$, and $c \approx 17.7$.

5-7

Practice

The Ambiguous Case for the Law of Sines

Determine the number of possible solutions for each triangle.

1. $A = 42°, a = 22, b = 12$

2. $a = 15, b = 25, A = 85°$

3. $A = 58°, a = 4.5, b = 5$

4. $A = 110°, a = 4, c = 4$

Find all solutions for each triangle. If no solutions exist, write none. Round to the nearest tenth.

5. $b = 50, a = 33, A = 132°$

6. $a = 125, A = 25°, b = 150$

7. $a = 32, c = 20, A = 112°$

8. $a = 12, b = 15, A = 55°$

9. $A = 42°, a = 22, b = 12$

10. $b = 15, c = 13, C = 50°$

11. *Property Maintenance* The McDougalls plan to fence a triangular parcel of their land. One side of the property is 75 feet in length. It forms a 38° angle with another side of the property, which has not yet been measured. The remaining side of the property is 95 feet in length. Approximate to the nearest tenth the length of fence needed to enclose this parcel of the McDougalls' lot.

92

5-8

Study Guide

The Law of Cosines

When we know the measures of two sides of a triangle and the included angle, we can use the **Law of Cosines** to find the measure of the third side. Often times we will use both the Law of Cosines and the Law of Sines to solve a triangle.

Law of Cosines	$a^2 = b^2 + c^2 - 2bc \cos A$ $b^2 = a^2 + c^2 - 2ac \cos B$ $c^2 = a^2 + b^2 - 2ab \cos C$

Example 1 **Solve $\triangle ABC$ if $B = 40°$, $a = 12$, and $c = 6$.**

$b^2 = a^2 + c^2 - 2ac \cos B$ *Law of Cosines*
$b^2 = 12^2 + 6^2 - 2(12)(6) \cos 40°$
$b^2 \approx 69.68960019$
$b \approx 8.348029719$
So, $b \approx 8.34$

$$\frac{b}{\sin B} = \frac{c}{\sin C} \qquad Law\ of\ Sines$$

$$\frac{8.3}{\sin 40°} \approx \frac{6}{\sin C}$$

$$\sin C \approx \frac{6 \sin 40°}{8.3}$$

$$C \approx \sin^{-1}\left(\frac{6 \sin 40°}{8.3}\right)$$

$$C \approx 27.68859159$$

So, $C \approx 27.7°$.
$A \approx 180° - (40° + 27.7°) \approx 112.3°$

The solution of this triangle is $b \approx 8.3$, $A \approx 112.3°$, and $C \approx 27.7°$.

Example 2 **Find the area of $\triangle ABC$ if $a = 5$, $b = 8$, and $c = 10$.**

First, find the semiperimeter of $\triangle ABC$.
$s = \frac{1}{2}(a + b + c)$

$s = \frac{1}{2}(5 + 8 + 10)$

$s = 11.5$

Now, apply Hero's Formula
$k = \sqrt{s(s - a)(s - b)(s - c)}$
$k = \sqrt{11.5(11.5 - 5)(11.5 - 8)(11.5 - 10)}$
$k = \sqrt{392.4375}$
$k = \approx 19.81003534$

The area of the triangle is about 19.8 square units.

5-8

Practice

The Law of Cosines

Solve each triangle. Round to the nearest tenth.

1. $a = 20, b = 12, c = 28$

2. $a = 10, c = 8, B = 100°$

3. $c = 49, b = 40, A = 53°$

4. $a = 5, b = 7, c = 10$

Find the area of each triangle. Round to the nearest tenth.

5. $a = 5, b = 12, c = 13$

6. $a = 11, b = 13, c = 16$

7. $a = 14, b = 9, c = 8$

8. $a = 8, b = 7, c = 3$

9. The sides of a triangle measure 13.4 centimeters, 18.7 centimeters, and 26.5 centimeters. Find the measure of the angle with the least measure.

10. **Orienteering** During an orienteering hike, two hikers start at point A and head in a direction 30° west of south to point B. They hike 6 miles from point A to point B. From point B, they hike to point C and then from point C back to point A, which is 8 miles directly north of point C. How many miles did they hike from point B to point C?

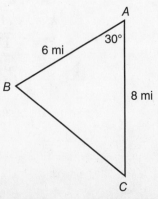

5-1 Practice

NAME _____ DATE _____ PERIOD _____

Angles and Degree Measure

Change each measure to degrees, minutes, and seconds.

1. 28.955°
28° 57′ 18″

2. −57.327°
−57° 19′ 37.2″

Write each measure as a decimal degree to the nearest thousandth.

3. 32° 28′ 10″
32.469°

4. −73° 14′ 35″
−73.243°

Give the angle measure represented by each rotation.

5. 1.5 rotations clockwise
−540°

6. 2.6 rotations counterclockwise
936°

Identify all angles that are coterminal with each angle. Then find one positive angle and one negative angle that are coterminal with each angle.

7. 43°
43° + 360k°;
sample answers:
763°; −317°

8. −30°
−30° + 360k°;
sample answers:
690°; −750°

If each angle is in standard position, determine a coterminal angle that is between 0° and 360°, and state the quadrant in which the terminal side lies.

9. 472°
112°; II

10. −995°
85°; I

Find the measure of the reference angle for each angle.

11. 227°
47°

12. 640°
80°

13. **Navigation** For an upcoming trip, Jackie plans to sail from Santa Barbara Island, located at 33° 28′ 32″ N, 119° 2′ 7″ W, to Santa Catalina Island, located at 33.386° N, 118.430° W. Write the latitude and longitude for Santa Barbara Island as decimals to the nearest thousandth and the latitude and longitude for Santa Catalina Island as degrees, minutes, and seconds.
Santa Barbara Island: 33.476° N, 119.035° W
Santa Catalina Island: 33° 23′ 9.6″ N, 118° 25′ 48″ W

5-2 Practice

NAME _____ DATE _____ PERIOD _____

Trigonometric Ratios in Right Triangles

Find the values of the sine, cosine, and tangent for each ∠B.

1.

$\sin B = \frac{3}{8}$; $\cos B = \frac{\sqrt{55}}{8}$;

$\tan B = \frac{3\sqrt{55}}{55}$

2.

$\sin B = \frac{2\sqrt{5}}{5}$; $\cos B = \frac{\sqrt{5}}{5}$;

$\tan B = 2$

3. If $\tan \theta = 5$, find $\cot \theta$.
$\frac{1}{5}$

4. If $\sin \theta = \frac{3}{8}$, find $\csc \theta$.
$\frac{8}{3}$

Find the values of the six trigonometric ratios for each ∠S.

5.

$\sin S = \frac{3\sqrt{10}}{10}$; $\cos S = \frac{\sqrt{10}}{10}$;

$\tan S = 3$; $\csc S = \frac{\sqrt{10}}{3}$;

$\sec S = \sqrt{10}$; $\cot S = \frac{1}{3}$

6.
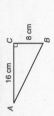

$\sin S = \frac{7}{19}$; $\cos S = \frac{2\sqrt{78}}{19}$;

$\tan S = \frac{7\sqrt{78}}{156}$; $\csc S = \frac{19}{7}$;

$\sec S = \frac{19\sqrt{78}}{156}$; $\cot S = \frac{2\sqrt{78}}{7}$

7. **Physics** Suppose you are traveling in a car when a beam of light passes from the air to the windshield. The measure of the angle of incidence is 55°, and the measure of the angle of refraction is 35° 15′. Use Snell's Law, $\frac{\sin \theta_i}{\sin \theta_r} = n$, to find the index of refraction n of the windshield to the nearest thousandth.
about 1.419

Answers (Lessons 5-3 and 5-4)

5-3 Practice

NAME _____ DATE _____ PERIOD _____

Trigonometric Functions on the Unit Circle

Use the unit circle to find each value.

1. csc 90°
   1

2. tan 270°
   undefined

3. sin (−90°)
   −1

Use the unit circle to find the values of the six trigonometric functions for each angle.

4. 45°

$\sin 45° = \dfrac{\sqrt{2}}{2}$ $\csc 45° = \sqrt{2}$

$\cos 45° = \dfrac{\sqrt{2}}{2}$ $\sec 45° = \sqrt{2}$

$\tan 45° = 1$ $\cot 45° = 1$

5. 120°

$\sin 120° = \dfrac{\sqrt{3}}{2}$ $\csc 120° = \dfrac{2\sqrt{3}}{3}$

$\cos 120° = -\dfrac{1}{2}$ $\sec 120° = -2$

$\tan 120° = -\sqrt{3}$ $\cot 120° = -\dfrac{\sqrt{3}}{3}$

Find the values of the six trigonometric functions for angle θ in standard position if a point with the given coordinates lies on its terminal side.

6. (−1, 5)

$\sin \theta = \dfrac{5\sqrt{26}}{26}$

$\cos \theta = -\dfrac{\sqrt{26}}{26}$

$\tan \theta = -5$

$\csc \theta = \dfrac{\sqrt{26}}{5}$

$\sec \theta = -\sqrt{26}$

$\cot \theta = -\dfrac{1}{5}$

7. (7, 0)

$\sin \theta = 0$

$\cos \theta = 1$

$\tan \theta = 0$

$\csc \theta = $ undefined

$\sec \theta = 1$

$\cot \theta = $ undefined

8. (−3, −4)

$\sin \theta = -\dfrac{4}{5}$

$\cos \theta = -\dfrac{3}{5}$

$\tan \theta = \dfrac{4}{3}$

$\csc \theta = -\dfrac{5}{4}$

$\sec \theta = -\dfrac{5}{3}$

$\cot \theta = \dfrac{3}{4}$

© Glencoe/McGraw-Hill 84 Advanced Mathematical Concepts

5-4 Practice

NAME _____ DATE _____ PERIOD _____

Applying Trigonometric Functions

Solve each problem. Round to the nearest tenth.

1. If $A = 55° 55'$ and $c = 16$, find a.
   13.3

2. If $a = 9$ and $B = 49°$, find b.
   10.4

3. If $B = 56° 48'$ and $c = 63.1$, find b.
   52.8

4. If $B = 64°$ and $b = 19.2$, find a.
   9.4

5. If $b = 14$ and $A = 16°$, find c.
   14.6

6. **Construction** A 30-foot ladder leaning against the side of a house makes a 70° 5′ angle with the ground.
   a. How far up the side of the house does the ladder reach?
   about 28.2 ft

   b. What is the horizontal distance between the bottom of the ladder and the house?
   about 10.2 ft

7. **Geometry** A circle is circumscribed about a regular hexagon with an apothem of 4.8 centimeters.
   a. Find the radius of the circumscribed circle. about 5.5 cm

   b. What is the length of a side of the hexagon? about 5.5 cm

   c. What is the perimeter of the hexagon? about 33 cm

8. **Observation** A person standing 100 feet from the bottom of a cliff notices a tower on top of the cliff. The angle of elevation to the top of the cliff is 30°. The angle of elevation to the top of the tower is 58°. How tall is the tower?
   about 102.3 ft

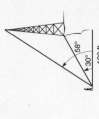

© Glencoe/McGraw-Hill 86 Advanced Mathematical Concepts

© Glencoe/McGraw-Hill 96 Advanced Mathematical Concepts

5-5 Practice
Solving Right Triangles

Solve each equation if $0° \leq x \leq 360°$.

1. $\cos x = \frac{\sqrt{2}}{2}$
45°, 315°

2. $\tan x = 1$
45°, 225°

3. $\sin x = \frac{1}{2}$
30°, 150°

Evaluate each expression. Assume that all angles are in Quadrant I.

4. $\tan\left(\tan^{-1} \frac{\sqrt{3}}{3}\right)$
$\frac{\sqrt{3}}{3}$

5. $\tan\left(\cos^{-1} \frac{2}{3}\right)$
$\frac{\sqrt{5}}{2}$

6. $\cos\left(\arcsin \frac{5}{13}\right)$
$\frac{12}{13}$

Solve each problem. Round to the nearest tenth.

7. If $q = 10$ and $s = 3$, find S.
17.5°

8. If $r = 12$ and $s = 4$, find R.
71.6°

9. If $q = 20$ and $r = 15$, find S.
41.4°

Solve each triangle described, given the triangle at the right. Round to the nearest tenth, if necessary.

10. $a = 9$, $B = 49°$
$A = 41°$, $b = 10.4$, $c = 13.7$

11. $A = 16°$, $c = 14$
$a = 3.9$, $b = 13.5$, $B = 74°$

12. $a = 2$, $b = 7$
$c = 7.3$, $A = 15.9°$, $B = 74.1°$

13. **Recreation** The swimming pool at Perris Hill Plunge is 50 feet long and 25 feet wide. The bottom of the pool is slanted so that the water depth is 3 feet at the shallow end and 15 feet at the deep end. What is the angle of elevation at the bottom of the pool? **about 13.5°**

5-6 Practice
The Law of Sines

Solve each triangle. Round to the nearest tenth.

1. $A = 38°$, $B = 63°$, $c = 15$
$C = 79°$, $a = 9.4$, $b = 13.6$

2. $A = 33°$, $B = 29°$, $b = 41$
$C = 118°$, $a = 46.1$, $c = 74.7$

3. $A = 150°$, $C = 20°$, $a = 200$
$B = 10°$, $b = 69.5$, $c = 136.8$

4. $A = 30°$, $B = 45°$, $a = 10$
$C = 105°$, $b = 14.1$, $c = 19.3$

Find the area of each triangle. Round to the nearest tenth.

5. $c = 4$, $A = 37°$, $B = 69°$
4.7 units²

6. $C = 85°$, $a = 2$, $B = 19°$
0.7 units²

7. $A = 50°$, $b = 12$, $c = 14$
64.3 units²

8. $b = 14$, $C = 110°$, $B = 25°$
154.1 units²

9. $b = 15$, $c = 20$, $A = 115°$
135.9 units²

10. $a = 68$, $c = 110$, $B = 42.5°$
2526.7 units²

11. **Street Lighting** A lamppost tilts toward the sun at a 2° angle from the vertical and casts a 25-foot shadow. The angle from the tip of the shadow to the top of the lamppost is 45°. Find the length of the lamppost. **about 25.9 ft**

5-7 Practice

NAME _____ DATE _____ PERIOD _____

The Ambiguous Case for the Law of Sines

Determine the number of possible solutions for each triangle.

1. $A = 42°$, $a = 22$, $b = 12$
1

2. $a = 15$, $b = 25$, $A = 85°$
0

3. $A = 58°$, $a = 4.5$, $b = 5$
2

4. $A = 110°$, $a = 4$, $c = 4$
0

Find all solutions for each triangle. If no solutions exist, write none. Round to the nearest tenth.

5. $b = 50$, $a = 33$, $A = 132°$
none

6. $a = 125$, $A = 25°$, $b = 150$
$B = 30.5°$, $C = 124.5°$, $c = 243.7$;
$B = 149.5°$, $C = 5.5°$, $c = 28.2$

7. $a = 32$, $c = 20$, $A = 112°$
$B = 32.6°$, $C = 35.4°$,
$b = 18.6$

8. $a = 12$, $b = 15$, $A = 55°$
none

9. $A = 42°$, $a = 22$, $b = 12$
$B = 21.4°$, $C = 116.6°$,
$c = 29.4$

10. $b = 15$, $c = 13$, $C = 50°$
$A = 67.9°$, $B = 62.1°$, $a = 15.7$;
$A = 12.1°$, $B = 117.9°$, $a = 3.6$

11. **Property Maintenance** The McDougalls plan to fence a triangular parcel of their land. One side of the property is 75 feet in length. It forms a 38° angle with another side of the property, which has not yet been measured. The remaining side of the property is 95 feet in length. Approximate to the nearest tenth the length of fence needed to enclose this parcel of the McDougalls' lot.
about 312.1 ft

5-8 Practice

NAME _____ DATE _____ PERIOD _____

The Law of Cosines

Solve each triangle. Round to the nearest tenth.

1. $a = 20$, $b = 12$, $c = 28$
$A = 38.2°$, $B = 21.8°$,
$C = 120.0°$

2. $a = 10$, $c = 8$, $B = 100°$
$b = 13.8$, $A = 45.3°$, $C = 34.7°$

3. $c = 49$, $b = 40$, $A = 53°$
$a = 40.5$, $B = 52.0°$,
$C = 75.0°$

4. $a = 5$, $b = 7$, $c = 10$
$A = 27.7°$, $B = 40.5°$, $C = 111.8°$

Find the area of each triangle. Round to the nearest tenth.

5. $a = 5$, $b = 12$, $c = 13$
30.0 units^2

6. $a = 11$, $b = 13$, $c = 16$
71.0 units^2

7. $a = 14$, $b = 9$, $c = 8$
33.7 units^2

8. $a = 8$, $b = 7$, $c = 3$
10.4 units^2

9. The sides of a triangle measure 13.4 centimeters, 18.7 centimeters, and 26.5 centimeters. Find the measure of the angle with the least measure.
about 28.3°

10. **Orienteering** During an orienteering hike, two hikers start at point A and head in a direction 30° west of south to point B. They hike 6 miles from point A to point B. From point B, they hike to point C and then from point C back to point A, which is 8 miles directly north of point C. How many miles did they hike from point B to point C?
4.1 mi

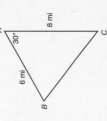

6-1

Study Guide

Angles and Radian Measure

An angle of one complete revolution can be represented either by 360° or by 2π radians. Thus, the following formulas can be used to relate degree and **radian** measures.

Degree/Radian Conversion Formulas	1 radian = $\frac{180}{\pi}$ degrees or about 57.3°
	1 degree = $\frac{\pi}{180}$ radians or about 0.017 radian

Example 1   a. **Change 36° to radian measure in terms of π.**
   b. **Change $-\frac{17\pi}{3}$ radians to degree measure.**

   a. $36° = 36° \times \frac{\pi}{180°}$
   $= \frac{\pi}{5}$

   b. $-\frac{17\pi}{3} = -\frac{17\pi}{3} \times \frac{180°}{\pi}$
   $= -1020°$

Example 2   **Evaluate $\sin \frac{3\pi}{4}$.**

The reference angle for $\frac{3\pi}{4}$ is $\frac{\pi}{4}$. Since $\frac{\pi}{4} = 45°$, the terminal side of the angle intersects the unit circle at a point with coordinates of $\left(\frac{\sqrt{2}}{2}, \frac{\sqrt{2}}{2}\right)$. Because the terminal side of $\frac{3\pi}{4}$ lies in Quadrant II, the x-coordinate is negative and the y-coordinate is positive. Therefore, $\sin \frac{3\pi}{4} = \frac{\sqrt{2}}{2}$.

Example 3   **Given a central angle of 147°, find the length of its intercepted arc in a circle of radius 10 centimeters. Round to the nearest tenth.**
First convert the measure of the central angle from degrees to radians.

$147° = 147° \times \frac{\pi}{180°}$ *1 degree* $= \frac{\pi}{180°}$
$= \frac{49\pi}{60}$

Then find the length of the arc.

$s = r\theta$ *Formula for the length of an arc*
$s = 10\left(\frac{49\pi}{60}\right)$ $r = 10, \theta = \frac{49\pi}{60}$
$s \approx 25.65634$

The length of the arc is about 25.7 cm.

6-1

Practice

Angles and Radian Measure

Change each degree measure to radian measure in terms of π.

1. $-250°$

2. $6°$

3. $-145°$

4. $870°$

5. $18°$

6. $-820°$

Change each radian measure to degree measure. Round to the nearest tenth, if necessary.

7. 4π

8. $\frac{13\pi}{30}$

9. -1

10. $\frac{3\pi}{16}$

11. -2.56

12. $-\frac{7\pi}{9}$

Evaluate each expression.

13. $\tan \frac{\pi}{4}$

14. $\cos \frac{3\pi}{2}$

15. $\sin \frac{3\pi}{2}$

16. $\tan \frac{11\pi}{6}$

17. $\cos \frac{3\pi}{4}$

18. $\sin \frac{5\pi}{3}$

Given the measurement of a central angle, find the length of its intercepted arc in a circle of radius 10 centimeters. Round to the nearest tenth.

19. $\frac{\pi}{6}$

20. $\frac{3\pi}{5}$

21. $\frac{\pi}{2}$

Find the area of each sector, given its central angle θ and the radius of the circle. Round to the nearest tenth.

22. $\theta = \frac{\pi}{6}, r = 14$

23. $\theta = \frac{7\pi}{4}, r = 4$

6-2

Study Guide

Linear and Angular Velocity

As a circular object rotates about its center, an object at the edge moves through an angle relative to the object's starting position. That is known as the **angular displacement,** or angle of rotation. **Angular velocity** ω is given by $\omega = \frac{\theta}{t}$, where θ is the angular displacement in radians and t is time. **Linear velocity** v is given by $v = r\frac{\theta}{t}$, where $\frac{\theta}{t}$ represents the angular velocity in radians per unit of time. Since $\omega = \frac{\theta}{t}$, this formula can also be written as $v = r\omega$.

Example 1 **Determine the angular displacement in radians of 3.5 revolutions. Round to the nearest tenth.**

Each revolution equals 2π radians. For 3.5 revolutions, the number of radians is $3.5 \times 2\pi$, or 7π. 7π radians equals about 22.0 radians.

Example 2 **Determine the angular velocity if 8.2 revolutions are completed in 3 seconds. Round to the nearest tenth.**

The angular displacement is $8.2 \times 2\pi$, or 16.4π radians.

$\omega = \frac{\theta}{t}$

$\omega = \frac{16.4\pi}{3}$ $\theta = 16.4\pi,\ t = 3$

$\omega \approx 17.17403984$ *Use a calculator.*

The angular velocity is about 17.2 radians per second.

Example 3 **Determine the linear velocity of a point rotating at an angular velocity of 13π radians per second at a distance of 7 centimeters from the center of the rotating object. Round to the nearest tenth.**

$v = r\omega$

$v = 7(13\pi)$ $r = 7,\ \omega = 13\pi$

$v \approx 285.8849315$ *Use a calculator.*

The linear velocity is about 285.9 centimeters per second.

6-2

Practice

Linear and Angular Velocity

Determine each angular displacement in radians. Round to the nearest tenth.

1. 6 revolutions

2. 4.3 revolutions

3. 85 revolutions

4. 11.5 revolutions

5. 7.7 revolutions

6. 17.8 revolutions

Determine each angular velocity. Round to the nearest tenth.

7. 2.6 revolutions in 6 seconds

8. 7.9 revolutions in 11 seconds

9. 118.3 revolutions in 19 minutes

10. 5.5 revolutions in 4 minutes

11. 22.4 revolutions in 15 seconds

12. 14 revolutions in 2 minutes

Determine the linear velocity of a point rotating at the given angular velocity at a distance r from the center of the rotating object. Round to the nearest tenth.

13. $\omega = 14.3$ radians per second, $r = 7$ centimeters

14. $\omega = 28$ radians per second, $r = 2$ feet

15. $\omega = 5.4\pi$ radians per minute, $r = 1.3$ meters

16. $\omega = 41.7\pi$ radians per second, $r = 18$ inches

17. $\omega = 234$ radians per minute, $r = 31$ inches

18. *Clocks* Suppose the second hand on a clock is 3 inches long.
    Find the linear velocity of the tip of the second hand.

6-3

Study Guide

Graphing Sine and Cosine Functions

If the values of a function are the same for each given interval of the domain, the function is said to be **periodic.** Consider the graphs of $y = \sin x$ and $y = \cos x$ shown below. Notice that for both graphs the period is 2π and the range is from -1 to 1, inclusive.

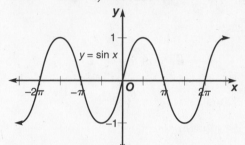
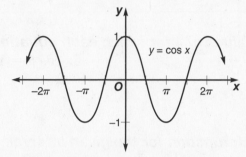

Properties of the Graph of $y = \sin x$	Properties of the Graph of $y = \cos x$
The x-intercepts are located at πn, where n is an integer.	The x-intercepts are located at $\frac{\pi}{2} + \pi n$, where n is an integer.
The y-intercept is 0.	The y-intercept is 1.
The maximum values are $y = 1$ and occur when $x = \frac{\pi}{2} + 2\pi n$, when n is an integer.	The maximum values are $y = 1$ and occur when $x = \pi n$, where n is an even integer.
The minimum values are $y = -1$ and occur when $x = \frac{3\pi}{2} + 2\pi n$, where n is an integer.	The minimum values are $y = -1$ and occur when $x = \pi n$, where n is an odd integer.

Example 1 **Find $\sin \frac{7\pi}{2}$ by referring to the graph of the sine function.**

The period of the sine function is 2π. Since $\frac{7\pi}{2} > 2\pi$, rewrite $\frac{7\pi}{2}$ as a sum involving 2π.

$\frac{7\pi}{2} = 2\pi(1) + \frac{3\pi}{2}$ *This is a form of $\frac{3\pi}{2} + 2\pi n$.*

So, $\sin \frac{7\pi}{2} = \sin \frac{3\pi}{2}$ or -1.

Example 2 **Find the values of θ for which $\cos \theta = 0$ is true.**

Since $\cos \theta = 0$ indicates the x-intercepts of the cosine function, $\cos \theta = 0$ if $\theta = \frac{\pi}{2} + \pi n$, where n is an integer.

Example 3 **Graph $y = \sin x$ for $6\pi \le x \le 8\pi$.**

The graph crosses the x-axis at 6π, 7π, and 8π. Its maximum value of 1 is at $x = \frac{13\pi}{2}$, and its minimum value of -1 is at $x = \frac{15\pi}{2}$. Use this information to sketch the graph.

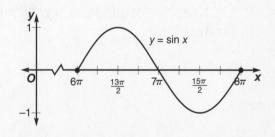

6-3

Practice

Graphing Sine and Cosine Functions

Find each value by referring to the graph of the sine or the cosine function.

1. $\cos \pi$

2. $\sin \frac{3\pi}{2}$

3. $\sin \left(-\frac{7\pi}{2}\right)$

Find the values of θ for which each equation is true.

4. $\sin \theta = 0$

5. $\cos \theta = 1$

6. $\cos \theta = -1$

Graph each function for the given interval.

7. $y = \sin x; -\frac{\pi}{2} \le x \le \frac{\pi}{2}$

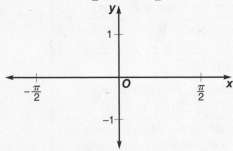

8. $y = \cos x; 7\pi \le x \le 9\pi$

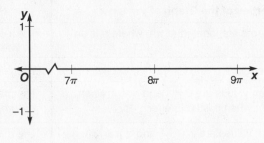

Determine whether each graph is y = sin x, y = cos x, or neither.

9.

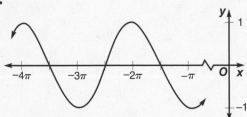

10.

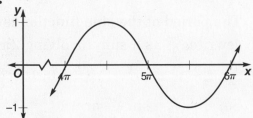

11. *Meteorology* The equation $y = 70.5 + 19.5 \sin \left[\frac{\pi}{6}(t - 4)\right]$ models the average monthly temperature for Phoenix, Arizona, in degrees Fahrenheit. In this equation, t denotes the number of months, with $t = 1$ representing January. What is the average monthly temperature for July?

6-4

Study Guide

Amplitude and Period of Sine and Cosine Functions

The **amplitude** of the functions $y = A \sin \theta$ and $y = A \cos \theta$ is the absolute value of A, or $|A|$. The period of the functions $y = \sin k\theta$ and $y = \cos k\theta$ is $\frac{2\pi}{k}$, where $k > 0$.

Example 1   **State the amplitude and period for the function**
$$y = -2 \cos \frac{\theta}{4}.$$

The definition of *amplitude* states that the amplitude of $y = A \cos \theta$ is $|A|$. Therefore, the amplitude of $y = -2 \cos \frac{\theta}{4}$ is $|-2|$, or 2.

The definition of *period* states that the period of $y = \cos k\theta$ is $\frac{2\pi}{k}$. Since $-2 \cos \frac{\theta}{4}$ equals $-2 \cos \left(\frac{1}{4}\theta\right)$, the period is $\frac{2\pi}{\frac{1}{4}}$ or 8π.

Example 2   **State the amplitude and period for the function $y = 3 \sin 2\theta$. Then graph the function.**

Since $A = 3$, the amplitude is $|3|$ or 3.
Since $k = 2$, the period is $\frac{2\pi}{2}$ or π.

Use the amplitude and period above and the basic shape of the sine function to graph the equation.

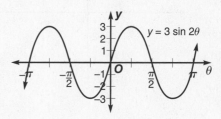

Example 3   **Write an equation of the sine function with amplitude 6.7 and period 3π.**

The form of the equation will be $y = A \sin k\theta$. First find the possible values of A for an amplitude of 6.7.

$|A| = 6.7$
$\quad A = 6.7$ or -6.7

Since there are two values of A, two possible equations exist.

Now find the value of k when the period is 3π.

$\frac{2\pi}{k} = 3\pi$ *The period of the sine function is $\frac{2\pi}{k}$.*

$\quad k = \frac{2\pi}{3\pi}$ or $\frac{2}{3}$

The possible equations are $y = 6.7 \sin \frac{2}{3}\theta$ or $y = -6.7 \sin \frac{2}{3}\theta$.

X **6-4**

Practice

Amplitude and Period of Sine and Cosine Functions

State the amplitude and period for each function. Then graph each function.

1. $y = -2 \sin \theta$

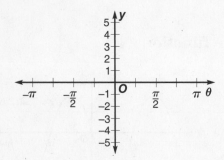

2. $y = 4 \cos \frac{\theta}{3}$

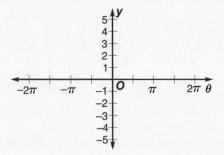

3. $y = 1.5 \cos 4\theta$

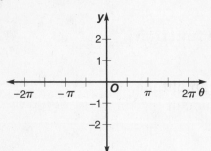

4. $y = -\frac{2}{3} \sin \frac{\theta}{2}$

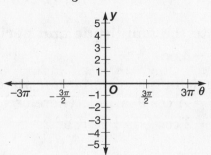

Write an equation of the sine function with each amplitude and period.

5. amplitude = 3, period = 2π

6. amplitude = 8.5, period = 6π

Write an equation of the cosine function with each amplitude and period.

7. amplitude = 0.5, period = 0.2π

8. amplitude = $\frac{1}{5}$, period = $\frac{2}{5}\pi$

9. *Music*   A piano tuner strikes a tuning fork for note A above middle C and sets in motion vibrations that can be modeled by the equation $y = 0.001 \sin 880\pi t$. Find the amplitude and period for the function.

6-5

Study Guide

Translations of Sine and Cosine Functions

A horizontal translation of a trigonometric function is called a **phase shift**. The phase shift of the functions $y = A \sin (k\theta + c)$
and $y = A \cos (k\theta + c)$ is $-\frac{c}{k}$, where $k > 0$. If $c > 0$, the shift is to the left. If $c < 0$, the shift is to the right. The **vertical shift** of the functions $y = A \sin (k\theta + c) + h$ and $y = A \cos (k\theta + c) + h$ is h. If $h > 0$, the shift is upward. If $h < 0$, the shift is downward. The **midline** about which the graph oscillates is $y = h$.

Example 1   **State the phase shift for $y = \sin (4\theta + \pi)$. Then graph the function.**

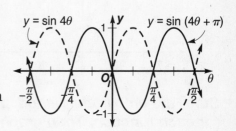

The phase shift of the function is $-\frac{c}{k}$ or $-\frac{\pi}{4}$.

To graph $y = \sin (4\theta + \pi)$, consider the graph of $y = \sin 4\theta$. The graph of $y = \sin 4\theta$ has an amplitude of 1 and a period of $\frac{\pi}{2}$. Graph this function, then shift the graph $-\frac{\pi}{4}$.

Example 2   **State the vertical shift and the equation of the midline for $y = 3 \cos \theta + 2$. Then graph the function.**

The vertical shift is 2 units upward. The midline is the graph of $y = 2$.

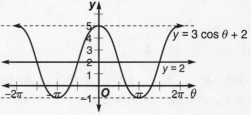

To graph the function, draw the midline. Since the amplitude of the function is $|3|$, or 3, draw dashed lines parallel to the midline which are 3 units above and below $y = 2$. That is, $y = 5$ and $y = -1$. Then draw the cosine curve with a period of 2π.

Example 3   **Write an equation of the cosine function with amplitude 2.9, period $\frac{2\pi}{5}$, phase shift $-\frac{\pi}{2}$, and vertical shift -3.**

The form of the equation will be $y = A \cos (k\theta + c) + h$. Find the values of A, k, c, and h.

A: $|A| = 2.9$
   $A = 2.9$ or -2.9

k: $\frac{2\pi}{k} = \frac{2\pi}{5}$ *The period is $\frac{2\pi}{5}$.*
   $k = 5$

c: $-\frac{c}{k} = -\frac{\pi}{2}$
   $-\frac{c}{5} = -\frac{\pi}{2}$
   $c = \frac{5\pi}{2}$

The phase shift is $-\frac{\pi}{2}$.
   $k = 5$

h: $h = -3$

The possible equations are $y = \pm 2.9 \cos \left(5\theta + \frac{5\pi}{2}\right) - 3$.

6-5

Practice

Translations of Sine and Cosine Functions

State the vertical shift and the equation of the midline for each function. Then graph each function.

1. $y = 4 \cos \theta + 4$

2. $y = \sin 2\theta - 2$

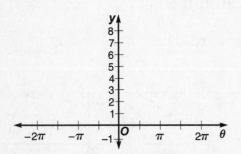

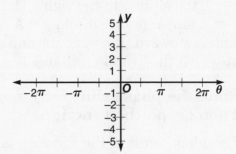

State the amplitude, period, phase shift, and vertical shift for each function. Then graph the function.

3. $y = 2 \sin \left(\theta + \frac{\pi}{2}\right) - 3$

4. $y = \frac{1}{2} \cos (2\theta - \pi) + 2$

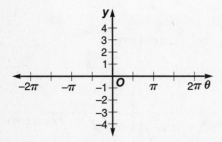

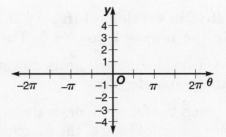

Write an equation of the specified function with each amplitude, period, phase shift, and vertical shift.

5. sine function: amplitude = 15, period = 4π, phase shift = $\frac{\pi}{2}$, vertical shift = -10

6. cosine function: amplitude = $\frac{2}{3}$, period = $\frac{\pi}{3}$, phase shift = $-\frac{\pi}{3}$, vertical shift = 5

7. sine function: amplitude = 6, period = π, phase shift = 0, vertical shift = $-\frac{3}{2}$

6-6

Study Guide

Modeling Real-World Data with Sinusoidal Functions

Example

The table shows the average monthly temperatures for Ann Arbor, Michigan. Write a sinusoidal function that models the average monthly temperatures, using $t = 1$ to represent January. Temperatures are in degrees Fahrenheit (°F).

Jan.	30°
Feb.	34°
Mar.	45°
Apr.	59°
May	71°
June	80°
July	84°
Aug.	81°
Sept.	74°
Oct.	62°
Nov.	48°
Dec.	35°

These data can be modeled by a function of the form $y = A \sin (kt + c) + h$, where t is the time in months.

First, find A, h, and k.

A: $A = \frac{84 - 30}{2}$ or 27   *A is half the difference between the greatest temperature and the least temperature.*

h: $h = \frac{84 + 30}{2}$ or 57   *h is half the sum of the greatest value and the least value.*

k: $\frac{2\pi}{k} = 12$ *The period is 12.*

     $k = \frac{\pi}{6}$

Substitute these values into the general form of the function.

$y = A \sin (kt + c) + h \qquad y = 27 \sin \left(\frac{\pi}{6}t + c\right) + 57$

To compute c, substitute one of the coordinate pairs into the equation.

$$y = 27 \sin \left(\frac{\pi}{6}t + c\right) + 57$$

$30 = 27 \sin \left[\frac{\pi}{6}(1) + c\right] + 57$ *Use $(t, y) = (1, 30)$.*

$-27 = 27 \sin \left(\frac{\pi}{6} + c\right)$ *Subtract 57 from each side.*

$-\frac{27}{27} = \sin \left(\frac{\pi}{6} + c\right)$ *Divide each side by 27.*

$\sin^{-1}(-1) = \frac{\pi}{6} + c$ *Definition of inverse*

$\sin^{-1}(-1) - \frac{\pi}{6} = c$ *Subtract $\frac{\pi}{6}$ from each side.*

$-2.094395102 \approx c$ *Use a calculator.*

The function $y = 27 \sin \left(\frac{\pi}{6}t - 2.09\right) + 57$ is one model for the average monthly temperature in Ann Arbor, Michigan.

6-6

Practice

Modeling Real-World Data with Sinusoidal Functions

1. *Meteorology*   The average monthly temperatures in degrees Fahrenheit (°F) for Baltimore, Maryland, are given below.

Jan.	Feb.	Mar.	Apr.	May	June	July	Aug.	Sept.	Oct.	Nov.	Dec.
32°	35°	44°	53°	63°	73°	77°	76°	69°	57°	47°	37°

   a. Find the amplitude of a sinusoidal function that models the monthly temperatures.

   b. Find the vertical shift of a sinusoidal function that models the monthly temperatures.

   c. What is the period of a sinusoidal function that models the monthly temperatures?

   d. Write a sinusoidal function that models the monthly temperatures, using $t = 1$ to represent January.

   e. According to your model, what is the average temperature in July? How does this compare with the actual average?

   f. According to your model, what is the average temperature in December? How does this compare with the actual average?

2. *Boating*   A buoy, bobbing up and down in the water as waves move past it, moves from its highest point to its lowest point and back to its highest point every 10 seconds. The distance between its highest and lowest points is 3 feet.

   a. What is the amplitude of a sinusoidal function that models the bobbing buoy?

   b. What is the period of a sinusoidal function that models the bobbing buoy?

   c. Write a sinusoidal function that models the bobbing buoy, using $t = 0$ at its highest point.

   d. According to your model, what is the height of the buoy at $t = 2$ seconds?

   e. According to your model, what is the height of the buoy at $t = 6$ seconds?

6-7

Study Guide

Graphing Other Trigonometric Functions

The period of functions $y = \csc k\theta$ and $y = \sec k\theta$ is $\frac{2\pi}{k}$, where $k > 0$. The period of functions $y = \tan k\theta$ and $y = \cot k\theta$ is $\frac{\pi}{k}$, where $k > 0$. The phase shift and vertical shift work the same way for all trigonometric functions. For example, the phase shift of the function $y = \tan(k\theta + c) + h$ is $-\frac{c}{k}$, and its vertical shift is h.

Example 1 **Graph $y = \tan x$.**

To graph $y = \tan x$, first draw the asymptotes located at $x = \frac{\pi}{2}n$, where n is an odd integer. Then plot the following coordinate pairs and draw the curves.

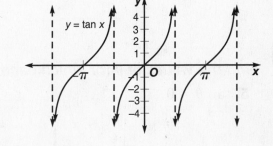

$\left(-\frac{5\pi}{4}, -1\right)$, $(-\pi, 0)$, $\left(-\frac{3\pi}{4}, 1\right)$, $\left(-\frac{\pi}{4}, -1\right)$,

$(0, 0)$, $\left(\frac{\pi}{4}, 1\right)$, $\left(\frac{3\pi}{4}, -1\right)$, $(\pi, 0)$, $\left(\frac{5\pi}{4}, 1\right)$

Notice that the range values for the interval $-\frac{3\pi}{2} \le x \le -\frac{\pi}{2}$ repeat for the intervals $-\frac{\pi}{2} \le x \le \frac{\pi}{2}$ and $\frac{\pi}{2} \le x \le \frac{3\pi}{2}$.

So, the tangent function is a periodic function with a period of $\frac{\pi}{k}$ or π.

Example 2 **Graph $y = \sec(2\theta + \pi) + 4$.**

Since $k = 2$, the period is $\frac{2\pi}{2}$ or π. Since $c = \pi$, the phase shift is $-\frac{\pi}{2}$. The vertical shift is 4.

Using this information, follow the steps for graphing a secant function.

Step 1 Draw the midline, which is the graph of $y = 4$.

Step 2 Draw dashed lines parallel to the midline, which are 1 unit above and below $y = 4$.

Step 3 Draw the secant curve with a period of π.

Step 4 Shift the graph $\frac{\pi}{2}$ units to the left.

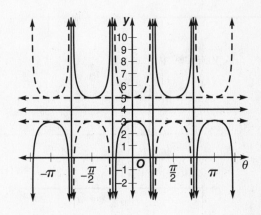

6-7

Practice

Graphing Other Trigonometric Functions

Find each value by referring to the graphs of the trigonometric functions.

1. $\tan\left(-\frac{3\pi}{2}\right)$

2. $\cot\left(\frac{3\pi}{2}\right)$

3. $\sec 4\pi$

4. $\csc\left(-\frac{7\pi}{2}\right)$

Find the values of θ for which each equation is true.

5. $\tan\theta = 0$

6. $\cot\theta = 0$

7. $\csc\theta = 1$

8. $\sec\theta = -1$

Graph each function.

9. $y = \tan(2\theta + \pi) + 1$

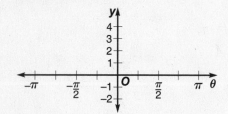

10. $y = \cot\left(\frac{\theta}{2} - \frac{\pi}{2}\right) - 2$

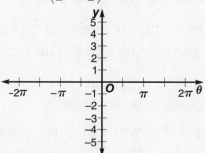

11. $y = \csc\theta + 3$

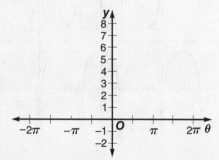

12. $y = \sec\left(\frac{\theta}{3} + \pi\right) - 1$

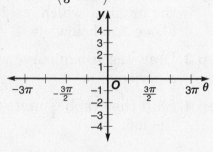

6-8

Study Guide

Trigonometric Inverses and Their Graphs

The inverses of the Sine, Cosine, and Tangent functions are called Arcsine, Arccosine, and Arctangent, respectively. The capital letters are used to represent the functions with restricted domains. The graphs of Arcsine, Arccosine, and Arctangent are defined as follows.

Arcsine Function	Given $y = \text{Sin } x$, the inverse Sine function is defined by the equation $y = \text{Sin}^{-1} x$ or $y = \text{Arcsin } x$.
Arccosine Function	Given $y = \text{Cos } x$, the inverse Cosine function is defined by the equation $y = \text{Cos}^{-1} x$ or $y = \text{Arccos } x$.
Arctangent Function	Given $y = \text{Tan } x$, the inverse Tangent function is defined by the equation $y = \text{Tan}^{-1} x$ or $y = \text{Arctan } x$.

Example 1 **Write the equation for the inverse of $y = \text{Arcsin } 2x$. Then graph the function and its inverse.**

$$y = \text{Arcsin } 2x$$
$$x = \text{Arcsin } 2y \qquad \textit{Exchange x and y.}$$
$$\text{Sin } x = 2y \qquad \textit{Definition of Arcsin function}$$
$$\tfrac{1}{2} \text{Sin } x = y \qquad \textit{Divide each side by 2.}$$

Now graph the functions.

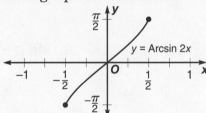 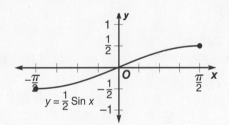

Example 2 **Find each value.**

   a. $\text{Arctan}\left(-\frac{\sqrt{3}}{3}\right)$

     Let $\theta = \text{Arctan}\left(-\frac{\sqrt{3}}{3}\right)$. $\textit{Arctan}\left(-\frac{\sqrt{3}}{3}\right)$ *means that angle whose tan is* $-\frac{\sqrt{3}}{3}$.

     $\text{Tan } \theta = -\frac{\sqrt{3}}{3}$ *Definition of Arctan function*

     $\theta = -\frac{\pi}{6}$

   b. $\text{Cos}^{-1}\left(\sin \frac{\pi}{2}\right)$

     If $y = \sin \frac{\pi}{2}$, then $y = 1$.

     $\text{Cos}^{-1}\left(\sin \frac{\pi}{2}\right) = \text{Cos}^{-1} 1$ *Replace sin $\frac{\pi}{2}$ with 1.*

                    $= 0$

6-8

Practice

Trigonometric Inverses and Their Graphs

Write the equation for the inverse of each function. Then graph the function and its inverse.

1. $y = \tan 2x$

2. $y = \frac{\pi}{2} + \text{Arccos } x$

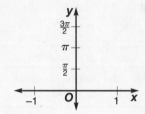

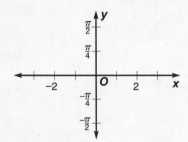

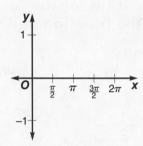

Find each value.

3. $\text{Arccos } (-1)$

4. $\text{Arctan } 1$

5. $\text{Arcsin } \left(-\frac{1}{2}\right)$

6. $\text{Sin}^{-1} \frac{\sqrt{3}}{2}$

7. $\text{Cos}^{-1} \left(\sin \frac{\pi}{3}\right)$

8. $\tan \left(\text{Sin}^{-1} 1 - \text{Cos}^{-1} \frac{1}{2}\right)$

9. *Weather* The equation $y = 10 \sin \left(\frac{\pi}{6}t - \frac{2\pi}{3}\right) + 57$ models the average monthly temperatures for Napa, California. In this equation, t denotes the number of months with January represented by $t = 1$. During which two months is the average temperature 62°?

Answers (Lessons 6-1 and 6-2)

6-1 Practice

Angles and Radian Measure

Change each degree measure to radian measure in terms of π.

1. $-250°$ $-\dfrac{25\pi}{18}$
2. $6°$ $\dfrac{\pi}{30}$
3. $-145°$ $-\dfrac{29\pi}{36}$
4. $870°$ $\dfrac{29\pi}{6}$
5. $18°$ $\dfrac{\pi}{10}$
6. $-820°$ $-\dfrac{41\pi}{9}$

Change each radian measure to degree measure. Round to the nearest tenth, if necessary.

7. 4π $720°$
8. $\dfrac{13\pi}{30}$ $78°$
9. -1 $-57.3°$
10. $\dfrac{3\pi}{16}$ $33.8°$
11. -2.56 $-146.7°$
12. $-\dfrac{7\pi}{9}$ $-140°$

Evaluate each expression.

13. $\tan \dfrac{\pi}{4}$ 1
14. $\cos \dfrac{3\pi}{2}$ 0
15. $\sin \dfrac{3\pi}{2}$ -1
16. $\tan \dfrac{11\pi}{6}$ $-\dfrac{\sqrt{3}}{3}$
17. $\cos \dfrac{3\pi}{4}$ $-\dfrac{\sqrt{2}}{2}$
18. $\sin \dfrac{5\pi}{3}$ $-\dfrac{\sqrt{3}}{2}$

Given the measurement of a central angle, find the length of its intercepted arc in a circle of radius 10 centimeters. Round to the nearest tenth.

19. $\dfrac{\pi}{6}$ 5.2 cm
20. $\dfrac{3\pi}{5}$ 18.8 cm
21. $\dfrac{\pi}{2}$ 15.7 cm

Find the area of each sector, given its central angle θ and the radius of the circle. Round to the nearest tenth.

22. $\theta = \dfrac{\pi}{6}, r = 14$ 51.3 units^2
23. $\theta = \dfrac{7\pi}{4}, r = 4$ 44.0 units^2

6-2 Practice

Linear and Angular Velocity

Determine each angular displacement in radians. Round to the nearest tenth.

1. 6 revolutions   **37.7 radians**
2. 4.3 revolutions   **27.0 radians**
3. 85 revolutions   **534.1 radians**
4. 11.5 revolutions   **72.3 radians**
5. 7.7 revolutions   **48.4 radians**
6. 17.8 revolutions   **111.8 radians**

Determine each angular velocity. Round to the nearest tenth.

7. 2.6 revolutions in 6 seconds   **2.7 radians/s**
8. 7.9 revolutions in 11 seconds   **4.5 radians/s**
9. 118.3 revolutions in 19 minutes   **39.1 radians/min**
10. 5.5 revolutions in 4 minutes   **8.6 radians/min**
11. 22.4 revolutions in 15 seconds   **9.4 radians/s**
12. 14 revolutions in 2 minutes   **44.0 radians/min**

Determine the linear velocity of a point rotating at the given angular velocity at a distance r from the center of the rotating object. Round to the nearest tenth.

13. $\omega = 14.3$ radians per second, $r = 7$ centimeters   **100.1 cm/s**
14. $\omega = 28$ radians per second, $r = 2$ feet   **56.0 ft/s**
15. $\omega = 5.4\pi$ radians per minute, $r = 1.3$ meters   **22.1 m/min**
16. $\omega = 41.7\pi$ radians per second, $r = 18$ inches   **2358.1 in/s**
17. $\omega = 234$ radians per minute, $r = 31$ inches   **7254.0 in./min**
18. **Clocks** Suppose the second hand on a clock is 3 inches long. Find the linear velocity of the tip of the second hand.   **0.3 in/s**

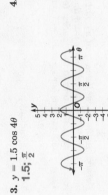

Answers (Lessons 6-3 and 6-4)

6-3

NAME _____ DATE _____ PERIOD _____

Practice

Graphing Sine and Cosine Functions

Find each value by referring to the graph of the sine or the cosine function.

1. $\cos \pi$

-1

2. $\sin \dfrac{3\pi}{2}$

-1

3. $\sin \left(-\dfrac{7\pi}{2}\right)$

1

Find the values of θ for which each equation is true.

4. $\sin \theta = 0$

πn, where n is any integer

5. $\cos \theta = 1$

πn, where n is an even integer

6. $\cos \theta = -1$

πn, where n is an odd integer

Graph each function for the given interval.

7. $y = \sin x$; $-\dfrac{\pi}{2} \leq x \leq \dfrac{\pi}{2}$

8. $y = \cos x$; $7\pi \leq x \leq 9\pi$

Determine whether each graph is $y = \sin x$, $y = \cos x$, or neither.

9.

$y = \cos x$

10.

$y = \sin x$

11. **Meteorology** The equation $y = 70.5 + 19.5 \sin \left[\dfrac{\pi}{6}(t - 4)\right]$ models the average monthly temperature for Phoenix, Arizona, in degrees Fahrenheit. In this equation, t denotes the number of months, with $t = 1$ representing January. What is the average monthly temperature for July? **90°F**

6-4

NAME _____ DATE _____ PERIOD _____

Practice

Amplitude and Period of Sine and Cosine Functions

State the amplitude and period for each function. Then graph each function.

1. $y = -2 \sin \theta$

2; 2π

2. $y = 4 \cos \dfrac{\theta}{3}$

4; 6π

3. $y = 1.5 \cos 4\theta$

1.5; $\dfrac{\pi}{2}$

4. $y = -\dfrac{2}{3} \sin \dfrac{\theta}{2}$

$\dfrac{2}{3}$; 4π

Write an equation of the sine function with each amplitude and period.

5. amplitude = 3, period = 2π

$y = \pm 3 \sin \theta$

6. amplitude = 8.5, period = 6π

$y = \pm 8.5 \sin \dfrac{\theta}{3}$

Write an equation of the cosine function with each amplitude and period.

7. amplitude = 0.5, period = 0.2π

$y = \pm 0.5 \cos 10\theta$

8. amplitude = $\dfrac{1}{5}$, period = $\dfrac{2}{5}\pi$

$y = \pm\dfrac{1}{5} \cos 5\theta$

9. **Music** A piano tuner strikes a tuning fork for note A above middle C and sets in motion vibrations that can be modeled by the equation $y = 0.001 \sin 880\pi t$. Find the amplitude and period for the function. **0.001; $\dfrac{1}{440}$**

6-5 Practice

Translations of Sine and Cosine Functions

State the vertical shift and the equation of the midline for each function. Then graph each function.

1. $y = 4 \cos \theta + 4$

4 units up; $y = 4$

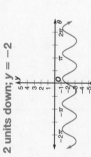

2. $y = \sin 2\theta - 2$

2 units down; $y = -2$

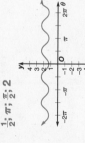

State the amplitude, period, phase shift, and vertical shift for each function. Then graph the function.

3. $y = 2 \sin \left(\theta + \frac{\pi}{2}\right) - 3$

2; 2π, $-\frac{\pi}{2}$; -3

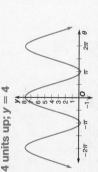

4. $y = \frac{1}{2} \cos (2\theta - \pi) + 2$

$\frac{1}{2}$; π; $\frac{\pi}{2}$; 2

Write an equation of the specified function with each amplitude, period, phase shift, and vertical shift.

5. sine function: amplitude = 15, period = 4π, phase shift = $\frac{\pi}{2}$, vertical shift = -10

$y = \pm 15 \sin \left(\frac{\theta}{2} - \frac{\pi}{4}\right) - 10$

6. cosine function: amplitude = $\frac{2}{3}$, period = $\frac{\pi}{3}$, phase shift = $-\frac{\pi}{3}$, vertical shift = 5

$y = \pm \frac{2}{3} \cos (6\theta + 2\pi) + 5$

7. sine function: amplitude = 6, period = π, phase shift = 0, vertical shift = $-\frac{3}{2}$

$y = \pm 6 \sin 2\theta - \frac{3}{2}$

6-6 Practice

Modeling Real-World Data with Sinusoidal Functions

1. **Meteorology** The average monthly temperatures in degrees Fahrenheit (°F) for Baltimore, Maryland, are given below.

Jan.	Feb.	Mar.	Apr.	May	June	July	Aug.	Sept.	Oct.	Nov.	Dec.
32°	35°	44°	53°	63°	73°	77°	76°	69°	57°	47°	37°

a. Find the amplitude of a sinusoidal function that models the monthly temperatures.

22.5°

b. Find the vertical shift of a sinusoidal function that models the monthly temperatures.

54.5°

c. What is the period of a sinusoidal function that models the monthly temperatures?

12 months

d. Write a sinusoidal function that models the monthly temperatures, using $t = 1$ to represent January.

Sample answer: $y = 22.5 \cos \left(\frac{\pi}{6}t + 2.62\right) + 54.5$

e. According to your model, what is the average temperature in July? How does this compare with the actual average?

Sample answer: 77°; the average temperature and the model are the same.

f. According to your model, what is the average temperature in December? How does this compare with the actual average?

Sample answer: 35°; the average temperature is 37°; the model is 2° less.

2. **Boating** A buoy, bobbing up and down in the water as waves move past it, moves from its highest point to its lowest point and back to its highest point every 10 seconds. The distance between its highest and lowest points is 3 feet.

a. What is the amplitude of a sinusoidal function that models the bobbing buoy? **1.5**

b. What is the period of a sinusoidal function that models the bobbing buoy? **10 s**

c. Write a sinusoidal function that models the bobbing buoy, using $t = 0$ at its highest point. **Sample answer: $1.5 \cos \left(\frac{\pi t}{5}\right)$**

d. According to your model, what is the height of the buoy at $t = 2$ seconds? **about 0.46 ft**

e. According to your model, what is the height of the buoy at $t = 6$ seconds? **about -1.21 ft**

Left page (6-7)

6-7

Practice

Graphing Other Trigonometric Functions

Find each value by referring to the graphs of the trigonometric functions.

1. $\tan\left(-\dfrac{3\pi}{2}\right)$
undefined

2. $\cot\left(\dfrac{3\pi}{2}\right)$
0

3. $\sec 4\pi$
1

4. $\csc\left(-\dfrac{7\pi}{2}\right)$
1

Find the values of θ for which each equation is true.

5. $\tan\theta = 0$
πn, where n is an integer

6. $\cot\theta = 0$
$\dfrac{\pi}{2}n$, where n is an odd integer

7. $\csc\theta = 1$
$\dfrac{\pi}{2} + 2\pi n$, where n is an integer

8. $\sec\theta = -1$
πn, where n is an odd integer

Graph each function.

9. $y = \tan(2\theta + \pi) + 1$

10. $y = \cot\left(\dfrac{\theta}{2} - \dfrac{\pi}{2}\right) - 2$

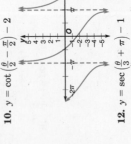

11. $y = \csc\theta + 3$

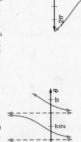

12. $y = \sec\left(\dfrac{\theta}{3} + \pi\right) - 1$

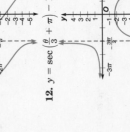

Right page (6-8)

6-8

Practice

Trigonometric Inverses and Their Graphs

Write the equation for the inverse of each function. Then graph the function and its inverse.

1. $y = \tan 2x$
$y = \dfrac{1}{2}\tan^{-1}x$

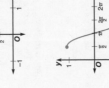

2. $y = \dfrac{\pi}{2} + \text{Arccos } x$
$y = \text{Cos}\left(x - \dfrac{\pi}{2}\right)$

Find each value.

3. $\text{Arccos}(-1)$
π

4. $\text{Arctan } 1$
$\dfrac{\pi}{4}$

5. $\text{Arcsin}\left(-\dfrac{1}{2}\right)$
$-\dfrac{\pi}{6}$

6. $\text{Sin}^{-1}\dfrac{\sqrt{3}}{2}$
$\dfrac{\pi}{3}$

7. $\text{Cos}^{-1}\left(\sin\dfrac{\pi}{3}\right)$
$\dfrac{\pi}{6}$

8. $\tan\left(\text{Sin}^{-1}1 - \text{Cos}^{-1}\dfrac{1}{2}\right)$
$\dfrac{\sqrt{3}}{3}$

9. Weather The equation $y = 10\sin\left(\dfrac{\pi}{6}t - \dfrac{2\pi}{3}\right) + 57$ models the average monthly temperatures for Napa, California. In this equation, t denotes the number of months with January represented by $t = 1$. During which two months is the average temperature 62°? **May and September**

7-1

Study Guide

Basic Trigonometric Identities

You can use the **trigonometric identities** to help find the values of trigonometric functions.

Example 1 **If $\sin \theta = \frac{3}{5}$, find $\tan \theta$.**

Use two identities to relate $\sin \theta$ and $\tan \theta$.

$\sin^2 \theta + \cos^2 \theta = 1$ *Pythagorean identity*

$\left(\frac{3}{5}\right)^2 + \cos^2 \theta = 1$ *Substitute $\frac{3}{5}$ for $\sin \theta$.*

$\cos^2 \theta = \frac{16}{25}$

$\cos \theta = \pm \sqrt{\frac{16}{25}}$ or $\pm\frac{4}{5}$

Now find $\tan \theta$.

$\tan \theta = \frac{\sin \theta}{\cos \theta}$ *Quotient identity*

$\tan \theta = \dfrac{\frac{3}{5}}{\pm\frac{4}{5}}$

$\tan \theta = \pm\frac{3}{4}$

To determine the sign of a function value, use the **symmetry identities** for sine and cosine. To use these identities with radian measure, replace 180° with π and 360° with 2π.

Case 1:	$\sin (A + 360k°) = \sin A$	$\cos (A + 360k°) = \cos A$
Case 2:	$\sin [A + 180°(2k - 1)] = -\sin A$	$\cos [A + 180°(2k - 1)] = -\cos A$
Case 3:	$\sin (360k° - A) = -\sin A$	$\cos (360k° - A) = \cos A$
Case 4:	$\sin [180°(2k - 1) - A] = \sin A$	$\cos [180°(2k - 1) - A] = -\cos A$

Example 2 Express $\tan \frac{11\pi}{3}$ as a trigonometric function of an angle in Quadrant I.

The sum of $\frac{11\pi}{3}$ and $\frac{\pi}{3}$, which is $\frac{12\pi}{3}$ or 4π, is a multiple of 2π.

$\frac{11\pi}{3} = 2(2\pi) - \frac{\pi}{3}$ *Case 3, with $A = \frac{\pi}{3}$ and $k = 2$*

$\tan \frac{11\pi}{3} = \dfrac{\sin \frac{11\pi}{3}}{\cos \frac{11\pi}{3}}$ *Quotient identity*

$= \dfrac{\sin \left[2(2\pi) - \frac{\pi}{3}\right]}{\cos \left[2(2\pi) - \frac{\pi}{3}\right]}$

$= \dfrac{-\sin \frac{\pi}{3}}{\cos \frac{\pi}{3}}$ *Symmetry identities*

$= -\tan \frac{\pi}{3}$ *Quotient identity*

7-1

Practice

Basic Trigonometric Identities

Use the given information to determine the exact trigonometric value if $0° < \theta < 90°$.

1. If $\cos \theta = \frac{1}{4}$, find $\tan \theta$.

2. If $\sin \theta = \frac{2}{3}$, find $\cos \theta$.

3. If $\tan \theta = \frac{7}{2}$, find $\sin \theta$.

4. If $\tan \theta = 2$, find $\cot \theta$.

Express each value as a trigonometric function of an angle in Quandrant I.

5. $\cos 892°$

6. $\csc 495°$

7. $\sin \frac{23\pi}{3}$

Simplify each expression.

8. $\cos x + \sin x \tan x$

9. $\frac{\cot A}{\tan A}$

10. $\sin^2 \theta \cos^2 \theta - \cos^2 \theta$

11. *Kite Flying* Brett and Tara are flying a kite. When the string is tied to the ground, the height of the kite can be determined by the formula $\frac{L}{H} = \csc \theta$, where L is the length of the string and θ is the angle between the string and the level ground. What formula could Brett and Tara use to find the height of the kite if they know the value of $\sin \theta$?

7-2

Study Guide

Verifying Trigonometric Identities

When verifying trigonometric identities, you cannot add or subtract quantities from each side of the identity. An unverified identity is not an equation, so the properties of equality do not apply.

Example 1 **Verify that $\dfrac{\sec^2 x - 1}{\sec^2 x} = \sin^2 x$ is an identity.**

Since the left side is more complicated, transform it into the expression on the right.

$$\frac{\sec^2 x - 1}{\sec^2 x} \stackrel{?}{=} \sin^2 x$$

$$\frac{(\tan^2 x + 1) - 1}{\sec^2 x} \stackrel{?}{=} \sin^2 x \qquad sec^2\ x = tan^2\ x + 1$$

$$\frac{\tan^2 x}{\sec^2 x} \stackrel{?}{=} \sin^2 x \qquad Simplify.$$

$$\frac{\dfrac{\sin^2 x}{\cos^2 x}}{\dfrac{1}{\cos^2 x}} \stackrel{?}{=} \sin^2 x \qquad tan^2\ x = \frac{sin^2\ x}{cos^2\ x},\ sec^2\ x = \frac{1}{cos^2\ x}$$

$$\frac{\sin^2 x}{\cos^2 x} \cdot \cos^2 x \stackrel{?}{=} \sin^2 x$$

$$\sin^2 x = \sin^2 x \qquad Multiply.$$

The techniques that you use to verify trigonometric identities can also be used to simplify trigonometric equations.

Example 2 **Find a numerical value of one trigonometric function of x if $\cos x \csc x = 3$.**

You can simplify the trigonometric epression on the left side by writing it in terms of sine and cosine.

$$\cos x \csc x = 3$$

$$\cos x \cdot \frac{1}{\sin x} = 3 \qquad csc\ x = \frac{1}{sin\ x}$$

$$\frac{\cos x}{\sin x} = 3 \qquad Multiply.$$

$$\cot x = 3 \qquad cot\ x = \frac{cos\ x}{sin\ x}$$

Therefore, if $\cos x \csc x = 3$, then $\cot x = 3$.

7-2

Practice

Verifying Trigonometric Identities

Verify that each equation is an identity.

1. $\dfrac{\csc x}{\cot x + \tan x} = \cos x$

2. $\dfrac{1}{\sin y - 1} - \dfrac{1}{\sin y + 1} = -2 \sec^2 y$

3. $\sin^3 x - \cos^3 x = (1 + \sin x \cos x)(\sin x - \cos x)$

4. $\tan \theta + \dfrac{\cos \theta}{1 + \sin \theta} = \sec \theta$

Find a numerical value of one trigonometric function of x.

5. $\sin x \cot x = 1$

6. $\sin x = 3 \cos x$

7. $\cos x = \cot x$

8. **Physics** The work done in moving an object is given by the formula $W = Fd \cos \theta$, where d is the displacement, F is the force exerted, and θ is the angle between the displacement and the force. Verify that $W = Fd \dfrac{\cot \theta}{\csc \theta}$ is an equivalent formula.

7-3

Study Guide

Sum and Difference Identities

You can use the **sum and difference identities** and the
values of the trigonometric functions of common angles to
find the values of trigonometric functions of other angles.
Notice how the addition and subtraction symbols are related
in the sum and difference identities.

Sum and Difference Identities	
Cosine function	$\cos(\alpha \pm \beta) = \cos \alpha \cos \beta \mp \sin \alpha \sin \beta$
Sine function	$\sin(\alpha \pm \beta) = \sin \alpha \cos \beta \pm \cos \alpha \sin \beta$
Tangent function	$\tan(\alpha \pm \beta) = \dfrac{\tan \alpha \pm \tan \beta}{1 \pm \tan \alpha \tan \beta}$

Example 1 **Use the sum or difference identity for cosine to
find the exact value of cos 375°.**

$375° = 360° + 15°$

$\cos 375° = \cos 15°$ *Symmetry identity, Case 1*

$\cos 15° = \cos(60° - 45°)$ *60° and 45° are two common
angles that differ by 15°.*

$\cos 15° = \cos 60° \cos 45° + \sin 60° \sin 45°$ *Difference identity for cosine*

$\cos 15° = \dfrac{1}{2} \cdot \dfrac{\sqrt{2}}{2} + \dfrac{\sqrt{3}}{2} \cdot \dfrac{\sqrt{2}}{2}$ or $\dfrac{\sqrt{2} + \sqrt{6}}{4}$

Example 2 **Find the value of $\sin(x + y)$ if $0 < x < \dfrac{\pi}{2}$, $0 < y < \dfrac{\pi}{2}$,
$\sin x = \dfrac{3}{5}$, and $\sin y = \dfrac{12}{37}$.**

In order to use the sum identity for sine, you
need to know $\cos x$ and $\cos y$. Use a Pythagorean
identity to determine the necessary values.

$\sin^2 \alpha + \cos^2 \alpha = 1 \Rightarrow \cos^2 \alpha = 1 - \sin^2 \alpha.$ *Pythagorean identity*

Since it is given that the angles are in Quadrant I,
the values of sine and cosine are positive. Therefore,
$\cos \alpha = \sqrt{1 - \sin^2 \alpha}$.

$\cos x = \sqrt{1 - \left(\dfrac{3}{5}\right)^2}$ $\cos y = \sqrt{1 - \left(\dfrac{12}{37}\right)^2}$

$= \sqrt{\dfrac{16}{25}}$ or $\dfrac{4}{5}$ $= \sqrt{\dfrac{1225}{1369}}$ or $\dfrac{35}{37}$

Now substitute these values into the sum
identity for sine.

$\sin(x + y) = \sin x \cos y + \cos x \sin y$

$= \left(\dfrac{3}{5}\right)\left(\dfrac{35}{37}\right) + \left(\dfrac{4}{5}\right)\left(\dfrac{12}{37}\right)$ or $\dfrac{153}{185}$

7-3

Practice

Sum and Difference Identities

Use sum or difference identities to find the exact value of each trigonometric function.

1. $\cos \frac{5\pi}{12}$

2. $\sin(-165°)$

3. $\tan 345°$

4. $\csc 915°$

5. $\tan\left(-\frac{7\pi}{12}\right)$

6. $\sec \frac{\pi}{12}$

Find each exact value if $0 < x < \frac{\pi}{2}$ and $0 < y < \frac{\pi}{2}$.

7. $\cos(x + y)$ if $\sin x = \frac{5}{13}$ and $\sin y = \frac{4}{5}$

8. $\sin(x - y)$ if $\cos x = \frac{8}{17}$ and $\cos y = \frac{3}{5}$

9. $\tan(x - y)$ if $\csc x = \frac{13}{5}$ and $\cot y = \frac{4}{3}$

Verify that each equation is an identity.

10. $\cos(180° - \theta) = -\cos \theta$

11. $\sin(360° + \theta) = \sin \theta$

12. *Physics* Sound waves can be modeled by equations of the form $y = 20 \sin(3t + \theta)$. Determine what type of interference results when sound waves modeled by the equations $y = 20 \sin(3t + 90°)$ and $y = 20 \sin(3t + 270°)$ are combined. (*Hint:* Refer to the application in Lesson 7-3.)

7-4

Study Guide

Double-Angle and Half-Angle Identities

Example 1 If $\sin \theta = \frac{1}{4}$ and θ has its terminal side in the first quadrant, find the exact value of $\sin 2\theta$.

To use the double-angle identity for $\sin 2\theta$, we must first find $\cos \theta$.

$$\sin^2 \theta + \cos^2 \theta = 1$$
$$\left(\frac{1}{4}\right)^2 + \cos^2 \theta = 1 \quad \sin \theta = \frac{1}{4}$$
$$\cos^2 \theta = \frac{15}{16}$$
$$\cos \theta = \frac{\sqrt{15}}{4}$$

Now find $\sin 2\theta$.

$$\sin 2\theta = 2 \sin \theta \cos \theta \qquad \textit{Double-angle identity for sine}$$
$$= 2\left(\frac{1}{4}\right)\frac{\sqrt{15}}{4} \qquad \sin \theta = \frac{1}{4}, \cos \theta = \frac{\sqrt{15}}{4}$$
$$= \frac{\sqrt{15}}{8}$$

Example 2 Use a half-angle identity to find the exact value of $\sin \frac{\pi}{12}$.

$$\sin \frac{\pi}{12} = \sin \frac{\frac{\pi}{6}}{2}$$

$$= \sqrt{\frac{1 - \cos \frac{\pi}{6}}{2}} \qquad \textit{Use } \sin \frac{\alpha}{2} = \pm\sqrt{\frac{1 - \cos \alpha}{2}}. \textit{ Since } \frac{\pi}{12} \textit{ is in Quadrant I, choose the positive sine value.}$$

$$= \sqrt{\frac{1 - \frac{\sqrt{3}}{2}}{2}}$$

$$= \sqrt{\frac{2 - \sqrt{3}}{4}}$$

$$= \frac{\sqrt{2 - \sqrt{3}}}{2}$$

7-4

Practice

Double-Angle and Half-Angle Identities

Use a half-angle identity to find the exact value of each function.

1. $\sin 105°$

2. $\tan \frac{\pi}{8}$

3. $\cos \frac{5\pi}{8}$

Use the given information to find $\sin 2\theta$, $\cos 2\theta$, and $\tan 2\theta$.

4. $\sin \theta = \frac{12}{13}, 0° < \theta < 90°$

5. $\tan \theta = \frac{1}{2}, \pi < \theta < \frac{3\pi}{2}$

6. $\sec \theta = -\frac{5}{2}, \frac{\pi}{2} < \theta < \pi$

7. $\sin \theta = \frac{3}{5}, 0 < \theta < \frac{\pi}{2}$

Verify that each equation is an identity.

8. $1 + \sin 2x = (\sin x + \cos x)^2$

9. $\cos x \sin x = \frac{\sin 2x}{2}$

10. **Baseball**   A batter hits a ball with an initial velocity v_0 of 100 feet per second at an angle θ to the horizontal. An outfielder catches the ball 200 feet from home plate. Find θ if the range of a projectile is given by the formula $R = \frac{1}{32}v_0{}^2 \sin 2\theta$.

7-5

Study Guide

Solving Trigonometric Equations

When you solve trigonometric equations for **principal values** of x, x is in the interval $-90° \leq x \leq 90°$ for $\sin x$ and $\tan x$. For $\cos x$, x is in the interval $0° \leq x \leq 180°$. If an equation cannot be solved easily by factoring, try writing the expressions in terms of only one trigonometric function.

Example 1 **Solve $\tan x \cos x - \cos x = 0$ for principal values of x. Express solutions in degrees.**

$$\tan x \cos x - \cos x = 0$$

$\cos x (\tan x - 1) = 0$	*Factor.*

$\cos x = 0$ or $\tan x - 1 = 0$	*Set each factor equal to 0.*

$$x = 90° \qquad\qquad \tan x = 1$$
$$x = 45°$$

When $x = 90°$, $\tan x$ is undefined, so the only principal value is 45°.

Example 2 **Solve $2 \tan^2 x - \sec^2 x + 3 = 1 - 2 \tan x$ for $0 \leq x < 2\pi$.**

This equation can be written in terms of $\tan x$ only.

$$2 \tan^2 x - \sec^2 x + 3 = 1 - 2 \tan x$$

$2 \tan^2 x - (\tan^2 x + 1) + 3 = 1 - 2 \tan x$	*$\sec^2 x = \tan^2 x + 1$*

$\tan^2 x + 2 = 1 - 2 \tan x$	*Simplify.*

$$\tan^2 x + 2 \tan x + 1 = 0$$

$(\tan x + 1)^2 = 0$	*Factor.*

$\tan x + 1 = 0$	*Take the square root of each side.*

$$\tan x = -1$$
$$x = \frac{3\pi}{4} \text{ or } x = \frac{7\pi}{4}$$

When you solve for all values of x, the solution should be represented as $x + 360°k$ or $x + 2\pi k$ for $\sin x$ and $\cos x$ and $x + 180°k$ or $x + \pi k$ for $\tan x$, where k is any integer.

Example 3 **Solve $\sin x + \sqrt{3} = -\sin x$ for all real values of x.**

$$\sin x + \sqrt{3} = -\sin x$$
$$2 \sin x + \sqrt{3} = 0$$
$$2 \sin x = -\sqrt{3}$$
$$\sin x = -\frac{\sqrt{3}}{2}$$
$$x = \frac{4\pi}{3} + 2\pi k \text{ or } x = \frac{5\pi}{3} + 2\pi k, \text{ where } k \text{ is any integer}$$

The solutions are $\frac{4\pi}{3} + 2\pi k$ and $\frac{5\pi}{3} + 2\pi k$.

7-5

Practice

Solving Trigonometric Equations

Solve each equation for principal values of x. Express solutions in degrees.

1. $\cos x = 3 \cos x - 2$

2. $2 \sin^2 x - 1 = 0$

Solve each equation for $0° \leq x < 360°$.

3. $\sec^2 x + \tan x - 1 = 0$

4. $\cos 2x + 3 \cos x - 1 = 0$

Solve each equation for $0 \leq x < 2\pi$.

5. $4 \sin^2 x - 4 \sin x + 1 = 0$

6. $\cos 2x + \sin x = 1$

Solve each equation for all real values of x.

7. $3 \cos 2x - 5 \cos x = 1$

8. $2 \sin^2 x - 5 \sin x + 2 = 0$

9. $3 \sec^2 x - 4 = 0$

10. $\tan x (\tan x - 1) = 0$

11. Aviation An airplane takes off from the ground and reaches a height of 500 feet after flying 2 miles. Given the formula $H = d \tan \theta$, where H is the height of the plane and d is the distance (along the ground) the plane has flown, find the angle of ascent θ at which the plane took off.

7-6

Study Guide

Normal Form of a Linear Equation

Normal Form	The normal form of a linear equation is $x \cos \phi + y \sin \phi - p = 0$, where p is the length of the normal from the line to the origin and ϕ is the positive angle formed by the positive x-axis and the normal.

You can write the standard form of a linear equation if you are given the values of ϕ and p.

Example 1 **Write the standard form of the equation of a line for which the length of the normal segment to the origin is 5 and the normal makes an angle of 135° with the positive x-axis.**

$$x \cos \phi + y \sin \phi - p = 0 \quad \textit{Normal form}$$
$$x \cos 135° + y \sin 135° - 5 = 0 \quad \textit{$\phi = 135°$ and $p = 5$}$$
$$-\frac{\sqrt{2}}{2}x + \frac{\sqrt{2}}{2}y - 5 = 0$$
$$\sqrt{2}x - \sqrt{2}y + 10 = 0 \quad \textit{Multiply each side by -2.}$$

The standard form of the equation is $\sqrt{2}x - \sqrt{2}y + 10 = 0$.

The standard form of a linear equation, $Ax + By + C = 0$, can be changed to the normal form by dividing each term of the equation by $\pm\sqrt{A^2 + B^2}$. The sign is chosen opposite the sign of C. You can then find the length of the normal, p units, and the angle ϕ.

Example 2 **Write $3x + 4y - 10 = 0$ in normal form. Then find the length of the normal and the angle it makes with the positive x-axis.**

Since C is negative, use $\sqrt{A^2 + B^2}$ to determine the normal form.

$$\sqrt{A^2 + B^2} = \sqrt{3^2 + 4^2} \text{ or } 5$$

The normal form is $\frac{3}{5}x + \frac{4}{5}y - \frac{10}{5} = 0$ or $\frac{3}{5}x + \frac{4}{5}y - 2 = 0$.

Therefore, $\cos \phi = \frac{3}{5}$, $\sin \phi = \frac{4}{5}$, and $p = 2$.

Since $\cos \phi$ and $\sin \phi$ are both positive, ϕ must lie in Quadrant I.

$$\tan \phi = \frac{\frac{4}{5}}{\frac{3}{5}} \text{ or } \frac{4}{3} \qquad \tan \phi = \frac{\sin \phi}{\cos \phi}$$
$$\phi \approx 53°$$

The normal segment has length 2 units and makes an angle of 53° with the positive x-axis.

7-6

Practice

Normal Form of a Linear Equation

Write the standard form of the equation of each line, given
p, the length of the normal segment, and φ, the angle the
normal segment makes with the positive x-axis.

1. $p = 4, \phi = 30°$ **2.** $p = 2\sqrt{2}, \phi = \dfrac{\pi}{4}$

3. $p = 3, \phi = 60°$ **4.** $p = 8, \phi = \dfrac{5\pi}{6}$

5. $p = 2\sqrt{3}, \phi = \dfrac{7\pi}{4}$ **6.** $p = 15, \phi = 225°$

Write each equation in normal form. Then find the length of
the normal and the angle it makes with the positive x-axis.

7. $3x - 2y - 1 = 0$

8. $5x + y - 12 = 0$

9. $4x + 3y - 4 = 0$

10. $y = x + 5$

11. $2x + y + 1 = 0$

12. $x + y - 5 = 0$

7-7

Study Guide

Distance from a Point to a Line

The distance from a point at (x_1, y_1) to a line with equation
$Ax + By + C = 0$ can be determined by using the formula
$d = \dfrac{Ax_1 + By_1 + C}{\pm\sqrt{A^2 + B^2}}$. The sign of the radical is chosen opposite
the sign of C.

Example 1   **Find the distance between $P(3, 4)$ and the line
with equation $4x + 2y = 10$.**

First, rewrite the equation of the line in standard form.

$$4x + 2y - 10 = 0$$

Then, use the formula for the distance from a point to a line.

$d = \dfrac{Ax_1 + By_1 + C}{\pm\sqrt{A^2 + B^2}}$

$d = \dfrac{4(3) + 2(4) - 10}{\pm\sqrt{4^2 + 2^2}}$ *$A = 4, B = 2, C = -10, x_1 = 3, y_1 = 4$*

$d = \dfrac{10}{2\sqrt{5}}$ or $\sqrt{5}$ *Since C is negative, use $+\sqrt{A^2 + B^2}$.*

$d \approx 2.24$ units

Therefore, P is approximately 2.24 units from the line
with equation $4x + 2y = 10$. Since d is positive, P is on
the opposite side of the line from the origin.

You can also use the formula to find the distance
between two parallel lines. To do this, choose any point
on one of the lines and use the formula to find the
distance from that point to the other line.

Example 2   **Find the distance between the lines with
equations $2x - 2y = 5$ and $y = x - 1$.**

Since $y = x - 1$ is in slope-intercept form, you
can see that it passes through the point at
$(0, -1)$. Use this point to find the distance to
the other line.

The standard form of the other equation is $2x - 2y - 5 = 0$.

$d = \dfrac{Ax_1 + By_1 + C}{\pm\sqrt{A^2 + B^2}}$

$d = \dfrac{2(0) - 2(-1) - 5}{\pm\sqrt{2^2 + (-2)^2}}$ *$A = 2, B = -2, C = -5, x_1 = 0, y_1 = -1$*

$d = -\dfrac{3}{2\sqrt{2}}$ or $-\dfrac{3\sqrt{2}}{4}$ *Since C is negative, use $+\sqrt{A^2 + B^2}$.*

≈ -1.06

The distance between the lines is about 1.06 units.

7-7

Practice

Distance From a Point to a Line

Find the distance between the point with the given coordinates and the line with the given equation.

1. $(-1, 5)$, $3x - 4y - 1 = 0$

2. $(2, 5)$, $5x - 12y + 1 = 0$

3. $(1, -4)$, $12x + 5y - 3 = 0$

4. $(-1, -3)$, $6x + 8y - 3 = 0$

Find the distance between the parallel lines with the given equations.

5. $2x - 3y + 4 = 0$
$y = \frac{2}{3}x + 5$

6. $4x - y + 1 = 0$
$4x - y - 8 = 0$

Find equations of the lines that bisect the acute and obtuse angles formed by the lines with the given equations.

7. $x + 2y - 3 = 0$
$x - y + 4 = 0$

8. $9x + 12y + 10 = 0$
$3x + 2y - 6 = 0$

NAME _____ DATE _____ PERIOD _____

7-1 Practice

Basic Trigonometric Identities

Use the given information to determine the exact trigonometric value if $0° < \theta < 90°$.

1. If $\cos \theta = \frac{1}{4}$, find $\tan \theta$.

$\sqrt{15}$

2. If $\sin \theta = \frac{2}{3}$, find $\cos \theta$.

$\frac{\sqrt{5}}{3}$

3. If $\tan \theta = \frac{7}{2}$, find $\sin \theta$.

$\frac{7\sqrt{53}}{53}$

4. If $\tan \theta = 2$, find $\cot \theta$.

$\frac{1}{2}$

Express each value as a trigonometric function of an angle in Quadrant I.

5. $\cos 892°$

$-\cos 8°$

6. $\csc 495°$

$\csc 45°$

7. $\sin \frac{23\pi}{3}$

$-\sin \frac{\pi}{3}$

Simplify each expression.

8. $\cos x + \sin x \tan x$

$\sec x$

9. $\dfrac{\cot A}{\tan A}$

$\cot^2 A$

10. $\sin^2 \theta \cos^2 \theta - \cos^2 \theta$

$-\cos^4 \theta$

11. Kite Flying Brett and Tara are flying a kite. When the string is tied to the ground, the height of the kite can be determined by the formula $\frac{L}{H} = \csc \theta$, where L is the length of the string and θ is the angle between the string and the level ground. What formula could Brett and Tara use to find the height of the kite if they know the value of $\sin \theta$?

$H = L \sin \theta$

NAME _____ DATE _____ PERIOD _____

7-2 Practice

Verifying Trigonometric Identities

Verify that each equation is an identity.

1. $\dfrac{\csc x}{\cot x + \tan x} = \cos x$

$\dfrac{\csc x}{\cot x + \tan x} = \dfrac{\frac{1}{\sin x}}{\frac{\cos x}{\sin x} + \frac{\sin x}{\cos x}} = \dfrac{\frac{1}{\sin x}}{\frac{\sin x \cos x}{\sin x \cos x}} = \dfrac{\cos x}{\cos^2 x + \sin^2 x} = \dfrac{\cos x}{1} = \cos x$

2. $\dfrac{1}{\sin y - 1} - \dfrac{1}{\sin y + 1} = -2 \sec^2 y$

$\dfrac{1}{\sin y - 1} - \dfrac{1}{\sin y + 1} = \dfrac{\sin y + 1 - \sin y + 1}{\sin^2 y - 1} = \dfrac{2}{-\cos^2 y} = -2 \sec^2 y$

3. $\sin^3 x - \cos^3 x = (1 + \sin x \cos x)(\sin x - \cos x)$

$\sin^3 x - \cos^3 x = (\sin x - \cos x)(\sin^2 x + \sin x \cos x + \cos^2 x)$
$= (\sin x - \cos x)(1 + \sin x \cos x)$
$= (1 + \sin x \cos x)(\sin x - \cos x)$

4. $\tan \theta + \dfrac{\cos \theta}{1 + \sin \theta} = \sec \theta$

$\tan \theta + \dfrac{\cos \theta}{1 + \sin \theta} = \dfrac{\sin \theta}{\cos \theta} + \dfrac{\cos \theta}{1 + \sin \theta} = \dfrac{\sin \theta + \sin^2 \theta + \cos^2 \theta}{(\cos \theta)(1 + \sin \theta)}$
$= \dfrac{1 + \sin \theta}{(\cos \theta)(1 + \sin \theta)} = \sec \theta$

Find a numerical value of one trigonometric function of x.

5. $\sin x \cot x = 1$

$\cos x = 1$

6. $\sin x = 3 \cos x$

$\tan x = 3$

7. $\cos x = \cot x$

$\csc x = 1$ or $\sin x = 1$

8. Physics The work done in moving an object is given by the formula $W = Fd \cos \theta$, where d is the displacement, F is the force exerted, and θ is the angle between the displacement and the force. Verify that $W = Fd \dfrac{\cot \theta}{\csc \theta}$ is an equivalent formula.

$W = Fd \dfrac{\cot \theta}{\csc \theta} = Fd \dfrac{\frac{\cos \theta}{\sin \theta}}{\frac{1}{\sin \theta}} = Fd \dfrac{\cos \theta}{\sin \theta} \cdot \dfrac{\sin \theta}{1} = Fd \cos \theta$

7-3

Practice

Sum and Difference Identities

Use sum or difference identities to find the exact value of each trigonometric function.

1. $\cos \frac{5\pi}{12}$

$\dfrac{\sqrt{6} - \sqrt{2}}{4}$

2. $\sin(-165°)$

$\dfrac{\sqrt{2} - \sqrt{6}}{4}$

3. $\tan 345°$

$\sqrt{3} - 2$

4. $\csc 915°$

$-\sqrt{6} - \sqrt{2}$

5. $\tan\left(-\frac{7\pi}{12}\right)$

$2 + \sqrt{3}$

6. $\sec \frac{\pi}{12}$

$\sqrt{6} - \sqrt{2}$

Find each exact value if $0 < x < \frac{\pi}{2}$ and $0 < y < \frac{\pi}{2}$.

7. $\cos(x + y)$ if $\sin x = \frac{5}{13}$ and $\sin y = \frac{4}{5}$

$\dfrac{16}{65}$

8. $\sin(x - y)$ if $\cos x = \frac{8}{17}$ and $\cos y = \frac{3}{5}$

$\dfrac{13}{85}$

9. $\tan(x - y)$ if $\csc x = \frac{13}{5}$ and $\cot y = \frac{4}{3}$

$-\dfrac{16}{63}$

Verify that each equation is an identity.

10. $\cos(180° - \theta) = -\cos\theta$

$\cos(180° - \theta)$

$= \cos 180° \cos\theta + \sin 180° \sin\theta$

$= (-1)\cos\theta + 0 \cdot \sin\theta$

$= -\cos\theta$

11. $\sin(360° + \theta) = \sin\theta$

$\sin(360° + \theta)$

$= \sin 360° \cos\theta + \cos 360° \sin\theta$

$= 0 \cdot \cos\theta + 1 \cdot \sin\theta$

$= \sin\theta$

12. *Physics* Sound waves can be modeled by equations of the form $y = 20\sin(3t + \theta)$. Determine what type of interference results when sound waves modeled by the equations $y = 20\sin(3t + 90°)$ and $y = 20\sin(3t + 270°)$ are combined. (*Hint*: Refer to the application in Lesson 7-3.) **The interference is destructive. The waves cancel each other out completely.**

7-4

Practice

Double-Angle and Half-Angle Identities

Use a half-angle identity to find the exact value of each function.

1. $\sin 105°$

$\dfrac{\sqrt{2 + \sqrt{3}}}{2}$

2. $\tan \frac{\pi}{8}$

$\sqrt{2} - 1$

3. $\cos \frac{5\pi}{8}$

$-\dfrac{\sqrt{2 - \sqrt{2}}}{2}$

Use the given information to find $\sin 2\theta$, $\cos 2\theta$, and $\tan 2\theta$.

4. $\sin\theta = \frac{12}{13}$, $0° < \theta < 90°$

$\dfrac{120}{169}$, $-\dfrac{119}{169}$, $-\dfrac{120}{119}$

5. $\tan\theta = \frac{1}{2}$, $\pi < \theta < \frac{3\pi}{2}$

$\dfrac{4}{5}$, $\dfrac{3}{5}$, $\dfrac{4}{3}$

6. $\sec\theta = -\frac{5}{2}$, $\frac{\pi}{2} < \theta < \pi$

$-\dfrac{4\sqrt{21}}{25}$, $-\dfrac{17}{25}$, $\dfrac{4\sqrt{21}}{17}$

7. $\sin\theta = \frac{3}{5}$, $0 < \theta < \frac{\pi}{2}$

$\dfrac{24}{25}$, $\dfrac{7}{25}$, $\dfrac{24}{7}$

Verify that each equation is an identity.

8. $1 + \sin 2x = (\sin x + \cos x)^2$

$1 + \sin 2x \stackrel{?}{=} (\sin x + \cos x)^2$

$1 + \sin 2x \stackrel{?}{=} \sin^2 x + 2\sin x \cos x + \cos^2 x$

$1 + \sin 2x \stackrel{?}{=} 1 + 2\sin x \cos x$

$1 + \sin 2x = 1 + \sin 2x$

9. $\cos x \sin x = \dfrac{\sin 2x}{2}$

$\cos x \sin x \stackrel{?}{=} \dfrac{\sin 2x}{2}$

$\cos x \sin x \stackrel{?}{=} \dfrac{2\sin x \cos x}{2}$

$\cos x \sin x = \cos x \sin x$

10. *Baseball* A batter hits a ball with an initial velocity v_0 of 100 feet per second at an angle θ to the horizontal. An outfielder catches the ball 200 feet from home plate. Find θ if the range of a projectile is given by the formula $R = \frac{1}{32}v_0^2 \sin 2\theta$. **about 20°**

7-5

Practice

Solving Trigonometric Equations

Solve each equation for principal values of x. Express solutions in degrees.

1. $\cos x = 3 \cos x - 2$
$0°$

2. $2 \sin^2 x - 1 = 0$
$\pm 45°$

Solve each equation for $0° \leq x < 360°$.

3. $\sec^2 x + \tan x - 1 = 0$
$0°, 135°, 180°, 315°$

4. $\cos 2x + 3 \cos x - 1 = 0$
$60°, 300°$

Solve each equation for $0 \leq x < 2\pi$.

5. $4 \sin^2 x - 4 \sin x + 1 = 0$
$\frac{\pi}{6}, \frac{5\pi}{6}$

6. $\cos 2x + \sin x = 1$
$0, \frac{\pi}{6}, \frac{5\pi}{6}, \pi$

Solve each equation for all real values of x.

7. $3 \cos 2x - 5 \cos x = 1$
$\frac{2\pi}{3} + 2\pi k, \frac{4\pi}{3} + 2\pi k$

8. $2 \sin^2 x - 5 \sin x + 2 = 0$
$\frac{\pi}{6} + 2\pi k, \frac{5\pi}{6} + 2\pi k$

9. $3 \sec^2 x - 4 = 0$
$\frac{\pi}{6} + \pi k, \frac{5\pi}{6} + \pi k$

10. $\tan x (\tan x - 1) = 0$
$\pi k, \frac{\pi}{4} + \pi k$

11. **Aviation** An airplane takes off from the ground and reaches a height of 500 feet after flying 2 miles. Given the formula $H = d \tan \theta$, where H is the height of the plane and d is the distance (along the ground) the plane has flown, find the angle of ascent θ at which the plane took off.
about 2.7°

7-6

Practice

Normal Form of a Linear Equation

Write the standard form of the equation of each line, given p, the length of the normal segment, and φ, the angle the normal segment makes with the positive x-axis.

1. $p = 4, \phi = 30°$
$\sqrt{3}x + y - 8 = 0$

2. $p = 2\sqrt{2}, \phi = \frac{\pi}{4}$
$x + y - 4 = 0$

3. $p = 3, \phi = 60°$
$x + \sqrt{3}y - 6 = 0$

4. $p = 8, \phi = \frac{5\pi}{6}$
$\sqrt{3}x - y + 16 = 0$

5. $p = 2\sqrt{3}, \phi = \frac{7\pi}{4}$
$\sqrt{2}x - \sqrt{2}y - 4\sqrt{3} = 0$

6. $p = 15, \phi = 225°$
$\sqrt{2}x + \sqrt{2}y + 30 = 0$

Write each equation in normal form. Then find the length of the normal and the angle it makes with the positive x-axis.

7. $3x - 2y - 1 = 0$
$\frac{3\sqrt{13}}{13}x - \frac{2\sqrt{13}}{13}y - \frac{\sqrt{13}}{13} = 0; \frac{\sqrt{13}}{13}, 326°$

8. $5x + y - 12 = 0$
$\frac{5\sqrt{26}}{26}x + \frac{\sqrt{26}}{26}y - \frac{6\sqrt{26}}{26} = 0; \frac{6\sqrt{26}}{13}, 11°$

9. $4x + 3y - 4 = 0$
$\frac{4}{5}x + \frac{3}{5}y - \frac{4}{5} = 0; \frac{4}{5}, 37°$

10. $y = x + 5$
$-\frac{\sqrt{2}}{2}x + \frac{\sqrt{2}}{2}y - \frac{5\sqrt{2}}{2} = 0; \frac{5\sqrt{2}}{2}, 135°$

11. $2x + y + 1 = 0$
$-\frac{2\sqrt{5}}{5}x - \frac{\sqrt{5}}{5}y - \frac{\sqrt{5}}{5} = 0; \frac{\sqrt{5}}{5}, 207°$

12. $x + y - 5 = 0$
$\frac{\sqrt{2}}{2}x + \frac{\sqrt{2}}{2}y - \frac{5\sqrt{2}}{2} = 0; \frac{5\sqrt{2}}{2}, 45°$

NAME _____ DATE _____ PERIOD _____

7-7 Practice

Distance From a Point to a Line

Find the distance between the point with the given coordinates and the line with the given equation.

1. $(-1, 5)$, $3x - 4y - 1 = 0$
$\dfrac{24}{5}$

2. $(2, 5)$, $5x - 12y + 1 = 0$
$\dfrac{49}{13}$

3. $(1, -4)$, $12x + 5y - 3 = 0$
$\dfrac{11}{13}$

4. $(-1, -3)$, $6x + 8y - 3 = 0$
$\dfrac{33}{10}$

Find the distance between the parallel lines with the given equations.

5. $2x - 3y + 4 = 0$
$y = \dfrac{2}{3}x + 5$
$\dfrac{11\sqrt{13}}{13}$

6. $4x - y + 1 = 0$
$4x - y - 8 = 0$
$\dfrac{9\sqrt{17}}{17}$

Find equations of the lines that bisect the acute and obtuse angles formed by the lines with the given equations.

7. $x + 2y - 3 = 0$
$x - y + 4 = 0$
$(\sqrt{2} + \sqrt{5})x + (2\sqrt{2} - \sqrt{5})y - 3\sqrt{2} + 4\sqrt{5} = 0$;
$(\sqrt{2} - \sqrt{5})x + (2\sqrt{2} + \sqrt{5})y - 3\sqrt{2} - 4\sqrt{5} = 0$

8. $9x + 12y + 10 = 0$
$3x + 2y - 6 = 0$
$(45 + 9\sqrt{13})x + (30 + 12\sqrt{13})y - 90 + 10\sqrt{13} = 0$;
$(9\sqrt{13} - 45)x + (12\sqrt{13} - 30)y + 90 + 10\sqrt{13} = 0$

132

Advanced Mathematical Concepts

8-1

Study Guide

Geometric Vectors

The **magnitude** of a **vector** is the length of a directed line segment. The **direction** of the vector is the directed angle between the positive x-axis and the vector. When adding or subtracting vectors, use either the parallelogram or the triangle method to find the **resultant**.

Example 1   **Use the parallelogram method to find the sum of $\vec{v}$ and $\vec{w}$.**

Copy $\vec{v}$ and $\vec{w}$, placing the initial points together.
Form a parallelogram that has $\vec{v}$ and $\vec{w}$ as two of its sides.
Draw dashed lines to represent the other two sides.

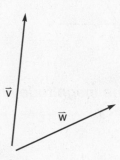

The resultant is the vector from the vertex of $\vec{v}$ and $\vec{w}$ to the opposite vertex of the parallelogram.

Use a ruler and protractor to measure the magnitude and direction of the resultant.

The magnitude is 6 centimeters, and the direction is 40°.

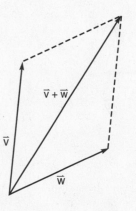

Example 2   **Use the triangle method to find $2\vec{v} - 3\vec{w}$.**

$2\vec{v} - 3\vec{w} = 2\vec{v} + (-3\vec{w})$

Draw a vector that is twice the magnitude of $\vec{v}$ to represent $2\vec{v}$. Then draw a vector with the opposite direction to $\vec{w}$ and three times its magnitude to represent $-3\vec{w}$. Place the initial point of $-3\vec{w}$ on the terminal point of $2\vec{v}$. *Tip-to-tail method.*

Draw the resultant from the initial point of the first vector to the terminal point of the second vector. The resultant is $2\vec{v} - 3\vec{w}$.

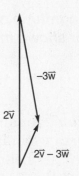

8-1

Practice

Geometric Vectors

Use a ruler and a protractor to determine the magnitude (in centimeters) and direction of each vector.

1. $\vec{x}$ 2.  $\vec{y}$ 3. $\vec{z}$

Find the magnitude and direction of each resultant.

4. $\vec{x} + \vec{y}$ 5. $\vec{x} - \vec{z}$

6. $2\vec{x} + \vec{y}$ 7. $\vec{y} + 3\vec{z}$

Find the magnitude of the horizontal and vertical components of each vector shown in Exercises 1-3.

8. $\vec{x}$ 9. $\vec{y}$ 10. $\vec{z}$

11. *Aviation*   An airplane is flying at a velocity of 500 miles per hour due north when it encounters a wind blowing out of the west at 50 miles per hour. What is the magnitude of the airplane's resultant velocity?

8-2

Study Guide

Algebraic Vectors

Vectors can be represented algebraically using ordered pairs
of real numbers.

Example 1 **Write the ordered pair that represents the vector
from $X(2, -3)$ to $Y(-4, 2)$. Then find the
magnitude of $\overrightarrow{XY}$.**

First represent $\overrightarrow{XY}$ as an ordered pair.
$$\overrightarrow{XY} = \langle x_2 - x_1, y_2 - y_1 \rangle$$
$$= \langle -4 - 2, 2 - (-3) \rangle$$
$$= \langle -6, 5 \rangle$$

Then determine the magnitude of $\overrightarrow{XY}$.

$$|\overrightarrow{XY}| = \sqrt{(x_2 - x_1)^2, (y_2 - y_1)^2}$$
$$= \sqrt{(-4 - 2)^2 + [2 - (-3)]^2}$$
$$= \sqrt{(-6)^2 + 5^2}$$
$$= \sqrt{61}$$

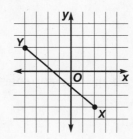

$\overrightarrow{XY}$ is represented by the ordered pair $\langle -6, 5 \rangle$
and has a magnitude of $\sqrt{61}$ units.

Example 2 **Let $\vec{s} = \langle 4, 2 \rangle$ and $\vec{t} = \langle -1, 3 \rangle$. Find each of the
following.**

a. $\vec{s} + \vec{t}$
$$\vec{s} + \vec{t} = \langle 4, 2 \rangle + \langle -1, 3 \rangle$$
$$= \langle 4 + (-1), 2 + 3 \rangle$$
$$= \langle 3, 5 \rangle$$

b. $\vec{s} - \vec{t}$
$$\vec{s} - \vec{t} = \langle 4, 2 \rangle - \langle -1, 3 \rangle$$
$$= \langle 4 - (-1), 2 - 3 \rangle$$
$$= \langle 5, -1 \rangle$$

c. $4\vec{s}$
$$4\vec{s} = 4\langle 4, 2 \rangle$$
$$= \langle 4 \cdot 4, 4 \cdot 2 \rangle$$
$$= \langle 16, 8 \rangle$$

d. $3\vec{s} + \vec{t}$
$$3\vec{s} + \vec{t} = 3\langle 4, 2 \rangle + \langle -1, 3 \rangle$$
$$= \langle 12, 6 \rangle + \langle -1, 3 \rangle$$
$$= \langle 11, 9 \rangle$$

A unit vector in the direction of the positive
x-axis is represented by $\vec{i}$, and a unit vector in
the direction of the positive y-axis is represented
by $\vec{j}$. Vectors represented as ordered pairs can be
written as the sum of unit vectors.

Example 3 **Write $\overrightarrow{MP}$ as the sum of unit vectors for $M(2, 2)$
and $P(5, 4)$.**

First write $\overrightarrow{MP}$ as an ordered pair.
$$\overrightarrow{MP} = \langle 5 - 2, 4 - 2 \rangle$$
$$= \langle 3, 2 \rangle$$

Then write $\overrightarrow{MP}$ as the sum of unit vectors.
$$\overrightarrow{MP} = 3\vec{i} + 2\vec{j}$$

8-2

Practice

Algebraic Vectors

Write the ordered pair that represents $\overline{AB}$. Then find the magnitude of $\overline{AB}$.

1. $A(2, 4), B(-1, 3)$ 　　 2. $A(4, -2), B(5, -5)$ 　　 3. $A(-3, -6), B(8, -1)$

Find an ordered pair to represent $\vec{u}$ in each equation if $\vec{v} = \langle 2, -1 \rangle$ and $\vec{w} = \langle -3, 5 \rangle$.

4. $\vec{u} = 3\vec{v}$ 　　　　　　　　　　 5. $\vec{u} = \vec{w} - 2\vec{v}$

6. $\vec{u} = 4\vec{v} + 3\vec{w}$ 　　　　　　　　 7. $\vec{u} = 5\vec{w} - 3\vec{v}$

Find the magnitude of each vector, and write each vector as the sum of unit vectors.

8. $\langle 2, 6 \rangle$ 　　　　　　　　　　 9. $\langle 4, -5 \rangle$

10. *Gardening* Nancy and Harry are lifting a stone statue and moving it to a new location in their garden. Nancy is pushing the statue with a force of 120 newtons (N) at a 60° angle with the horizontal while Harry is pulling the statue with a force of 180 newtons at a 40° angle with the horizontal. What is the magnitude of the combined force they exert on the statue?

8-3

Study Guide

Vectors in Three-Dimensional Space

Ordered triples, like ordered pairs, can be used to represent vectors. Operations on vectors respresented by ordered triples are similar to those on vectors represented by ordered pairs. For example, an extension of the formula for the distance between two points in a plane allows us to find the distance between two points in space.

Example 1   **Locate the point at $(-1, 3, 1)$.**

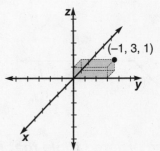

Locate -1 on the x-axis, 3 on the y-axis, and 1 on the z-axis.

Now draw broken lines for parallelograms to represent the three planes.

The planes intersect at $(-1, 3, 1)$.

Example 2   **Write the ordered triple that represents the vector from $X(-4, 5, 6)$ to $Y(-2, 6, 3)$. Then find the magnitude of $\overrightarrow{XY}$.**

$$\overrightarrow{XY} = (-2, 6, 3) - (-4, 5, 6)$$
$$= \langle -2 - (-4), 6 - 5, 3 - 6 \rangle$$
$$= \langle 2, 1, -3 \rangle$$

$$|\overrightarrow{XY}| = \sqrt{(x_2 - x_1)^2 + (y_2 - y_1)^2 + (z_2 - z_1)^2}$$
$$= \sqrt{[-2 - (-4)]2 + (6 - 5)2 + (3 - 6)2}$$
$$= \sqrt{(2)^2 + (1)^2 + (-3)^2}$$
$$= \sqrt{14} \text{ or } 3.7$$

Example 3   **Find an ordered triple that represents $2\vec{s} + 3\vec{t}$ if $\vec{s} = \langle 5, -1, 2 \rangle$ and $\vec{t} = \langle 4, 3, -2 \rangle$.**

$$2\vec{s} + 3\vec{t} = 2\langle 5, -1, 2 \rangle + 3\langle 4, 3, -2 \rangle$$
$$= \langle 10, -2, 4 \rangle + \langle 12, 9, -6 \rangle$$
$$= \langle 22, 7, -2 \rangle$$

Example 4   **Write $\overrightarrow{AB}$ as the sum of unit vectors for $A(5, -2, 3)$ and $B(-4, 2, 1)$.**

First express $\overrightarrow{AB}$ as an ordered triple. Then write the sum of the unit vectors $\vec{i}$, $\vec{j}$, and $\vec{k}$.

$$\overrightarrow{AB} = (-4, 2, 1) - (5, -2, 3)$$
$$= \langle -4 - 5, 2 - (-2), 1 - 3 \rangle$$
$$= \langle -9, 4, -2 \rangle$$
$$= -9\vec{i} + 4\vec{j} - 2\vec{k}$$

8-3

Practice

Vectors in Three-Dimensional Space

Locate point B in space. Then find the magnitude of a vector from the origin to B.

1. $B(4, 7, 6)$

2. $B(4, -2, 6)$

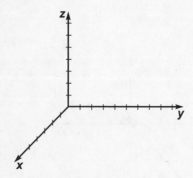

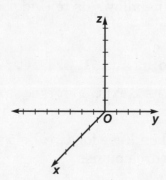

Write the ordered triple that represents $\overrightarrow{AB}$. Then find the magnitude of $\overrightarrow{AB}$.

3. $A(2, 1, 3), B(-4, 5, 7)$

4. $A(4, 0, 6), B(7, 1, -3)$

5. $A(-4, 5, 8), B(7, 2, -9)$

6. $A(6, 8, -5), B(7, -3, 12)$

Find an ordered triple to represent $\vec{u}$ in each equation if $\vec{v} = \langle 2, -4, 5 \rangle$ and $\vec{w} = \langle 6, -8, 9 \rangle$.

7. $\vec{u} = \vec{v} + \vec{w}$

8. $\vec{u} = \vec{v} - \vec{w}$

9. $\vec{u} = 4\vec{v} + 3\vec{w}$

10. $\vec{u} = 5\vec{v} - 2\vec{w}$

11. *Physics* Suppose that the force acting on an object can be expressed by the vector $\langle 85, 35, 110 \rangle$, where each measure in the ordered triple represents the force in pounds. What is the magnitude of this force?

8-4

Study Guide

Perpendicular Vectors

Two vectors are perpendicular if and only if their **inner product** is zero.

Example 1 Find each inner product if $\vec{u} = \langle 5, 1 \rangle$, $\vec{v} = \langle -3, 15 \rangle$, and $\vec{w} = \langle 2, -1 \rangle$. Is either pair of vectors perpendicular?

a. $\vec{u} \cdot \vec{v}$

$$\begin{aligned} \vec{u} \cdot \vec{v} &= 5(-3) + 1(15) \\ &= -15 + 15 \\ &= 0 \end{aligned}$$

$\vec{u}$ and $\vec{v}$ are perpendicular.

b. $\vec{v} \cdot \vec{w}$

$$\begin{aligned} \vec{v} \cdot \vec{w} &= -3(2) + 15(-1) \\ &= -6 + (-15) \\ &= -21 \end{aligned}$$

$\vec{v}$ and $\vec{w}$ are not perpendicular.

Example 2 Find the inner product of $\vec{r}$ and $\vec{s}$ if $\vec{r} = \langle 3, -1, 0 \rangle$ and $\vec{s} = \langle 2, 6, 4 \rangle$. Are $\vec{r}$ and $\vec{s}$ perpendicular?

$$\begin{aligned} \vec{r} \cdot \vec{s} &= (3)(2) + (-1)(6) + (0)(4) \\ &= 6 + (-6) + 0 \\ &= 0 \end{aligned}$$

$\vec{r}$ and $\vec{s}$ are perpendicular since their inner product is zero.

Unlike the inner product, the **cross product** of two vectors is a vector. This vector does not lie in the plane of the given vectors but is perpendicular to the plane containing the two vectors.

Example 3 Find the cross product of $\vec{v}$ and $\vec{w}$ if $\vec{v} = \langle 0, 4, 1 \rangle$ and $\vec{w} = \langle 0, 1, 3 \rangle$. Verify that the resulting vector is perpendicular to $\vec{v}$ and $\vec{w}$.

$$\vec{v} \times \vec{w} = \begin{vmatrix} \vec{i} & \vec{j} & \vec{k} \\ 0 & 4 & 1 \\ 0 & 1 & 3 \end{vmatrix}$$

$$\begin{aligned} &= \begin{vmatrix} 4 & 1 \\ 1 & 3 \end{vmatrix} \vec{i} - \begin{vmatrix} 0 & 1 \\ 0 & 3 \end{vmatrix} \vec{j} + \begin{vmatrix} 0 & 4 \\ 0 & 1 \end{vmatrix} \vec{k} \quad \textit{Expand by minors.} \\ &= 11\vec{i} - 0\vec{j} + 0\vec{k} \\ &= 11\vec{i} \text{ or } \langle 11, 0, 0 \rangle \end{aligned}$$

Find the inner products.

$\langle 11, 0, 0 \rangle \cdot \langle 0, 4, 1 \rangle$ $\langle 11, 0, 0 \rangle \cdot \langle 0, 1, 3 \rangle$

$11(0) + 0(4) + 0(1) = 0$ $11(0) + 0(1) + 0(3) = 0$

Since the inner products are zero, the cross product $\vec{v} \times \vec{w}$ is perpendicular to both $\vec{v}$ and $\vec{w}$.

8-4

Practice

Perpendicular Vectors

Find each inner product and state whether the vectors are perpendicular. Write yes or no.

1. $\langle 3, 6 \rangle \cdot \langle -4, 2 \rangle$ **2.** $\langle -1, 4 \rangle \cdot \langle 3, -2 \rangle$ **3.** $\langle 2, 0 \rangle \cdot \langle -1, -1 \rangle$

4. $\langle -2, 0, 1 \rangle \cdot \langle 3, 2, -3 \rangle$ **5.** $\langle -4, -1, 1 \rangle \cdot \langle 1, -3, 4 \rangle$ **6.** $\langle 0, 0, 1 \rangle \cdot \langle 1, -2, 0 \rangle$

Find each cross product. Then verify that the resulting vector is perpendicular to the given vectors.

7. $\langle 1, 3, 4 \rangle \times \langle -1, 0, -1 \rangle$ **8.** $\langle 3, 1, -6 \rangle \times \langle -2, 4, 3 \rangle$

9. $\langle 3, 1, 2 \rangle \times \langle 2, -3, 1 \rangle$ **10.** $\langle 4, -1, 0 \rangle \times \langle 5, -3, -1 \rangle$

11. $\langle -6, 1, 3 \rangle \times \langle -2, -2, 1 \rangle$ **12.** $\langle 0, 0, 6 \rangle \times \langle 3, -2, -4 \rangle$

13. *Physics*   Janna is using a force of 100 pounds to push a cart up a ramp. The ramp is 6 feet long and is at a 30° angle with the horizontal. How much work is Janna doing in the vertical direction? (*Hint:* Use the sine ratio and the formula $W = \vec{\mathbf{F}} \cdot \vec{\mathbf{d}}$.)

8-5

Study Guide

Applications with Vectors

Vectors can be used to represent any quantity that has
direction and magnitude, such as force, velocity, and weight.

Example   Suppose Jamal and Mike pull on the ends of a
rope tied to a dinghy. Jamal pulls with a force
of 60 newtons and Mike pulls with a force of
50 newtons. The angle formed when Jamal and
Mike pull on the rope is 60°.

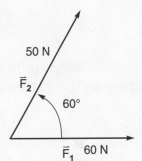

a. **Draw a labeled diagram that represents
the forces.**

Let $\vec{\mathbf{F}}_1$ and $\vec{\mathbf{F}}_2$ represent the two forces.

b. **Determine the magnitude of the
resultant force.**
First find the horizontal (x) and vertical (y)
components of each force.
Given that we place $\vec{\mathbf{F}}_1$ on the x-axis, the unit
vector is $1\vec{\mathbf{i}} + 0\vec{\mathbf{j}}$.
Therefore, the x- and y-components of $\vec{\mathbf{F}}_1$ are
$60\vec{\mathbf{i}} + 0\vec{\mathbf{j}}$.
$\vec{\mathbf{F}}_2 = x\vec{\mathbf{i}} + y\vec{\mathbf{j}}$

$\cos 60° = \frac{x}{50}$ $\sin 60° = \frac{y}{50}$
$\quad\quad x = 50 \cos 60°$ $\quad\quad y = 50 \sin 60°$
$\quad\quad\quad = 25$ $\quad\quad\quad \approx 43.3$

Thus, $\vec{\mathbf{F}}_2 = 25\vec{\mathbf{i}} + 43.3\vec{\mathbf{j}}$.

Then add the unit components.

$(60\vec{\mathbf{i}} + 0\vec{\mathbf{j}}) + (25\vec{\mathbf{i}} + 43.3\vec{\mathbf{j}}) = 85\vec{\mathbf{i}} + 43.3\vec{\mathbf{j}}$

$\vec{\mathbf{F}} \approx \sqrt{85^2 + 43.3^2}$
$\quad \approx \sqrt{9099.89}$
$\quad \approx 95.39$
The magnitude of the resultant force is
95.39 newtons.

c. **Determine the direction of the resultant force.**
$\tan \theta = \frac{43.3}{85}$ *Use the tangent ratio.*
$\quad \theta = \tan^{-1}\frac{43.3}{85}$
$\quad \theta \approx 27°$

The direction of the resultant force is 27° with
respect to the vector on the x-axis.

8-5

Practice

Applications with Vectors

Make a sketch to show the given vectors.

1. a force of 97 newtons acting on an object while a force of 38 newtons acts on the same object at an angle of 70° with the first force

2. a force of 85 pounds due north and a force of 100 pounds due west acting on the same object

Find the magnitude and direction of the resultant vector for each diagram.

3.

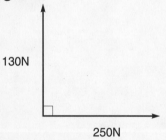

130N

250N

4.

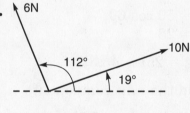

6N

10N

112°

19°

5. What would be the force required to push a 200-pound object up a ramp inclined at 30° with the ground?

6. Nadia is pulling a tarp along level ground with a force of 25 pounds directed along the tarp. If the tarp makes an angle of 50° with the ground, find the horizontal and vertical components of the force.

7. *Aviation*   A pilot flies a plane east for 200 kilometers, then 60° south of east for 80 kilometers. Find the plane's distance and direction from the starting point.

146

8-6

Study Guide

Vectors and Parametric Equations

Vector equations and **parametric equations** allow us to model movement.

Example 1 **Write a vector equation describing a line passing through $P_1(8, 4)$ and parallel to $\vec{a} = \langle 6, -1 \rangle$. Then write parametric equations of the line.**

Let the line ℓ through $P_1(8, 4)$ be parallel to $\vec{a}$.
For any point $P_2(x, y)$ on ℓ, $\overrightarrow{P_1P_2}\langle x - 8, y - 4 \rangle$.
Since $\overrightarrow{P_1P_2}$ is on ℓ and is parallel to $\vec{a}$, $\overrightarrow{P_1P_2} = t\vec{a}$,
for some value t. By substitution, we have
$\langle x - 8, y - 4 \rangle = t\langle 6, -1 \rangle$.

Therefore, the equation $\langle x - 8, y - 4 \rangle = t\langle 6, -1 \rangle$
is a vector equation describing all of the points (x, y)
on ℓ parallel to $\vec{a}$ through $P_1(8, 4)$.

Use the general form of the parametric equations
of a line with $\langle a_1, a_2 \rangle = \langle 6, -1 \rangle$
and $\langle x_1, y_1 \rangle = \langle 8, 4 \rangle$.

$$x = x_1 + ta_1 \qquad\qquad y = y_1 + ta_2$$
$$x = 8 + t(6) \qquad\qquad y = 4 + t(-1)$$
$$x = 8 + 6t \qquad\qquad y = 4 - t$$

Parametric equations for the line are $x = 8 + 6t$
and $y = 4 - t$.

Example 2 **Write an equation in slope-intercept form of the line whose parametric equations are $x = -3 + 4t$ and $y = 3 + 4t$.**

Solve each parametric equation for t.

$$x = -3 + 4t \qquad\qquad y = 3 + 4t$$
$$x + 3 = 4t \qquad\qquad y - 3 = 4t$$
$$\frac{x + 3}{4} = t \qquad\qquad \frac{y - 3}{4} = t$$

Use substitution to write an equation for the line
without the variable t.

$$\frac{x + 3}{4} = \frac{y - 3}{4} \qquad \textit{Substitute.}$$
$$(x + 3)(4) = 4(y - 3) \qquad \textit{Cross multiply.}$$
$$4x + 12 = 4y - 12 \qquad \textit{Simplify.}$$
$$y = x + 6 \qquad \textit{Solve for y.}$$

8-6

Practice

Vectors and Parametric Equations

Write a vector equation of the line that passes through point P and is parallel to $\vec{a}$. Then write parametric equations of the line.

1. $P(-2, 1), \vec{a} = \langle 3, -4 \rangle$

2. $P(3, 7), \vec{a} = \langle 4, 5 \rangle$

3. $P(2, -4), \vec{a} = \langle 1, 3 \rangle$

4. $P(5, -8), \vec{a} = \langle 9, 2 \rangle$

Write parametric equations of the line with the given equation.

5. $y = 3x - 8$

6. $y = -x + 4$

7. $3x - 2y = 6$

8. $5x + 4y = 20$

Write an equation in slope-intercept form of the line with the given parametric equations.

9. $x = 2t + 3$
    $y = t - 4$

10. $x = t + 5$
     $y = -3t$

11. *Physical Education*   Brett and Chad are playing touch football in gym class. Brett has to tag Chad before he reaches a 20-yard marker. Chad follows a path defined by $\langle x - 1, y - 19 \rangle = t\langle 0, 1 \rangle$, and Brett follows a path defined by $\langle x - 12, y - 0 \rangle = t\langle -11, 19 \rangle$. Write parametric equations for the paths of Brett and Chad. Will Brett tag Chad before he reaches the 20-yard marker?

8-7

Study Guide

Modeling Motion Using Parametric Equations

We can use the horizontal and vertical components of a
projectile to find parametric equations that represent the
path of the projectile.

Example 1 **Find the initial horizontal and vertical velocities
of a soccer ball kicked with an initial velocity of
33 feet per second at an angle of 29° with the
ground.**

$$|\vec{v}_x| = |\vec{v}| \cos \theta \qquad |\vec{v}_y| = |\vec{v}| \sin \theta$$
$$|\vec{v}_x| = 33 \cos 29° \qquad |\vec{v}_y| = 33 \sin 29°$$
$$|\vec{v}_x| \approx 29 \qquad |\vec{v}_y| \approx 16$$

The initial horizontal velocity is about 29 feet
per second and the initial vertical velocity is
about 16 feet per second.

The path of a projectile launched from the ground may be
described by the parametric equations $x = t|\vec{v}| \cos \theta$ for
horizontal distance and $y = t|\vec{v}| \sin \theta - \frac{1}{2}gt^2$ for vertical
distance, where t is time and g is acceleration due to gravity.
Use $g \approx 9.8$ m/s^2 or 32 ft/s^2.

Example 2 **A rock is tossed at an initial velocity of
50 meters per second at an angle of 8° with
the ground. After 0.8 second, how far has
the rock traveled horizontally and vertically?**

First write the position of the rock as a pair of
parametric equations defining the postition of
the rock for any time t in seconds.

$$x = t|\vec{v}| \cos \theta \qquad y = t|\vec{v}| \sin \theta - \frac{1}{2}gt^2$$
$$x = t(50) \cos 8° \qquad y = t(50) \sin 8° - \frac{1}{2}(9.8)t^2 \quad |\vec{v}| = 50 \ m/s$$
$$x = 50t \cos 8° \qquad y = 50t \sin 8° - 4.9gt^2$$

Then find x and y when $t = 0.8$ second.

$$x = 50(0.8) \cos 8° \qquad y = 50(0.8) \sin 8° - 4.9(0.8)^2$$
$$\approx 39.61 \qquad \approx 2.43$$

After 0.8 second, the rock has traveled about
39.61 meters horizontally and is about 2.43 meters
above the ground.

8-7

Practice

Modeling Motion Using Parametric Equations

Find the initial horizontal and vertical velocity for each situation.

1. a soccer ball kicked with an initial velocity of 39 feet per second at an angle of 44° with the ground

2. a toy rocket launched from level ground with an initial velocity of 63 feet per second at an angle of 84° with the horizontal

3. a football thrown at a velocity of 10 yards per second at an angle of 58° with the ground

4. a golf ball hit with an initial velocity of 102 feet per second at an angle of 67° with the horizontal

5. ***Model Rocketry*** Manuel launches a toy rocket from ground level with an initial velocity of 80 feet per second at an angle of 80° with the horizontal.

   a. Write parametric equations to represent the path of the rocket.

   b. How long will it take the rocket to travel 10 feet horizontally from its starting point? What will be its vertical distance at that point?

6. ***Sports*** Jessica throws a javelin from a height of 5 feet with an initial velocity of 65 feet per second at an angle of 45° with the ground.

   a. Write parametric equations to represent the path of the javelin.

   b. After 0.5 seconds, how far has the javelin traveled horizontally and vertically?

8-8

Study Guide

Transformation Matrices in Three-Dimensional Space

Example 1   Find the coordinates of the vertices of the
pyramid and represent them as a vertex matrix.

$A(-2, -2, -2)$
$B(2, -2, -2)$
$C(2, 2, -2)$
$D(-2, 2, -2)$
$E(0, 0, 2)$

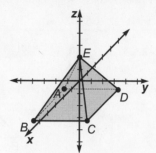

The vertex matrix for the pyramid is
$$\begin{array}{c} \\ x \\ y \\ z \end{array}\begin{array}{ccccc} A & B & C & D & E \\ \left[\begin{array}{ccccc} -2 & 2 & 2 & -2 & 0 \\ -2 & -2 & 2 & 2 & 0 \\ -2 & -2 & -2 & -2 & 2 \end{array}\right] \end{array}.$$

Example 2   Let M represent the vertex matrix of the pyramid
in Example 1.

a. Find TM if $T = \begin{bmatrix} 1 & 0 & 0 \\ 0 & -1 & 0 \\ 0 & 0 & 1 \end{bmatrix}$.

b. Graph the resulting image and describe the
transformation represented by matrix T.

a. First find TM.

$$TM = \begin{bmatrix} 1 & 0 & 0 \\ 0 & -1 & 0 \\ 0 & 0 & 1 \end{bmatrix} \cdot \begin{bmatrix} -2 & 2 & 2 & -2 & 0 \\ -2 & -2 & 2 & 2 & 0 \\ -2 & -2 & -2 & -2 & 2 \end{bmatrix} = \begin{array}{c} \\ \\ \end{array}\begin{array}{ccccc} A' & B' & C' & D' & E' \\ \left[\begin{array}{ccccc} -2 & 2 & 2 & -2 & 0 \\ 2 & 2 & -2 & -2 & 0 \\ -2 & -2 & -2 & -2 & 2 \end{array}\right] \end{array}$$

b. Then graph the points
represented by the resulting
matrix.

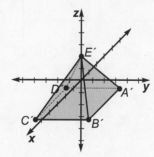

The transformation matrix reflects the image
of the pyramid over the xz-plane.

8-8

Practice

Transformation Matrices in Three-Dimensional Space

Write the matrix for each figure.

1.

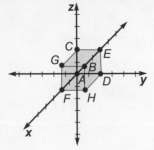

2.

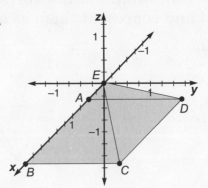

Translate the figure in Question 1 using the given vectors. Graph each image and write the translated matrix.

3. $\vec{a}\ \langle 1, 2, 0 \rangle$

4. $\vec{b}\ \langle -1, 2, -2 \rangle$

Transform the figure in Question 2 using each matrix. Graph each image and describe the result.

5. $\begin{bmatrix} 2 & 0 & 0 \\ 0 & 2 & 0 \\ 0 & 0 & 2 \end{bmatrix}$

6. $\begin{bmatrix} 1 & 0 & 0 \\ 0 & 1 & 0 \\ 0 & 0 & -1 \end{bmatrix}$

8-1 Practice — Geometric Vectors

NAME _____ DATE _____ PERIOD _____

Use a ruler and a protractor to determine the magnitude (in centimeters) and direction of each vector.

1.

2cm; 60°

2.

3 cm; 140°

3.

1cm; 310°

Find the magnitude and direction of each resultant.

4. $\bar{x} + \bar{y}$

3.9 cm; 110°

5. $\bar{x} - \bar{z}$

2.5 cm; 83°

6. $2\bar{x} + \bar{y}$

5.4 cm; 93°

7. $\bar{y} + 3\bar{z}$

0.6 cm; 217°

Find the magnitude of the horizontal and vertical components of each vector shown in Exercises 1–3.

8. $\bar{x}$

1.00 cm, 1.73 cm

9. $\bar{y}$

2.30 cm, 1.93 cm

10. $\bar{z}$

0.64 cm, 0.77 cm

11. **Aviation** An airplane is flying at a velocity of 500 miles per hour due north when it encounters a wind blowing out of the west at 50 miles per hour. What is the magnitude of the airplane's resultant velocity? **502.49 mph**

8-2 Practice — Algebraic Vectors

NAME _____ DATE _____ PERIOD _____

Write the ordered pair that represents $\overrightarrow{AB}$. Then find the magnitude of $\overrightarrow{AB}$.

1. $A(2, 4), B(-1, 3)$

$\langle -3, -1\rangle; \sqrt{10}$

2. $A(4, -2), B(5, -5)$

$\langle 1, -3\rangle; \sqrt{10}$

3. $A(-3, -6), B(8, -1)$

$\langle 11, 5\rangle; \sqrt{146}$

Find an ordered pair to represent $\bar{u}$ in each equation if $\bar{v} = \langle 2, -1\rangle$ and $\bar{w} = \langle -3, 5\rangle$.

4. $\bar{u} = 3\bar{v}$

$\langle 6, -3\rangle$

5. $\bar{u} = \bar{w} - 2\bar{v}$

$\langle -7, 7\rangle$

6. $\bar{u} = 4\bar{v} + 3\bar{w}$

$\langle -1, 11\rangle$

7. $\bar{u} = 5\bar{w} - 3\bar{v}$

$\langle -21, 28\rangle$

Find the magnitude of each vector, and write each vector as the sum of unit vectors.

8. $\langle 2, 6\rangle$

$2\sqrt{10}; 2\bar{i} + 6\bar{j}$

9. $\langle 4, -5\rangle$

$\sqrt{41}; 4\bar{i} - 5\bar{j}$

10. **Gardening** Nancy and Harry are lifting a stone statue and moving it to a new location in their garden. Nancy is pushing the statue with a force of 120 newtons (N) at a 60° angle with the horizontal while Harry is pulling the statue with a force of 180 newtons at a 40° angle with the horizontal. What is the magnitude of the combined force they exert on the statue? **295.62 N**

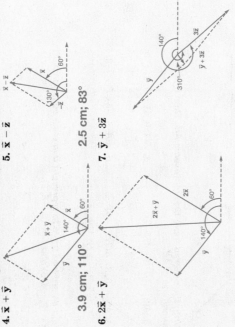

8-3 Practice

Vectors in Three-Dimensional Space

NAME _____ DATE _____ PERIOD _____

Locate point B in space. Then find the magnitude of a vector from the origin to B.

1. $B(4, 7, 6)$
$\sqrt{101}$

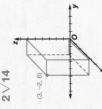

2. $B(4, -2, 6)$
$2\sqrt{14}$

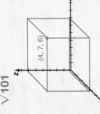

Write the ordered triple that represents $\overline{AB}$. Then find the magnitude of $\overline{AB}$.

3. $A(2, 1, 3), B(-4, 5, 7)$
$\langle -6, 4, 4 \rangle; 2\sqrt{17}$

4. $A(4, 0, 6), B(7, 1, -3)$
$\langle 3, 1, -9 \rangle; \sqrt{91}$

5. $A(-4, 5, 8), B(7, 2, -9)$
$\langle 11, -3, -17 \rangle; \sqrt{419}$

6. $A(6, 8, -5), B(7, -3, 12)$
$\langle 1, -11, 17 \rangle; \sqrt{411}$

Find an ordered triple to represent $\vec{u}$ in each equation if $\vec{v} = \langle 2, -4, 5 \rangle$ and $\vec{w} = \langle 6, -8, 9 \rangle$.

7. $\vec{u} = \vec{v} + \vec{w}$
$\langle 8, -12, 14 \rangle$

8. $\vec{u} = \vec{v} - \vec{w}$
$\langle -4, 4, -4 \rangle$

9. $\vec{u} = 4\vec{v} + 3\vec{w}$
$\langle 26, -40, 47 \rangle$

10. $\vec{u} = 5\vec{v} - 2\vec{w}$
$\langle -2, -4, 7 \rangle$

11. **Physics** Suppose that the force acting on an object can be expressed by the vector $\langle 85, 35, 110 \rangle$, where each measure in pounds. What is the magnitude of this force? ≈ 143 lb

8-4 Practice

Perpendicular Vectors

NAME _____ DATE _____ PERIOD _____

Find each inner product and state whether the vectors are perpendicular. Write yes or no.

1. $\langle 3, 6 \rangle \cdot \langle -4, 2 \rangle$
0; yes

2. $\langle -1, 4 \rangle \cdot \langle 3, -2 \rangle$
-11; no

3. $\langle 2, 0 \rangle \cdot \langle -1, -1 \rangle$
-2; no

4. $\langle -2, 0, 1 \rangle \cdot \langle 3, 2, -3 \rangle$
-9; no

5. $\langle -4, -1, 1 \rangle \cdot \langle 1, -3, 4 \rangle$
3; no

6. $\langle 0, 0, 1 \rangle \cdot \langle 1, -2, 0 \rangle$
0; yes

Find each cross product. Then verify that the resulting vector is perpendicular to the given vectors.

7. $\langle 1, 3, 4 \rangle \times \langle -1, 0, -1 \rangle$
$\langle -3, -3, 3 \rangle$; yes

8. $\langle 3, 1, -6 \rangle \times \langle -2, 4, 3 \rangle$
$\langle 27, 3, 14 \rangle$; yes

9. $\langle 3, 1, 2 \rangle \times \langle 2, -3, 1 \rangle$
$\langle 7, 1, -11 \rangle$; yes

10. $\langle 4, -1, 0 \rangle \times \langle 5, -3, -1 \rangle$
$\langle 1, 4, -7 \rangle$; yes

11. $\langle -6, 1, 3 \rangle \times \langle -2, -2, 1 \rangle$
$\langle 7, 0, 14 \rangle$; yes

12. $\langle 0, 0, 6 \rangle \times \langle 3, -2, -4 \rangle$
$\langle 12, 18, 0 \rangle$; yes

13. **Physics** Janna is using a force of 100 pounds to push a cart up a ramp. The ramp is 6 feet long and is at a 30° angle with the horizontal. How much work is Janna doing in the vertical direction? (*Hint:* Use the sine ratio and the formula $W = \vec{F} \cdot \vec{d}$.) 300 ft-lb

NAME _____ DATE _____ PERIOD _____

8-5 Practice

Applications with Vectors

Make a sketch to show the given vectors.

1. a force of 97 newtons acting on an object while a force of 38 newtons acts on the same object at an angle of 70° with the first force

2. a force of 85 pounds due north and a force of 100 pounds due west acting on the same object

Find the magnitude and direction of the resultant vector for each diagram.

3.

281.78 N; 27.47°

4.

11.39 N; 50.74°

5. What would be the force required to push a 200-pound object up a ramp inclined at 30° with the ground? **at least 100 lb**

6. Nadia is pulling a tarp along level ground with a force of 25 pounds directed along the tarp. If the tarp makes an angle of 50° with the ground, find the horizontal and vertical components of the force. **16.07 lb; 19.15 lb**

7. *Aviation* A pilot flies a plane east for 200 kilometers, then 60° south of east for 80 kilometers. Find the plane's distance and direction from the starting point. **249.80 km; 16.10° south of east**

NAME _____ DATE _____ PERIOD _____

8-6 Practice

Vectors and Parametric Equations

Write a vector equation of the line that passes through point P and is parallel to $\vec{a}$. Then write parametric equations of the line.

1. $P(-2, 1)$, $\vec{a} = \langle 3, -4 \rangle$
$\langle x + 2, y - 1 \rangle = t\langle 3, -4 \rangle$
$x = -2 + 3t$
$y = 1 - 4t$

2. $P(3, 7)$, $\vec{a} = \langle 4, 5 \rangle$
$\langle x - 3, y - 7 \rangle = t\langle 4, 5 \rangle$
$x = 3 + 4t$
$y = 7 + 5t$

3. $P(2, -4)$, $\vec{a} = \langle 1, 3 \rangle$
$\langle x - 2, y + 4 \rangle = t\langle 1, 3 \rangle$
$x = 2 + t$
$y = -4 + 3t$

4. $P(5, -8)$, $\vec{a} = \langle 9, 2 \rangle$
$\langle x - 5, y + 8 \rangle = t\langle 9, 2 \rangle$
$x = 5 + 9t$
$y = -8 + 2t$

Write parametric equations of the line with the given equation.

5. $y = 3x - 8$
$x = t$
$y = 3t - 8$

6. $y = -x + 4$
$x = t$
$y = -t + 4$

7. $3x - 2y = 6$
$x = t$
$y = \frac{3}{2}t - 3$

8. $5x + 4y = 20$
$x = t$
$y = -\frac{5}{4}t + 5$

Write an equation in slope-intercept form of the line with the given parametric equations.

9. $x = 2t + 3$
$y = t - 4$
$y = \frac{1}{2}x - \frac{11}{2}$

10. $x = t + 5$
$y = -3t$
$y = -3x + 15$

11. *Physical Education* Brett and Chad are playing touch football in gym class. Brett has to tag Chad before he reaches a 20-yard marker. Chad follows a path defined by $(x - 1, y - 19) = t(0, 1)$, and Brett follows a path defined by $(x - 12, y - 0) = t(-11, 19)$. Write parametric equations for the paths of Brett and Chad. Will Brett tag Chad before he reaches the 20-yard marker?
Chad $x = 1$, $y = 19 + t$; Brett $x = 12 - 11t$, $y = 19t$; yes

NAME _____ DATE _____ PERIOD _____

8-7 Practice

Modeling Motion Using Parametric Equations

Find the initial horizontal and vertical velocity for each situation.

1. a soccer ball kicked with an initial velocity of 39 feet per second at an angle of 44° with the ground
28.05 ft/s, 27.09 ft/s

2. a toy rocket launched from level ground with an initial velocity of 63 feet per second at an angle of 84° with the horizontal
6.59 ft/s, 62.65 ft/s

3. a football thrown at a velocity of 10 yards per second at an angle of 58° with the ground
5.30 yd/s, 8.48 yd/s

4. a golf ball hit with an initial velocity of 102 feet per second at an angle of 67° with the horizontal
39.85 ft/s, 93.89 ft/s

5. *Model Rocketry* Manuel launches a toy rocket from ground level with an initial velocity of 80 feet per second at an angle of 80° with the horizontal.
a. Write parametric equations to represent the path of the rocket.
$x = 80t \cos 80°; y = 80t \sin 80° - 16t^2$

b. How long will it take the rocket to travel 10 feet horizontally from its starting point? What will be its vertical distance at that point?
0.72 s; 48.43 ft

6. *Sports* Jessica throws a javelin from a height of 5 feet with an initial velocity of 65 feet per second at an angle of 45° with the ground.
a. Write parametric equations to represent the path of the javelin.
$x = 65t \cos 45°; y = 65t \sin 45° - 16t^2 + 5$

b. After 0.5 seconds, how far has the javelin traveled horizontally and vertically?
22.98 ft; 23.98 ft

© Glencoe/McGraw-Hill   150   *Advanced Mathematical Concepts*

NAME _____ DATE _____ PERIOD _____

8-8 Practice

Transformation Matrices in Three-Dimensional Space

Write the matrix for each figure.

1.

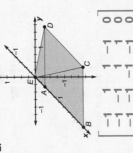

$$\begin{bmatrix} 0 & 2 & 0 & 0 & 0 & 2 & 2 & 2 \\ 0 & 2 & 2 & 0 & 0 & 0 & 0 & 2 \\ 0 & 2 & 2 & 0 & 2 & 0 & 2 & 0 \end{bmatrix}$$

2.

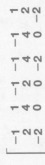

$$\begin{bmatrix} -1 & 1 & 1 & 1 & -1 & 0 \\ -1 & -1 & 1 & 1 & 1 & 0 \\ -1 & -1 & -1 & -1 & -1 & 0 \end{bmatrix}$$

Translate the figure in Question 1 using the given vectors. Graph each image and write the translated matrix.

3. $\vec{a}\,\langle 1, 2, 0\rangle$

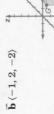

$$\begin{bmatrix} 1 & 3 & 1 & 1 & 1 & 3 & 3 & 3 \\ 2 & 4 & 4 & 2 & 2 & 2 & 2 & 4 \\ 0 & 2 & 2 & 0 & 2 & 0 & 2 & 0 \end{bmatrix}$$

4. $\vec{b}\,\langle -1, 2, -2\rangle$

$$\begin{bmatrix} -1 & 1 & -1 & -1 & -1 & 1 & 1 & 1 \\ -2 & 4 & 2 & 4 & 4 & 2 & 2 & 4 \\ -2 & 0 & 0 & -2 & 0 & -2 & 0 & -2 \end{bmatrix}$$

Transform the figure in Question 2 using each matrix. Graph each image and describe the result.

5. $\begin{bmatrix} 2 & 0 & 0 \\ 0 & 2 & 0 \\ 0 & 0 & 2 \end{bmatrix}$

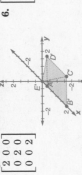

dimensions increased by a factor of 2

6. $\begin{bmatrix} 1 & 0 & 0 \\ 0 & 1 & 0 \\ 0 & 0 & -1 \end{bmatrix}$

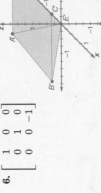

reflection over xy-plane

© Glencoe/McGraw-Hill   152   *Advanced Mathematical Concepts*

9-1

Study Guide

Polar Coordinates

A **polar coordinate system** uses distances and angles to record the position of a point. The location of a point P can be identified by polar coordinates in the form (r, θ), where $|r|$ is the distance from the **pole**, or origin, to point P and θ is the measure of the angle formed by the ray from the pole to point P and the **polar axis.**

Example 1 **Graph each point.**

  a. $P\left(3, \dfrac{\pi}{4}\right)$

  Sketch the terminal side of an angle measuring $\dfrac{\pi}{4}$ radians in standard position.

  Since r is positive ($r = 3$), find the point on the terminal side of the angle that is 3 units from the pole. *Notice point P is on the third circle from the pole.*

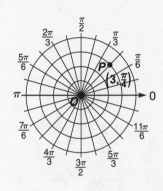

  b. $Q(-2.5, -120°)$

  Negative angles are measured clockwise. Sketch the terminal side of an angle of $-120°$ in standard position.

  Since r is negative, extend the terminal side of the angle in the opposite direction. Find the point Q that is 2.5 units from the pole along this extended ray.

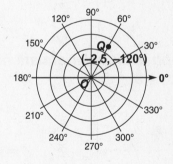

Example 2 **Find the distance between $P_1(3, 70°)$ and $P_2(5, 120°)$.**

$$P_1P_2 = \sqrt{r_1^2 + r_2^2 - 2r_1r_2 \cos(\theta_2 - \theta_1)}$$
$$= \sqrt{3^2 + 5^2 - 2(3)(5) \cos(120° - 70°)}$$
$$\approx 3.84$$

9-1

Practice

Polar Coordinates

Graph each point.

1. $(2.5, 0°)$

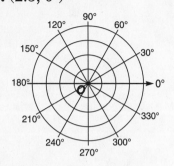

2. $(3, -135°)$

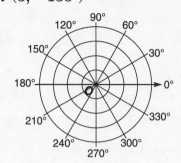

3. $(-1, -30°)$

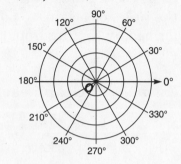

4. $\left(-2, \dfrac{\pi}{4}\right)$

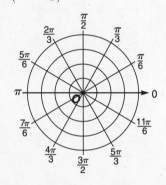

5. $\left(1, \dfrac{5\pi}{4}\right)$

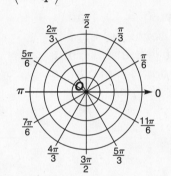

6. $\left(2, -\dfrac{2\pi}{3}\right)$

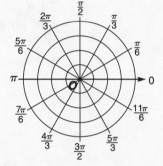

Graph each polar equation.

7. $r = 3$

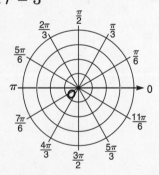

8. $\theta = 60°$

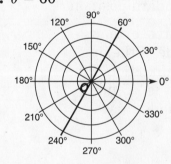

9. $r = 4$

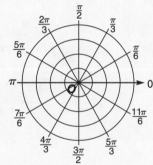

Find the distance between the points with the given polar coordinates.

10. $P_1(6, 90°)$ and $P_2(2, 130°)$

11. $P_1(-4, 85°)$ and $P_2(1, 105°)$

9-2

Study Guide

Graphs of Polar Equations

A **polar graph** is the set of all points whose coordinates (r, θ) satisfy a given polar equation. The position and shape of polar graphs can be altered by multiplying the function by a number or by adding to the function. You can also alter the graph by multiplying θ by a number or by adding to it.

Example 1   **Graph the polar equation $r = 2 \cos 2\theta$.**

Make a table of values. Graph the ordered pairs and connect them with a smooth curve.

θ	$2 \cos 2\theta$	(r, θ)
0°	2	(2, 0°)
30°	1	(1, 30°)
45°	0	(0, 45°)
60°	−1	(−1, 60°)
90°	−2	(−2, 90°)
120°	−1	(−1, 120°)
135°	0	(0, 135°)
150°	1	(1, 150°)
180°	2	(2, 180°)
210°	1	(1, 210°)
225°	0	(0, 225°)
240°	−1	(−1, 240°)
270°	−2	(−2, 270°)
300°	−1	(−1, 300°)
315°	0	(0, 315°)
330°	1	(1, 330°)

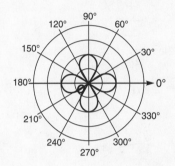

This type of curve is called a *rose*. Notice that the farthest points are 2 units from the pole and the rose has 4 petals.

Example 2   **Graph the system of polar equations. Solve the system using algebra and trigonometry, and compare the solutions to those on your graph.**

$r = 2 + 2 \cos \theta$
$r = 2 - 2 \cos \theta$

To solve the system of equations, substitute $2 + 2 \cos \theta$ for r in the second equation.

$2 + 2 \cos \theta = 2 - 2 \cos \theta$
     $\cos \theta = 0$
         $\theta = \dfrac{\pi}{2}$ or $\theta = \dfrac{3\pi}{2}$

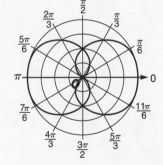

Substituting each angle into either of the original equations gives $r = 2$. The solutions of the system are therefore $\left(2, \dfrac{\pi}{2}\right)$ and $\left(2, \dfrac{3\pi}{2}\right)$.
Tracing on the curves shows that these solutions correspond with two of the intersection points on the graph. The curves also intersect at the pole.

9-2

Practice

Graphs of Polar Equations

Graph each polar equation. Identify the type of curve each represents.

1. $r = 1 + \cos \theta$

2. $r = 3 \sin 3\theta$

3. $r = 1 + 2 \cos \theta$

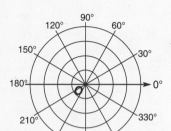

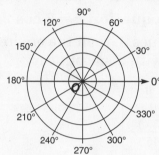

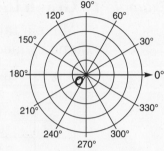

4. $r = 2 + 2 \sin \theta$

5. $r = 0.5\theta$

6. $r^2 = 16 \cos 2\theta$

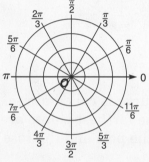

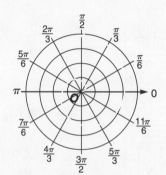

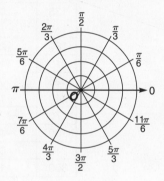

Graph each system of polar equations. Solve the system using algebra and trigonometry. Assume $0 \le \theta < 2\pi$.

7. $r = 1 + 2 \sin \theta$
  $r = 2 + \sin \theta$

8. $r = 1 + \cos \theta$
  $r = 3 \cos \theta$

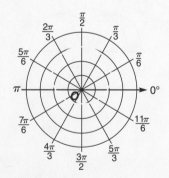

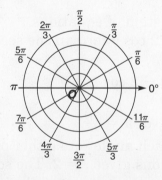

9. *Design* Mikaela is designing a border for her stationery. Suppose she uses a rose curve. Determine an equation for designing a rose that has 8 petals with each petal 4 units long.

160

9-3

Study Guide

Polar and Rectangular Coordinates

Use the conversion formulas in the following examples to convert coordinates and equations from one coordinate system to the other.

Example 1 **Find the rectangular coordinates of each point.**

a. $P\left(3, \frac{3\pi}{4}\right)$

For $P\left(3, \frac{3\pi}{4}\right)$, $r = 3$ and $\theta = \frac{3\pi}{4}$.
Use the conversion formulas
$x = r \cos \theta$ and $y = r \sin \theta$.

$x = r \cos \theta \qquad y = r \sin \theta$
$\quad = 3 \cos \frac{3\pi}{4} \qquad = 3 \sin \frac{3\pi}{4}$
$\quad = 3\left(-\frac{\sqrt{2}}{2}\right) \qquad = 3\left(\frac{\sqrt{2}}{2}\right)$
$\quad \text{or} -\frac{3\sqrt{2}}{2} \qquad \text{or} \frac{3\sqrt{2}}{2}$

The rectangular coordinates of P are $\left(-\frac{3\sqrt{2}}{2}, \frac{3\sqrt{2}}{2}\right)$, or $(-2.12, 2.12)$ to the nearest hundredth.

b. $Q(20, -60°)$

For $Q(20, -60°)$, $r = 20$ and $\theta = -60°$.

$x = r \cos \theta \qquad y = r \sin \theta$
$\quad = 20\cos(-60°) \qquad = 20 \sin(-60°)$
$\quad = 20(0.5) \qquad = 20\left(-\frac{\sqrt{3}}{2}\right)$
$\quad = 10 \qquad\qquad = -10\sqrt{3}$

The rectangular coordinates of Q are $(10, -10\sqrt{3})$, or approximately $(10, -17.32)$

Example 2 **Find the polar coordinates of $R(5, -9)$.**

For $R(5, -9)$, $x = 5$ and $y = -9$.

$r = \sqrt{x^2 + y^2} \qquad\qquad \theta = \text{Arctan} \frac{y}{x} \qquad x > 0$
$\quad = \sqrt{5^2 + (-9)^2} \qquad\qquad = \text{Arctan} \frac{-9}{5}$
$\quad = \sqrt{106} \text{ or about } 10.30 \qquad \approx -1.06$

To obtain an angle between 0 and 2π you can add 2π to the θ-value. This results in $\theta = 5.22$.

The polar coordinates of R are approximately $(10.30, 5.22)$.

Example 3 **Write the polar equation $r = 5 \cos \theta$ in rectangular form.**

$\qquad r = 5 \cos \theta$
$\qquad r^2 = 5r \cos \theta \qquad$ *Multiply each side by r.*
$\quad x^2 + y^2 = 5x \qquad\qquad r^2 = x^2 + y^2 \text{ and } r \cos \theta = x$

9-3

Practice

Polar and Rectangular Coordinates

Find the rectangular coordinates of each point with the given polar coordinates.

1. $(6, 120°)$

2. $(-4, 45°)$

3. $\left(4, \dfrac{\pi}{6}\right)$

4. $\left(0, \dfrac{13\pi}{3}\right)$

Find the polar coordinates of each point with the given rectangular coordinates. Use $0 \le \theta < 2\pi$ and $r \ge 0$.

5. $(2, 2)$

6. $(2, -3)$

7. $(-3, \sqrt{3})$

8. $(-5, -8)$

Write each polar equation in rectangular form.

9. $r = 4$

10. $r\cos\theta = 5$

Write each rectangular equation in polar form.

11. $x^2 + y^2 = 9$

12. $y = 3$

13. *Surveying* A surveyor records the polar coordinates of the location of a landmark as $(40, 62°)$. What are the rectangular coordinates?

9-4

Study Guide

Polar Form of a Linear Equation

Example 1 **Write the equation $x + 3y = 6$ in polar form.**

The standard form of the equation is $x + 3y - 6 = 0$. To find the values of p and ϕ, write the equation in normal form. To convert to normal form, find the value of $\pm\sqrt{A^2 + B^2}$.

$\pm\sqrt{A^2 + B^2} = \pm\sqrt{1^2 + 3^2}$ or $\pm\sqrt{10}$

Since C is negative, use $+\sqrt{10}$.

The normal form of the equation is
$\frac{1}{\sqrt{10}}x + \frac{3}{\sqrt{10}}y - \frac{6}{\sqrt{10}} = 0$ or $\frac{\sqrt{10}}{10}x + \frac{3\sqrt{10}}{10}y - \frac{3\sqrt{10}}{5} = 0$.

Using the normal form $x \cos \phi + y \sin \phi - p = 0$,
we can see that $p = \frac{6}{\sqrt{10}}$ or $\frac{3\sqrt{10}}{5}$. Since $\cos \phi$ and $\sin \phi$
are both positive, the normal lies in Quadrant I.

$\tan \phi = \frac{\sin \phi}{\cos \phi}$

$\tan \phi = 3 \qquad\qquad \frac{3}{\sqrt{10}} \div \frac{1}{\sqrt{10}} = 3$

$\phi \approx 1.25 \qquad$ *Use the Arctangent function.*

Substitute the values for p and ϕ into the polar form.
$\quad p = r \cos(\theta - \phi)$
$\frac{3\sqrt{10}}{5} = r \cos(\theta - 1.25) \qquad$ *Polar form of $x + 3y = 6$*

Example 2 **Write $3 = r \cos(\theta - 30°)$ in rectangular form.**

$3 = r \cos(\theta - 30°)$
$3 = r(\cos \theta \cos 30° + \sin \theta \sin 30°) \qquad$ *Difference identity for cosine*

$3 = r\left(\frac{\sqrt{3}}{2} \cos \theta + \frac{1}{2} \sin \theta\right) \qquad$ *$\cos 30° = \frac{\sqrt{3}}{2}, \sin 30° = \frac{1}{2}$*

$3 = \frac{\sqrt{3}}{2}r \cos \theta + \frac{1}{2}r \sin \theta \qquad$ *Distributive property*

$3 = \frac{\sqrt{3}}{2}x + \frac{1}{2}y \qquad$ *$r \cos \theta = x, r \sin \theta = y$*

$6 = \sqrt{3}x + y \qquad$ *Multiply each side by 2.*
$0 = \sqrt{3}x + y - 6 \qquad$ *Subtract 6 from each side.*

The rectangular form of $3 = r\cos(\theta - 30°)$ is $\sqrt{3}x + y - 6 = 0$.

9-4

Practice

Polar Form of a Linear Equation

Write each equation in polar form. Round ϕ to the nearest degree.

1. $3x + 2y = 16$

2. $3x + 4y = 15$

3. $3x - 4y = 12$

4. $y = 2x - 1$

Write each equation in rectangular form.

5. $4 = r \cos \left(\theta + \frac{5\pi}{6}\right)$

6. $2 = r \cos (\theta - 90°)$

7. $1 = r \cos \left(\theta - \frac{\pi}{4}\right)$

8. $3 = r \cos (\theta + 240°)$

Graph each polar equation.

9. $3 = r \cos (\theta - 60°)$

10. $1 = r \cos \left(\theta + \frac{\pi}{3}\right)$

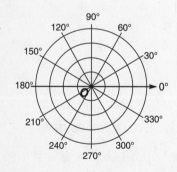

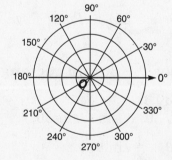

11. *Landscaping* A landscaper is designing a garden with hedges through which a straight path will lead from the exterior of the garden to the interior. If the polar coordinates of the endpoints of the path are $(20, 90°)$ and $(10, 150°)$, where r is measured in feet, what is the equation for the path?

9-5

Study Guide

Simplifying Complex Numbers

Add and subtract complex numbers by performing the chosen
operation on both the **real** and **imaginary parts.** Find the
product of two or more complex numbers by using the same
procedures used to multiply binomials. To simplify the
quotient of two complex numbers, multiply the numerator
and denominator by the complex conjugate of the
denominator.

To find the value of i^n, let R be the remainder when n is divided by 4.	
if R = 0	$i^n = 1$
if R = 1	$i^n = i$
if R = 2	$i^n = -1$
if R = 3	$i^n = -i$

Powers of i	
$i^1 = i$	$i^2 = -1$
$i^3 = i^2 \cdot i = -i$	$i^4 = (i^2)^2 = 1$
$i^5 = i^4 \cdot i = i$	$i^6 = i^4 \cdot i^2 = -1$
$i^7 = i^4 \cdot i^3 = -i$	$i^8 = (i^2)^4 = 1$

Example 1 Simplify each power of i.

   a. i^{30} **b.** i^{-11}

Method 1	**Method 2**	**Method 1**	**Method 2**
$30 \div 4 = 7 \text{ R } 2$	$i^{30} = (i^4)^7 \cdot i^2$	$-11 \div 4 = -3 \text{ R } 1$	$i^{-11} = (i^4)^{-3} \cdot i^1$
If R = 2, $i^n = -1$.	$= (1)^7 \cdot i^2$	If R = 1, $i^n = i$.	$= (1)^{-3} \cdot i^1$
$i^{30} = -1$	$= -1$	$i^{-11} = i$	$= i$

Example 2 Simplify each expression.

   a. $(3 + 2i) + (5 - 3i)$ **b.** $(8 - 4i) - (9 - 7i)$
   $\quad (3 + 2i) + (5 - 3i)$ $\quad (8 - 4i) - (9 - 7i)$
   $\quad = (3 + 5) + (2i - 3i)$ $\quad = 8 - 4i - 9 + 7i$
   $\quad = 8 - i$ $\quad = -1 + 3i$

Example 3 Simplify $(4 - 2i)(5 - 3i)$.

   $(4 - 2i)(5 - 3i) = 5(4 - 2i) - 3i(4 - 2i)$ *Distributive property*
   $\qquad\qquad\quad = 20 - 10i - 12i + 6i^2$ *Distributive property*
   $\qquad\qquad\quad = 20 - 10i - 12i + 6(-1)$ $i^2 = -1$
   $\qquad\qquad\quad = 14 - 22i$

Example 4 Simplify $(4 - 5i) \div (2 + i)$.

   $(4 - 5i) \div (2 + i) = \dfrac{4 - 5i}{2 + i}$

   $\qquad\qquad\qquad = \dfrac{4 - 5i}{2 + i} \cdot \dfrac{2 - i}{2 - i}$ *$2 - i$ is the conjugate of $2 + i$.*

   $\qquad\qquad\qquad = \dfrac{8 - 10i - 4i + 5i^2}{4 - i^2}$

   $\qquad\qquad\qquad = \dfrac{8 - 14i + 5(-1)}{4 - (-1)}$ $i^2 = -1$

   $\qquad\qquad\qquad = \dfrac{3 - 14i}{5}$

   $\qquad\qquad\qquad = \dfrac{3}{5} - \dfrac{14}{5}i$ *Write the answer in the form $a + bi$.*

9-5

Practice

Simplifying Complex Numbers

Simplify.

1. i^{38}

2. i^{-17}

3. $(3 + 2i) + (4 + 5i)$

4. $(-6 - 2i) - (-8 - 3i)$

5. $(8 - i) - (4 - i)$

6. $(1 + i)(3 - 2i)$

7. $(2 - 3i)(5 + i)$

8. $(4 + 5i)(4 - 5i)$

9. $(3 + 4i)^2$

10. $(4 + 3i) \div (1 - 2i)$

11. $(2 + i) \div (2 - i)$

12. $\dfrac{8 - 7i}{1 - 2i}$

13. *Physics*   A fence post wrapped in two wires has two forces acting on it. Once force exerts 5.3 newtons due north and 4.1 newtons due east. The second force exerts 6.2 newtons due north and 2.8 newtons due east. Find the resultant force on the fence post. Write your answer as a complex number. (*Hint:* A vector with a horizontal component of magnitude a and a vertical component of magnitude b can be represented by the complex number $a + bi$.)

9-6

Study Guide

The Complex Plane and Polar Form of Complex Numbers

In the **complex plane,** the real axis is horizontal and the imaginary axis is vertical. The **absolute value** of a complex number is its distance from zero in the complex plane.

The polar form of the complex number $a + bi$ is $r(\cos \theta + i \sin \theta)$, which is often abbreviated as r cis θ. In polar form, r represents the absolute value, or **modulus,** of the complex number. The angle θ is called the **amplitude** or **argument** of the complex number.

Example 1 Graph each number in the complex plane and find its absolute value.

  a. $z = 4 + 3i$
  $$|z| = \sqrt{4^2 + 3^2}$$
  $$= 5$$

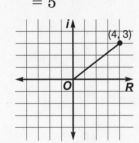

  b. $z = -2i$
  $$z = 0 - 2i$$
  $$|z| = \sqrt{0^2 + (-2)^2}$$
  $$= 2$$

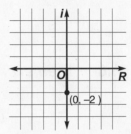

Example 2 Express the complex number $2 + 3i$ in polar form.

First plot the number in the complex plane.

Then find the modulus.

$$r = \sqrt{2^2 + 3^2} \text{ or } \sqrt{13}$$

Now find the amplitude. Notice that θ is in Quadrant I.

$$\theta = \text{Arctan } \frac{3}{2} \qquad \theta = \text{Arctan } \frac{b}{a} \text{ if } a > 0$$
$$\approx 0.98$$

Therefore, $2 + 3i \approx \sqrt{13}(\cos 0.98 + i \sin 0.98)$ or $\sqrt{13}$ cis 0.98.

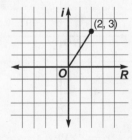

9-6

Practice

The Complex Plane and Polar Form of Complex Numbers

Graph each number in the complex plan and find its absolute value.

1. $z = 3i$ **2.** $z = 5 + i$ **3.** $z = -4 - 4i$

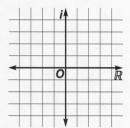   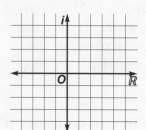   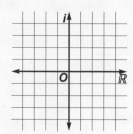

Express each complex number in polar form.

4. $3 + 4i$ **5.** $-4 + 3i$

6. $-1 + i$ **7.** $1 - i$

Graph each complex number. Then express it in rectangular form.

8. $2\left(\cos \frac{3\pi}{4} + i \sin \frac{3\pi}{4}\right)$ **9.** $4\left(\cos \frac{5\pi}{6} + i \sin \frac{5\pi}{6}\right)$ **10.** $3\left(\cos \frac{4\pi}{3} + i \sin \frac{4\pi}{3}\right)$

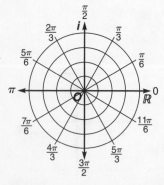   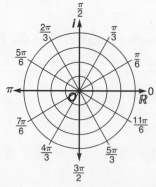   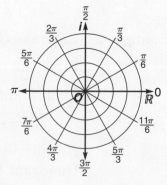

11. Vectors   The force on an object is represented by the complex number $8 + 21i$, where the components are measured in pounds. Find the magnitude and direction of the force.

9-7

Study Guide

Products and Quotients of Complex Numbers in Polar Form

Example 1 Find the product $2\left(\cos \frac{\pi}{2} + i \sin \frac{\pi}{2}\right) \cdot 4\left(\cos \frac{\pi}{3} + i \sin \frac{\pi}{3}\right)$.
Then express the product in rectangular form.

Find the modulus and amplitude of the product.

$$r = r_1 r_2 \qquad\qquad \theta = \theta_1 + \theta_2$$
$$= 2(4) \qquad\qquad\quad = \frac{\pi}{2} + \frac{\pi}{3}$$
$$= 8 \qquad\qquad\qquad\quad = \frac{5\pi}{6}$$

The product is $8\left(\cos \frac{5\pi}{6} + i \sin \frac{5\pi}{6}\right)$.

Now find the rectangular form of the product.
$$8\left(\cos \frac{5\pi}{6} + i \sin \frac{5\pi}{6}\right) = 8\left(-\frac{\sqrt{3}}{2} + \frac{1}{2}i\right) \qquad \cos \frac{5\pi}{6} = -\frac{\sqrt{3}}{2}, \; \sin \frac{5\pi}{6} = \frac{1}{2}$$
$$= -4\sqrt{3} + 4i$$

The rectangular form of the product is $-4\sqrt{3} + 4i$.

Example 2 Find the quotient $21\left(\cos \frac{7\pi}{6} + i \sin \frac{7\pi}{6}\right) \div$
$7\left(\cos \frac{4\pi}{3} + i \sin \frac{4\pi}{3}\right)$. **Then express the quotient in**
rectangular form.

Find the modulus and amplitude of the quotient.

$$r = \frac{r_1}{r_2} \qquad\qquad \theta = \theta_1 - \theta_2$$
$$= \frac{21}{7} \qquad\qquad\quad = \frac{7\pi}{6} - \frac{4\pi}{3}$$
$$= 3 \qquad\qquad\qquad = -\frac{\pi}{6}$$

The quotient is $3\left[\cos\left(-\frac{\pi}{6}\right) + i \sin\left(-\frac{\pi}{6}\right)\right]$.

Now find the rectangular form of the quotient.
$$3\left[\cos\left(-\frac{\pi}{6}\right) + i \sin\left(-\frac{\pi}{6}\right)\right] = 3\left[\frac{\sqrt{3}}{2} + \left(-\frac{1}{2}\right)i\right] \qquad \cos\left(-\frac{\pi}{6}\right) = \frac{\sqrt{3}}{2}, \; \sin\left(-\frac{\pi}{6}\right) = -\frac{1}{2}$$
$$= \frac{3\sqrt{3}}{2} - \frac{3}{2}i$$

The rectangular form of the quotient is $\frac{3\sqrt{3}}{2} - \frac{3}{2}i$.

169

9-7

Practice

Products and Quotients of Complex Numbers in Polar Form

Find each product or quotient. Express the result in rectangular form.

1. $3\left(\cos \frac{\pi}{3} + i \sin \frac{\pi}{3}\right) \cdot 3\left(\cos \frac{5\pi}{3} + i \sin \frac{5\pi}{3}\right)$

2. $6\left(\cos \frac{\pi}{2} + i \sin \frac{\pi}{2}\right) \div 2\left(\cos \frac{\pi}{3} + i \sin \frac{\pi}{3}\right)$

3. $14\left(\cos \frac{5\pi}{4} + i \sin \frac{5\pi}{4}\right) \div 2\left(\cos \frac{\pi}{2} + i \sin \frac{\pi}{2}\right)$

4. $3\left(\cos \frac{5\pi}{6} + i \sin \frac{5\pi}{6}\right) \cdot 6\left(\cos \frac{\pi}{3} + i \sin \frac{\pi}{3}\right)$

5. $2\left(\cos \frac{\pi}{2} + i \sin \frac{\pi}{2}\right) \cdot 2\left(\cos \frac{4\pi}{3} + i \sin \frac{4\pi}{3}\right)$

6. $15(\cos \pi + i \sin \pi) \div 3\left(\cos \frac{\pi}{2} + i \sin \frac{\pi}{2}\right)$

7. *Electricity*   Find the current in a circuit with a voltage of 12 volts and an impedance of $2 - 4j$ ohms. Use the formula, $E = I \cdot Z$, where E is the voltage measured in volts, I is the current measured in amperes, and Z is the impedance measured in ohms.
(*Hint:* Electrical engineers use j as the imaginary unit, so they write complex numbers in the form $a + bj$. Express each number in polar form, substitute values into the formula, and then express the current in rectangular form.)

9-8

Study Guide

Powers and Roots of Complex Numbers

You can use De Moivre's Theorem, $[r(\cos \theta + i \sin \theta)]^n = r^n(\cos n\theta + i \sin n\theta)$, to find the powers and roots of complex numbers in polar form.

Example 1 **Find $(-1 + \sqrt{3}i)^3$.**

First, write $-1 + \sqrt{3}i$ in polar form. Note that its graph is in Quadrant II of the complex plane.

$$r = \sqrt{(-1)^2 + (\sqrt{3})^2} \qquad \theta = \text{Arctan } \frac{\sqrt{3}}{-1} + \pi$$
$$= \sqrt{1 + 3} \text{ or } 2 \qquad = -\frac{\pi}{3} + \pi \text{ or } \frac{2\pi}{3}$$

The polar form of $-1 + \sqrt{3}i$ is $2\left(\cos \frac{2\pi}{3} + i \sin \frac{2\pi}{3}\right)$.

Now use De Moivre's Theorem to find the third power.

$$(-1 + \sqrt{3}i)^3 = \left[2\left(\cos \frac{2\pi}{3} + i \sin \frac{2\pi}{3}\right)\right]^3$$
$$= 2^3\left[\cos 3\left(\frac{2\pi}{3}\right) + i \sin 3\left(\frac{2\pi}{3}\right)\right] \qquad \textit{De Moivre's Theorem}$$
$$= 8(\cos 2\pi + i \sin 2\pi)$$
$$= 8(1 + 0i) \qquad\qquad \textit{Write the result in}$$
$$= 8 \qquad\qquad\qquad\quad \textit{rectangular form.}$$

Therefore, $(-1 + \sqrt{3}i)^3 = 8$.

Example 2 **Find $\sqrt[3]{64i}$.**

$$\sqrt[3]{64i} = (0 + 64i)^{\frac{1}{3}} \qquad\qquad a = 0, b = 64$$
$$= \left[64\left(\cos \frac{\pi}{2} + i \sin \frac{\pi}{2}\right)\right]^{\frac{1}{3}} \qquad \textit{Polar form: } r = \sqrt{0^2 + 64^2} \text{ or } 64;$$
$$\theta = \frac{\pi}{2} \textit{ since } a = 0.$$
$$= 64^{\frac{1}{3}}\left[\cos\left(\frac{1}{3}\right)\left(\frac{\pi}{2}\right) + i \sin\left(\frac{1}{3}\right)\left(\frac{\pi}{2}\right)\right] \quad \textit{De Moivre's Theorem}$$
$$= 4\left(\cos \frac{\pi}{6} + i \sin \frac{\pi}{6}\right)$$
$$= 4\left(\frac{\sqrt{3}}{2} + \frac{1}{2}i\right)$$
$$= 2\sqrt{3} + 2i$$

Therefore, $2\sqrt{3} + 2i$ is the principal cube root of $64i$.

9-8

Practice

Powers and Roots of Complex Numbers

Find each power. Express the result in rectangular form.

1. $(-2 - 2\sqrt{3}i)^3$

2. $(1 - i)^5$

3. $(-1 + \sqrt{3}i)^{12}$

4. $\left[1\left(\cos\frac{\pi}{4} + i\sin\frac{\pi}{4}\right)\right]^{-3}$

5. $(2 + 3i)^6$

6. $(1 + i)^8$

Find each principal root. Express the result in the form $a + bi$ with a and b rounded to the nearest hundredth.

7. $(-27i)^{\frac{1}{3}}$

8. $(8 - 8i)^{\frac{1}{3}}$

9. $\sqrt[5]{-243i}$

10. $(-i)^{\frac{1}{3}}$

11. $\sqrt[8]{-8i}$

12. $\sqrt[4]{-2 - 2\sqrt{3}i}$

Answers (Lessons 9-1 and 9-2)

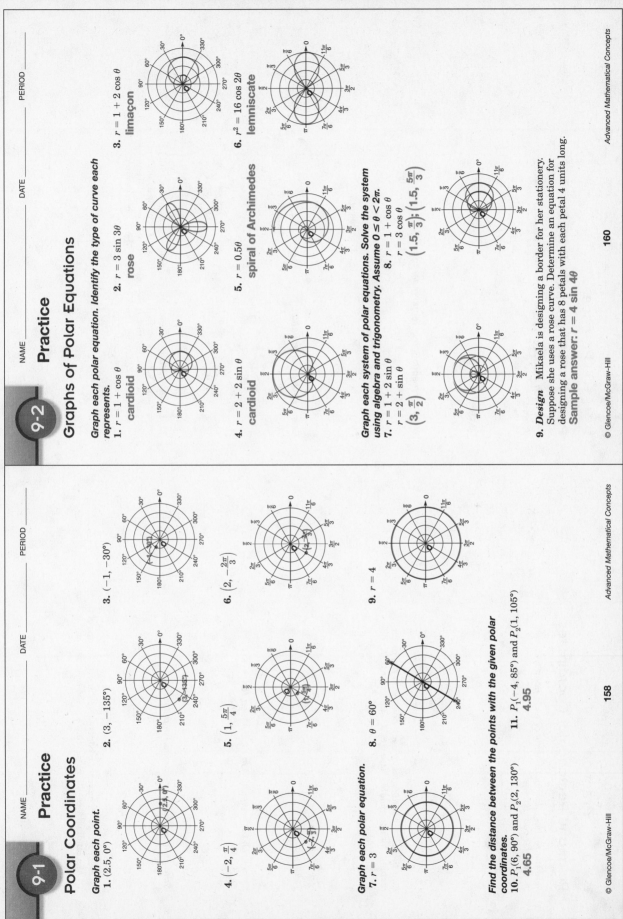

9-2 Practice

Graphs of Polar Equations

Graph each polar equation. Identify the type of curve each represents.

1. $r = 1 + \cos \theta$
cardioid

2. $r = 3 \sin 3\theta$
rose

3. $r = 1 + 2 \cos \theta$
limaçon

4. $r = 2 + 2 \sin \theta$
cardioid

5. $r = 0.5\theta$
spiral of Archimedes

6. $r^2 = 16 \cos 2\theta$
lemniscate

Graph each system of polar equations. Solve the system using algebra and trigonometry. Assume $0 \le \theta < 2\pi$.

7. $r = 1 + 2 \sin \theta$
$r = 2 + \sin \theta$
$\left(3, \frac{\pi}{2}\right)$

8. $r = 1 + \cos \theta$
$r = 3 \cos \theta$
$\left(1.5, \frac{\pi}{3}\right); \left(1.5, \frac{5\pi}{3}\right)$

9. **Design** Mikaela is designing a border for her stationery. Suppose she uses a rose curve. Determine an equation for designing a rose that has 8 petals with each petal 4 units long.
Sample answer: $r = 4 \sin 4\theta$

9-1 Practice

Polar Coordinates

Graph each point.

1. $(2.5, 0°)$

2. $(3, -135°)$

3. $(-1, -30°)$

4. $\left(-2, \frac{\pi}{4}\right)$

5. $\left(1, \frac{5\pi}{4}\right)$

6. $\left(2, -\frac{2\pi}{3}\right)$

Graph each polar equation.

7. $r = 3$

8. $\theta = 60°$

9. $r = 4$

Find the distance between the points with the given polar coordinates.

10. $P_1(6, 90°)$ and $P_2(2, 130°)$
4.65

11. $P_1(-4, 85°)$ and $P_2(1, 105°)$
4.95

Answers (Lessons 9-3 and 9-4)

Left page — Lesson 9-3

9-3

Practice

Polar and Rectangular Coordinates

Find the rectangular coordinates of each point with the given polar coordinates.

1. $(6, 120°)$
   $(-3, 3\sqrt{3})$

2. $(-4, 45°)$
   $(-2\sqrt{2}, -2\sqrt{2})$

3. $\left(4, \dfrac{\pi}{6}\right)$
   $(2\sqrt{3}, 2)$

4. $\left(0, \dfrac{13\pi}{3}\right)$
   $(0, 0)$

Find the polar coordinates of each point with the given rectangular coordinates. Use $0 \le \theta < 2\pi$ and $r \ge 0$.

5. $(2, 2)$
   $\left(2\sqrt{2}, \dfrac{\pi}{4}\right)$

6. $(2, -3)$
   $(3.61, 5.30)$

7. $(-3, \sqrt{3})$
   $\left(2\sqrt{3}, \dfrac{5\pi}{6}\right)$

8. $(-5, -8)$
   $(9.43, 4.15)$

Write each polar equation in rectangular form.

9. $r = 4$
   $x^2 + y^2 = 16$

10. $r \cos \theta = 5$
    $x = 5$

Write each rectangular equation in polar form.

11. $x^2 + y^2 = 9$
    $r = \pm 3$

12. $y = 3$
    $r \sin \theta = 3$ or
    $r = 3 \csc \theta$

13. *Surveying* A surveyor records the polar coordinates of the location of a landmark as $(40, 62°)$. What are the rectangular coordinates?
    $(18.78, 35.32)$

Right page — Lesson 9-4

9-4

Practice

Polar Form of a Linear Equation

Write each equation in polar form. Round ϕ to the nearest degree.

1. $3x + 2y = 16$
   $\dfrac{16\sqrt{13}}{13} = r \cos(\theta - 34°)$

2. $3x + 4y = 15$
   $3 = r \cos(\theta - 53°)$

3. $3x - 4y = 12$
   $-\dfrac{12}{5} = r \cos(\theta - 127°)$

4. $y = 2x - 1$
   $-\dfrac{\sqrt{5}}{5} = r \cos(\theta - 153°)$

Write each equation in rectangular form.

5. $4 = r \cos\left(\theta + \dfrac{5\pi}{6}\right)$
   $\sqrt{3}x + y + 8 = 0$

6. $2 = r \cos(\theta - 90°)$
   $y = 2$

7. $1 = r \cos\left(\theta - \dfrac{\pi}{4}\right)$
   $\sqrt{2}x + \sqrt{2}y - 2 = 0$

8. $3 = r \cos(\theta + 240°)$
   $x - \sqrt{3}y + 6 = 0$

Graph each polar equation.

9. $3 = r \cos(\theta - 60°)$

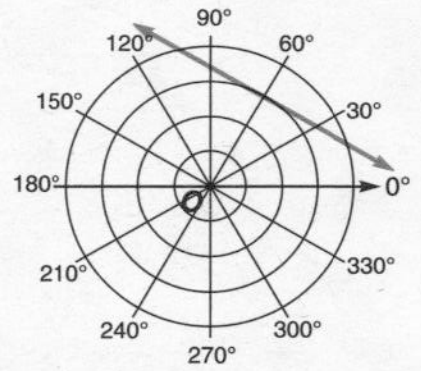

10. $1 = r \cos\left(\theta + \dfrac{\pi}{3}\right)$

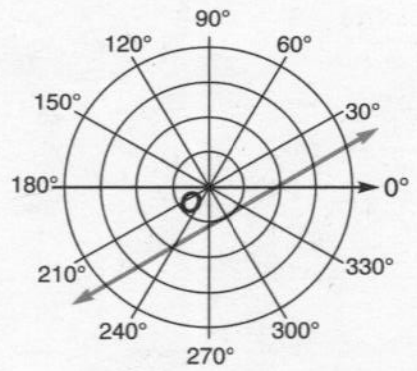

11. *Landscaping* A landscaper is designing a garden with hedges through which a straight path will lead from the exterior of the garden to the interior. If the polar coordinates of the endpoints of the path are $(20, 90°)$ and $(10, 150°)$, where r is measured in feet, what is the equation for the path?
    $10 = r \cos(\theta - 150°)$

9-5 Practice

Simplifying Complex Numbers

Simplify.

1. i^{38}

   -1

2. i^{-17}

   $-i$

3. $(3 + 2i) + (4 + 5i)$

   $7 + 7i$

4. $(-6 - 2i) - (-8 - 3i)$

   $2 + i$

5. $(8 - i) - (4 - i)$

   4

6. $(1 + i)(3 - 2i)$

   $5 + i$

7. $(2 - 3i)(5 + i)$

   $13 - 13i$

8. $(4 + 5i)(4 - 5i)$

   41

9. $(3 + 4i)^2$

   $-7 + 24i$

10. $(4 + 3i) \div (1 - 2i)$

   $-\dfrac{2}{5} + \dfrac{11}{5}i$

11. $(2 + i) \div (2 - i)$

   $\dfrac{3}{5} + \dfrac{4}{5}i$

12. $\dfrac{8 - 7i}{1 - 2i}$

   $\dfrac{22}{5} + \dfrac{9}{5}i$

13. **Physics** A fence post wrapped in two wires has two forces acting on it. One force exerts 5.3 newtons due north and 4.1 newtons due east. The second force exerts 6.2 newtons due north and 2.8 newtons due east. Find the resultant force on the fence post. Write your answer as a complex number. (*Hint:* A vector with a horizontal component of magnitude a and a vertical component of magnitude b can be represented by the complex number $a + bi$.)

   $(4.1 + 5.3i) + (2.8 + 6.2i) = 6.9 + 11.5i$ N

9-6 Practice

The Complex Plane and Polar Form of Complex Numbers

Graph each number in the complex plan and find its absolute value.

1. $z = 3i$

   $|z| = 3$

2. $z = 5 + i$

   $|z| = \sqrt{26}$

   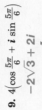

3. $z = -4 - 4i$

   $|z| = 4\sqrt{2}$

Express each complex number in polar form.

4. $3 + 4i$

   $5(\cos 0.93 + i \sin 0.93)$

5. $-4 + 3i$

   $5(\cos 2.5 + i \sin 2.5)$

6. $-1 + i$

   $\sqrt{2}\left(\cos \dfrac{3\pi}{4} + i \sin \dfrac{3\pi}{4}\right)$

7. $1 - i$

   $\sqrt{2}\left(\cos \dfrac{7\pi}{4} + i \sin \dfrac{7\pi}{4}\right)$

Graph each complex number. Then express it in rectangular form.

8. $2\left(\cos \dfrac{3\pi}{4} + i \sin \dfrac{3\pi}{4}\right)$

   $-\sqrt{2} + \sqrt{2}i$

9. $4\left(\cos \dfrac{5\pi}{6} + i \sin \dfrac{5\pi}{6}\right)$

   $-2\sqrt{3} + 2i$

10. $3\left(\cos \dfrac{4\pi}{3} + i \sin \dfrac{4\pi}{3}\right)$

   $-\dfrac{3}{2} - \dfrac{3\sqrt{3}}{2}i$

11. **Vectors** The force on an object is represented by the complex number $8 + 21i$, where the components are measured in pounds. Find the magnitude and direction of the force.

   22.47 lb; 69.15°

9-8 Practice

Powers and Roots of Complex Numbers

Find each power. Express the result in rectangular form.

1. $(-2 - 2\sqrt{3}i)^3$

 64

2. $(1 - i)^5$

 $-4 + 4i$

3. $(-1 + \sqrt{3}i)^{12}$

 4096

4. $\left[1\left(\cos\frac{\pi}{4} + i\sin\frac{\pi}{4}\right)\right]^{-3}$

 $-\frac{\sqrt{2}}{2} - \frac{\sqrt{2}}{2}i$

5. $(2 + 3i)^6$

 $2035 - 828i$

6. $(1 + i)^8$

 16

Find each principal root. Express the result in the form a + bi with a and b rounded to the nearest hundredth.

7. $(-27i)^{\frac{1}{3}}$

 $2.60 - 1.5i$

8. $(8 - 8i)^{\frac{1}{3}}$

 $2.17 - 0.58i$

9. $\sqrt[5]{-243i}$

 $2.85 - 0.93i$

10. $(-i)^{\frac{1}{3}}$

 $0.87 + 0.5i$

11. $\sqrt[8]{-8i}$

 $1.27 - 0.25i$

12. $\sqrt[4]{-2 - 2\sqrt{3}i}$

 $0.71 + 1.22i$

172 *Advanced Mathematical Concepts*

9-7 Practice

Products and Quotients of Complex Numbers in Polar Form

Find each product or quotient. Express the result in rectangular form.

1. $3\left(\cos\frac{\pi}{3} + i\sin\frac{\pi}{3}\right) \cdot 3\left(\cos\frac{5\pi}{3} + i\sin\frac{5\pi}{3}\right)$

 9

2. $6\left(\cos\frac{\pi}{2} + i\sin\frac{\pi}{2}\right) \div 2\left(\cos\frac{\pi}{3} + i\sin\frac{\pi}{3}\right)$

 $\frac{3\sqrt{3}}{2} + \frac{3}{2}i$

3. $14\left(\cos\frac{5\pi}{4} + i\sin\frac{5\pi}{4}\right) \div 2\left(\cos\frac{\pi}{2} + i\sin\frac{\pi}{2}\right)$

 $-\frac{7\sqrt{2}}{2} + \frac{7\sqrt{2}}{2}i$

4. $3\left(\cos\frac{5\pi}{6} + i\sin\frac{5\pi}{6}\right) \cdot 6\left(\cos\frac{\pi}{3} + i\sin\frac{\pi}{3}\right)$

 $-9\sqrt{3} - 9i$

5. $2\left(\cos\frac{\pi}{2} + i\sin\frac{\pi}{2}\right) \cdot 2\left(\cos\frac{4\pi}{3} + i\sin\frac{4\pi}{3}\right)$

 $2\sqrt{3} - 2i$

6. $15(\cos\pi + i\sin\pi) \div 3\left(\cos\frac{\pi}{2} + i\sin\frac{\pi}{2}\right)$

 $5i$

7. **Electricity** Find the current in a circuit with a voltage of 12 volts and an impedance of 2 − 4*j* ohms. Use the formula, $E = I \cdot Z$, where *E* is the voltage measured in volts, *I* is the current measured in amperes, and *Z* is the impedance measured in ohms.

 (*Hint:* Electrical engineers use *j* as the imaginary unit, so they write complex numbers in the form *a* + *bj*. Express each number in polar form, substitute values into the formula, and then express the current in rectangular form.)

 1.2 + 2.4*j* amps

170 *Advanced Mathematical Concepts*

10-1

Study Guide

Introduction to Analytic Geometry

Example 1 **Find the distance between points at (−2, 2) and (5, −4). Then find the midpoint of the segment that has endpoints at the given coordinates.**

$d = \sqrt{(x_2 - x_1)^2 + (y_2 - y_1)^2}$ *Distance Formula*

$d = \sqrt{[5 - (-2)]^2 + [(-4) - 2]^2}$ *Let $(x_1, y_1) = (-2, 2)$ and $(x_2, y_2) = (5, -4)$.*

$d = \sqrt{7^2 + (-6)^2}$ or $\sqrt{85}$

midpoint $= \left(\dfrac{x_1 + x_2}{2}, \dfrac{y_1 + y_2}{2}\right)$ *Midpoint Formula*

The midpoint is at $\left(\dfrac{-2 + 5}{2}, \dfrac{2 + (-4)}{2}\right)$ or $\left(\dfrac{3}{2}, -1\right)$.

Example 2 **Determine whether quadrilateral *ABCD* with vertices *A*(1, 1), *B*(0, −1), *C*(−2, 0), and *D*(−1, 2) is a parallelogram.**

First, graph the figure.

To determine if $\overline{DA} \parallel \overline{CB}$, find the slopes of $\overline{DA}$ and $\overline{CB}$.

slope of $\overline{DA}$

$m = \dfrac{y_2 - y_1}{x_2 - x_1}$ *Slope formula*

$= \dfrac{1 - 2}{1 - (-1)}$ *D(−1, 2) and A(1, 1)*

$= -\dfrac{1}{2}$

slope of $\overline{CB}$

$m = \dfrac{y_2 - y_1}{x_2 - x_1}$ *Slope formula*

$= \dfrac{-1 - 0}{0 - (-2)}$ *C(−2, 0) and B(0, −1)*

$= -\dfrac{1}{2}$

Their slopes are equal. Therefore, $\overline{DA} \parallel \overline{CB}$.

To determine if $\overline{DA} \cong \overline{CB}$, use the distance formula to find $\overline{DA}$ and $\overline{CB}$.

$DA = \sqrt{[1 - (-1)]^2 + (1 - 2)^2}$

$\quad = \sqrt{5}$

$CB = \sqrt{[0 - (-2)]^2 + (-1 - 0)^2}$

$\quad = \sqrt{5}$

The measures of $\overline{DA}$ and $\overline{CB}$ are equal. Therefore, $\overline{DA} \cong \overline{CB}$.

Since $\overline{DA} \parallel \overline{CB}$ and $\overline{DA} \cong \overline{CB}$, quadrilateral *ABCD* is a parallelogram.

10-1

Practice

Introduction to Analytic Geometry

Find the distance between each pair of points with the given coordinates. Then find the midpoint of the segment that has endpoints at the given coordinates.

1. $(-2, 1), (3, 4)$

2. $(1, 1), (9, 7)$

3. $(3, -4), (5, 2)$

4. $(-1, 2), (5, 4)$

5. $(-7, -4), (2, 8)$

6. $(-4, 10), (4, -5)$

Determine whether the quadrilateral having vertices with the given coordinates is a parallelogram.

7. $(4, 4), (2, -2), (-5, -1), (-3, 5)$

8. $(3, 5), (-1, 1), (-6, 2), (-3, 7)$

9. $(4, -1), (2, -5), (-3, -3), (-1, 1)$

10. $(2, 6), (1, 2), (-4, 4), (-3, 9)$

11. *Hiking*   Jenna and Maria are hiking to a campsite located at $(2, 1)$ on a map grid, where each side of a square represents 2.5 miles. If they start their hike at $(-3, 1)$, how far must they hike to reach the campsite?

10-2

Study Guide

Circles

The standard form of the equation of a **circle** with **radius** r and **center** at (h, k) is $(x - h)^2 + (y - k)^2 = r^2$.

Example 1   **Write the standard form of the equation of the circle that is tangent to the x-axis and has its center at $(-4, 3)$. Then graph the equation.**

Since the circle is tangent to the x-axis, the distance from the center to the x-axis is the radius. The center is 3 units above the x-axis. Therefore, the radius is 3.

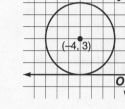

$$(x - h)^2 + (y - k)^2 = r^2 \quad \textit{Standard form}$$
$$[x - (-4)]^2 + (y - 3)^2 = 3^2 \quad \textit{(h, k) = (-4, 3) and r = 3}$$
$$(x + 4)^2 + (y - 3)^2 = 9$$

Example 2   **Write the standard form of the equation of the circle that passes through the points at $(1, -1)$, $(5, 3)$, and $(-3, 3)$. Then identify the center and radius of the circle.**

Substitute each ordered pair (x, y) in the general form $x^2 + y^2 + Dx + Ey + F = 0$ to create a system of equations.

$$(1)^2 + (-1)^2 + D(1) + E(-1) + F = 0 \quad \textit{(x, y) = (1, -1)}$$
$$(5)^2 + (3)^2 + D(5) + E(3) + F = 0 \quad \textit{(x, y) = (5, 3)}$$
$$(-3)^2 + (3)^2 + D(-3) + E(3) + F = 0 \quad \textit{(x, y) = (-3, 3)}$$

Simplify the system of equations.

$$D - E + F + 2 = 0$$
$$5D + 3E + F + 34 = 0$$
$$-3D + 3E + F + 18 = 0$$

The solution to the system is $D = -2$, $E = -6$, and $F = -6$.

The general form of the equation of the circle is $x^2 + y^2 - 2x - 6y - 6 = 0$.

$$x^2 + y^2 - 2x - 6y - 6 = 0$$
$$(x^2 - 2x + ?) + (y^2 - 6y + ?) = 6 \quad \textit{Group to form perfect square trinomials.}$$
$$(x^2 - 2x + 1) + (y^2 - 6y + 9) = 6 + 1 + 9 \quad \textit{Complete the square.}$$
$$(x - 1)^2 + (y - 3)^2 = 16 \quad \textit{Factor the trinomials.}$$

After completing the square, the standard form of the circle is $(x - 1)^2 + (y - 3)^2 = 16$. Its center is at $(1, 3)$, and its radius is 4.

179   *Advanced Mathematical Concepts*

10-2

Practice

Circles

Write the standard form of the equation of each circle described. Then graph the equation.

1. center at $(3, 3)$ tangent to the x-axis

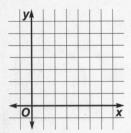

2. center at $(2, -1)$, radius 4

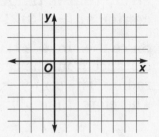

Write the standard form of each equation. Then graph the equation.

3. $x^2 + y^2 - 8x - 6y + 21 = 0$

4. $4x^2 + 4y^2 + 16x - 8y - 5 = 0$

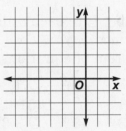

Write the standard form of the equation of the circle that passes through the points with the given coordinates. Then identify the center and radius.

5. $(-3, -2), (-2, -3), (-4, -3)$

6. $(0, -1), (2, -3), (4, -1)$

7. *Geometry* A square inscribed in a circle and centered at the origin has points at $(2, 2)$, $(-2, 2)$, $(2, -2)$ and $(-2, -2)$. What is the equation of the circle that circumscribes the square?

10-3

Study Guide

Ellipses

The standard form of the equation of an **ellipse** is
$\dfrac{(x-h)^2}{a^2} + \dfrac{(y-k)^2}{b^2} = 1$ when the **major axis** is horizontal.
In this case, a^2 is in the denominator of the x term. The
standard form is $\dfrac{(y-k)^2}{a^2} + \dfrac{(x-h)^2}{b^2} = 1$ when the major
axis is vertical. In this case, a^2 is in the denominator of
the y term. In both cases, $c^2 = a^2 - b^2$.

Example **Find the coordinates of the center, the foci,
and the vertices of the ellipse with the equation
$4x^2 + 9y^2 + 24x - 36y + 36 = 0$. Then graph the
equation.**

First write the equation in standard form.

$$4x^2 + 9y^2 + 24x - 36y + 36 = 0$$

$$4(x^2 + 6x + ?) + 9(y^2 - 4y + ?) = -36 + ? + ?$$
*GCF of x terms is 4;
GCF of y terms is 9.*

$$4(x^2 + 6x + 9) + 9(y^2 - 4y + 4) = -36 + 4(9) + 9(4)$$ *Complete the square.*

$$4(x+3)^2 + 9(y-2)^2 = 36$$ *Factor.*

$$\frac{(x+3)^2}{9} + \frac{(y+2)^2}{4} = 1$$ *Divide each side by 36.*

Now determine the values of a, b, c, h, and k. In all
ellipses, $a^2 > b^2$. Therefore, $a^2 = 9$ and $b^2 = 4$. Since a^2
is the denominator of the x term, the major axis is
parallel to the x-axis.

$a = 3$ $b = 2$ $c = \sqrt{a^2 - b^2}$ or $\sqrt{5}$ $h = -3$ $k = 2$

center: $(-3, 2)$ (h, k)
foci: $(-3 \pm \sqrt{5}, 2)$ $(h \pm c, k)$

major axis vertices:
$(0, 2)$ and $(-6, 2)$ $(h \pm a, k)$

minor axis vertices:
$(-3, 4)$ and $(-3, 0)$ $(h, k \pm b)$

Graph these ordered pairs. Then complete the ellipse.

10-3

Practice

Ellipses

Write the equation of each ellipse in standard form. Then find the coordinates of its foci.

1.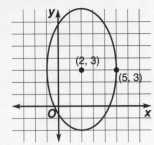

2.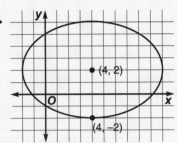

For the equation of each ellipse, find the coordinates of the center, foci, and vertices. Then graph the equation.

3. $4x^2 + 9y^2 - 8x - 36y + 4 = 0$

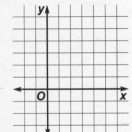

4. $25x^2 + 9y^2 - 50x - 90y + 25 = 0$

Write the equation of the ellipse that meets each set of conditions.

5. The center is at $(1, 3)$, the major axis is parallel to the y-axis, and one vertex is at $(1, 8)$, and $b = 3$.

6. The foci are at $(-2, 1)$ and $(-2, -7)$, and $a = 5$.

7. ***Construction*** A semi elliptical arch is used to design a headboard for a bed frame. The headboard will have a height of 2 feet at the center and a width of 5 feet at the base. Where should the craftsman place the foci in order to sketch the arch?

10-4

Study Guide

Hyperbolas

The standard form of the equation of a **hyperbola** is $\frac{(x-h)^2}{a^2} - \frac{(y-k)^2}{b^2} = 1$ when the **transverse axis** is horizontal, and $\frac{(y-k)^2}{a^2} - \frac{(x-h)^2}{b^2} = 1$ when the transverse axis is vertical. In both cases, $b^2 = c^2 - a^2$.

Example   **Find the coordinates of the center, foci, and vertices, and the equations of the asymptotes of the graph of $25x^2 - 9y^2 + 100x - 54y - 206 = 0$. Then graph the equation.**

Write the equation in standard form.

$$25x^2 - 9y^2 + 100x - 54y - 206 = 0$$
$$25(x^2 + 4x + ?) - 9(y^2 + 6y + ?) = 206 + ? + ? \quad \textit{GCF of x terms is 25;}$$
$$\textit{GCF of y terms is 9.}$$
$$25(x^2 + 4x + 4) - 9(y^2 + 6y + 9) = 206 + 25(4) + (-9)(9) \quad \textit{Complete the square.}$$
$$25(x + 2)^2 - 9(y + 3)^2 = 225 \quad \textit{Factor.}$$
$$\frac{(x + 2)^2}{9} - \frac{(y + 3)^2}{25} = 1 \quad \textit{Divide each side by 225.}$$

From the equation, $h = -2$, $k = -3$, $a = 3$, $b = 5$, and $c = \sqrt{34}$. The center is at $(-2, -3)$.

Since the x terms are in the first expression, the hyperbola has a horizontal transverse axis.

The vertices are at $(h \pm a, k)$ or $(1, -3)$ and $(-5, -3)$.

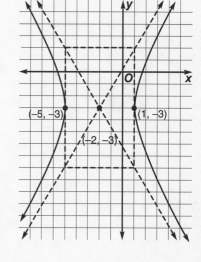

The foci are at $(h \pm c, k)$ or $(-2 \pm \sqrt{34}, -3)$.

The equations of the asymptotes are $y - k = \pm\frac{b}{a}(x - h)$ or $y + 3 = \pm\frac{5}{3}(x + 2)$.

Graph the center, the vertices, and the rectangle guide, which is $2a$ units by $2b$ units. Next graph the asymptotes. Then sketch the hyperbola.

10-4

Practice

Hyperbolas

For each equation, find the coordinates of the center, foci, and vertices, and the equations of the asymptotes of its graph. Then graph the equation.

1. $x^2 - 4y^2 - 4x + 24y - 36 = 0$

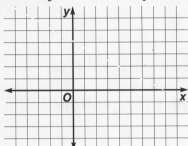

2. $y^2 - 4x^2 + 8x = 20$

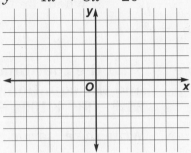

Write the equation of each hyperbola.

3.

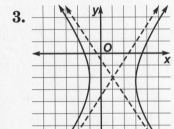

4.

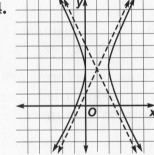

5. Write an equation of the hyperbola for which the length of the transverse axis is 8 units, and the foci are at $(6, 0)$ and $(-4, 0)$.

6. *Environmental Noise* Two neighbors who live one mile apart hear an explosion while they are talking on the telephone. One neighbor hears the explosion two seconds before the other. If sound travels at 1100 feet per second, determine the equation of the hyperbola on which the explosion was located.

10-5

Study Guide

Parabolas

The standard form of the equation of the **parabola** is $(y - k)^2 = 4p(x - h)$ when the parabola opens to the right. When p is negative, the parabola opens to the left. The standard form is $(x - h)^2 = 4p(y - k)$ when the parabola opens upward. When p is negative, the parabola opens downward.

Example 1 Given the equation $x^2 = 12y + 60$, find the coordinates of the focus and the vertex and the equations of the directrix and the axis of symmetry. Then graph the equation of the parabola.

First write the equation in the form $(x - h)^2 = 4p(y - k)$.

$$x^2 = 12y + 60$$
$$x^2 = 12(y + 5) \quad \textit{Factor.}$$
$$(x - 0)^2 = 4(3)(y + 5) \quad \textit{4p = 12, so p = 3.}$$

In this form, we can see that $h = 0$, $k = -5$, and $p = 3$.
Vertex: $(0, -5)$ (h, k) Focus: $(0, -2)$ $(h, k + p)$
Directrix: $y = -8$ $y = k - p$ Axis of Symmetry: $x = 0$ $x = h$

The axis of symmetry is the y-axis. Since p is positive, the parabola opens upward. Graph the directrix, the vertex, and the focus. To determine the shape of the parabola, graph several other ordered pairs that satisfy the equation and connect them with a smooth curve.

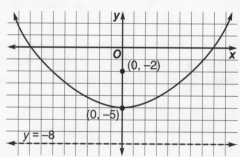

Example 2 Write the equation $y^2 + 6y + 8x + 25 = 0$ in standard form. Find the coordinates of the focus and the vertex, and the equations of the directrix and the axis of symmetry. Then graph the parabola.

$$y^2 + 6y + 8x + 25 = 0$$
$$y^2 + 6y = -8x - 25 \quad \textit{Isolate the x terms and the y terms.}$$
$$y^2 + 6y + ? = -8x - 25 + ?$$
$$y^2 + 6y + 9 = -8x - 25 + 9 \quad \textit{Complete the square.}$$
$$(y + 3)^2 = -8(x + 2) \quad \textit{Simplify and factor.}$$

From the standard form, we can see that $h = -2$ and $k = -3$. Since $4p = -8$, $p = -2$. Since y is squared, the directrix is parallel to the y-axis. The axis of symmetry is the x-axis. Since p is negative, the parabola opens to the left.

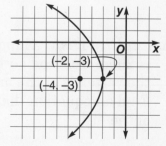

Vertex: $(-2, -3)$ (h, k)
Focus: $(-4, -3)$ $(h + p, k)$
Directrix: $x = 0$ $x = h - p$
Axis of Symmetry: $y = -3$ $y = k$

10-5

Practice

Parabolas

For the equation of each parabola, find the coordinates of the vertex and focus, and the equations of the directrix and axis of symmetry. Then graph the equation.

1. $x^2 - 2x - 8y + 17 = 0$

2. $y^2 + 6y + 9 = 12 - 12x$

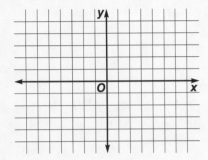

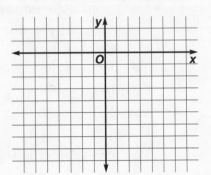

Write the equation of the parabola that meets each set of conditions. Then graph the equation.

3. The vertex is at $(-2, 4)$ and the focus is at $(-2, 3)$.

4. The focus is at $(2, 1)$, and the equation of the directrix is $x = -2$.

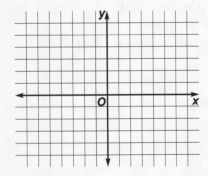

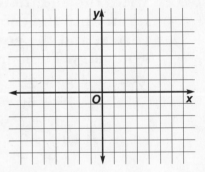

5. *Satellite Dish* Suppose the receiver in a parabolic dish antenna is 2 feet from the vertex and is located at the focus. Assume that the vertex is at the origin and that the dish is pointed upward. Find an equation that models a cross section of the dish.

10-6

Study Guide

Rectangular and Parametric Forms of Conic Sections

Use the table to identify a conic section given its equation in general form.

conic	$Ax^2 + Bxy + Cy^2 + Dx + Ey + F = 0$
circle	$A = C$
parabola	Either A or C is zero.
ellipse	A and C have the same sign and $A \neq C$.
hyperbola	A and C have opposite signs.

Example 1 **Identify the conic section represented by the equation $5x^2 + 4y^2 - 10x - 8y + 18 = 0$.**

$A = 5$ and $C = 4$. Since A and C have the same signs and are not equal, the conic is an ellipse.

Example 2 **Find the rectangular equation of the curve whose parametric equations are $x = 2t$ and $y = 4t^2 + 4t - 1$. Then identify the conic section represented by the equation.**

First, solve the equation $x = 2t$ for t.

$x = 2t$

$\dfrac{x}{2} = t$

Then substitute $\dfrac{x}{2}$ for t in the equation $y = 4t^2 + 4t - 1$.

$y = 4t^2 + 4t - 1$

$y = 4\left(\dfrac{x}{2}\right)^2 + 4\left(\dfrac{x}{2}\right) - 1 \qquad t = \dfrac{x}{2}$

$y = x^2 + 2x - 1$

Since $C = 0$, the equation $y = x^2 + 2x - 1$ is the equation of a parabola.

Example 3 **Find the rectangular equation of the curve whose parametric equations are $x = 3 \cos t$ and $y = 5 \sin t$, where $0 \le t \le 2\pi$. Then graph the equation using arrows to indicate orientation.**

Solve the first equation for $\cos t$ and the second equation for $\sin t$.

$\cos t = \dfrac{x}{3}$ and $\sin t = \dfrac{y}{5}$

Use the trigonometric identity $\cos^2 t + \sin^2 t = 1$ to eliminate t.

$\cos^2 t + \sin^2 t = 1$

$\left(\dfrac{x}{3}\right)^2 + \left(\dfrac{y}{5}\right)^2 = 1 \qquad Substitution$

$\dfrac{x^2}{9} + \dfrac{y^2}{25} = 1$

This is the equation of an ellipse with the center at $(0, 0)$. As t increases from 0 to 2π, the curve is traced in a counterclockwise motion.

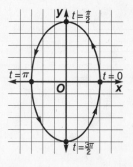

10-6

Practice

Rectangular and Parametric Forms of Conic Sections

Identify the conic section represented by each equation. Then write the equation in standard form and graph the equation.

1. $x^2 - 4y + 4 = 0$

2. $x^2 + y^2 - 6x - 6y - 18 = 0$

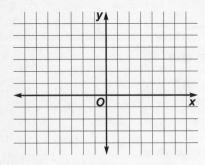

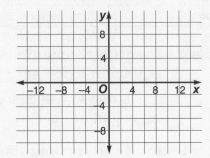

3. $4x^2 - y^2 - 8x + 6y = 9$

4. $9x^2 + 5y^2 + 18x = 36$

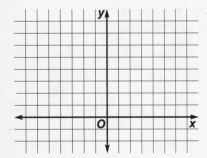

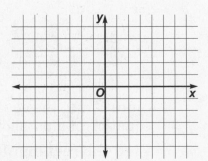

Find the rectangular equation of the curve whose parametric equations are given. Then graph the equation using arrows to indicate orientation.

5. $x = 3 \cos t, y = 3 \sin t, 0 \le t \le 2\pi$

6. $x = -4 \cos t, y = 5 \sin t, 0 \le t \le 2\pi$

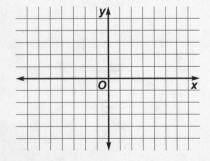

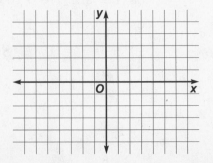

Advanced Mathematical Concepts

10-7

Study Guide

Transformation of Conics

Translations are often written in the form $T_{(h, k)}$. To find the equation of a rotated conic, replace x with $x' \cos \theta + y' \sin \theta$ and y with $-x' \sin \theta + y' \cos \theta$.

Example **Identify the graph of each equation. Write an equation of the translated or rotated graph in general form.**

  a. $4x^2 + y^2 = 12$ for $T_{(-2, 3)}$

   The graph of this equation is an ellipse. To write the equation of $4x^2 + y^2 = 12$ for $T_{(-2, 3)}$, let $h = -2$ and $k = 3$. Then replace x with $x - h$ and y with $y - k$.

   $x^2 \Rightarrow (x - (-2))^2$ or $(x + 2)^2$
   $y^2 \Rightarrow (y - 3)^2$

   Thus, the translated equation is $4(x + 2)^2 + (y - 3)^2 = 12$.

   Write the equation in general form.

   $$4(x + 2)^2 + (y - 3)^2 = 12$$
   $$4(x^2 + 4x + 4) + y^2 - 6y + 9 = 12 \quad \textit{Expand the binomial.}$$
   $$4x^2 + y^2 + 16x - 6y + 25 = 12 \quad \textit{Simplify.}$$
   $$4x^2 + y^2 + 16x - 6y + 13 = 0 \quad \textit{Subtract 12 from both sides.}$$

  b. $x^2 - 4y = 0$, $\theta = 45°$

   The graph of this equation is a parabola. Find the expressions to replace x and y.

   Replace x with $x' \cos 45° + y' \sin 45°$ or $\frac{\sqrt{2}}{2}x' + \frac{\sqrt{2}}{2}y'$.

   Replace y with $-x' \sin 45° + y' \cos 45°$ or $-\frac{\sqrt{2}}{2}x' + \frac{\sqrt{2}}{2}y'$.

   $$x^2 - 4y = 0$$
   $$\left(\frac{\sqrt{2}}{2}x' + \frac{\sqrt{2}}{2}y'\right)^2 - 4\left(-\frac{\sqrt{2}}{2}x' + \frac{\sqrt{2}}{2}y'\right) = 0 \quad \textit{Replace x and y.}$$
   $$\left[\frac{1}{2}(x')^2 + x'y' + \frac{1}{2}(y')^2\right] - 4\left(-\frac{\sqrt{2}}{2}x' + \frac{\sqrt{2}}{2}y'\right) = 0 \quad \textit{Expand the binomial.}$$
   $$\frac{1}{2}(x')^2 + x'y' + \frac{1}{2}(y')^2 + 2\sqrt{2}x' - 2\sqrt{2}y' = 0 \quad \textit{Simplify.}$$

   The equation of the parabola after the 45° rotation is

   $$\frac{1}{2}(x')^2 + x'y' + \frac{1}{2}(y')^2 + 2\sqrt{2}x' - 2\sqrt{2}y' = 0$$

10-7

Practice

Transformations of Conics

Identify the graph of each equation. Write an equation of the translated or rotated graph in general form.

1. $2x^2 + 5y^2 = 9$ for $T_{(-2, 1)}$

2. $2x^2 - 4x + 3 - y = 0$ for $T_{(1, -1)}$

3. $xy = 1$, $\theta = \frac{\pi}{4}$

4. $x^2 - 4y = 0$, $\theta = 90°$

Identify the graph of each equation. Then find θ to the nearest degree.

5. $2x^2 + 2y^2 - 2x = 0$

6. $3x^2 + 8xy + 4y^2 - 7 = 0$

7. $16x^2 - 24xy + 9y^2 - 30x - 40y = 0$

8. $13x^2 - 8xy + 7y^2 - 45 = 0$

9. *Communications* Suppose the orientation of a satellite dish that monitors radio waves is modeled by the equation $4x^2 + 2xy + 4y^2 + \sqrt{2}x - \sqrt{2}y = 0$. What is the angle of rotation of the satellite dish about the origin?

10-8

Study Guide

Systems of Second-Degree Equations and Inequalities

To find the exact solution to a system of second-degree equations, you must use algebra. Graph systems of inequalities involving second-degree equations to find solutions for the inequality.

Example

a. Solve the system of equations algebraically. Round to the nearest tenth.

$$x^2 + 2y^2 = 9$$
$$3x^2 - y^2 = 1$$

Since both equations contain a single term involving y, you can solve the system as follows.

First, multiply each side of the second equation by 2.

$$2(3x^2 - y^2) = 2(1)$$
$$6x^2 - 2y^2 = 2$$

Then, add the equations.

$$6x^2 - 2y^2 = 2$$
$$\underline{x^2 + 2y^2 = 9}$$
$$7x^2 \quad = 11$$
$$x = \pm\sqrt{\frac{11}{7}}$$

Now find y by substituting $\pm\sqrt{\frac{11}{7}}$ for x in one of the original equations.

$$x^2 + 2y^2 = 9 \rightarrow \left(\pm\sqrt{\frac{11}{7}}\right)^2 + 2y^2 = 9$$
$$11 + 14y^2 = 63$$
$$y^2 = \frac{26}{7}$$
$$y \approx \pm 1.9$$

The solutions are $(1.3, \pm 1.9)$, and $(-1.3, \pm 1.9)$.

b. Graph the solutions for the system of inequalities.

$$x^2 + 2y^2 < 9$$
$$3x^2 - y^2 \geq 1$$

First graph $x^2 + 2y^2 < 9$. The ellipse should be dashed. Test a point either inside or outside the ellipse to see if its coordinates satisfy the inequality. Since $(0, 0)$ satisfies the inequality, shade the interior of the ellipse.

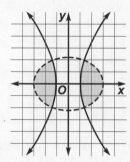

Then graph $3x^2 - y^2 \geq 1$. The hyperbola should be a solid curve. Test a point inside the branches of the hyperbola or outside its branches. Since $(0, 0)$ does not satisfy the inequality, shade the regions inside the branches. The intersection of the two graphs represents the solution of the system.

10-8

Practice

Systems of Second-Degree Equations and Inequalities

Solve each system of equations algebraically. Round to the nearest tenth. Check the solutions by graphing each system.

1. $2x - y = 8$
$x^2 + y^2 = 9$

2. $x^2 - y^2 = 4$
$y = 1$

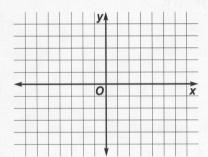

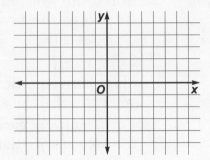

3. $xy = 4$
$x^2 = y^2 + 1$

4. $x^2 + y^2 = 4$
$4x^2 + 9y^2 = 36$

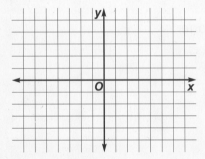

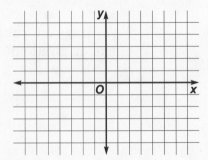

Graph each system of inequalities.

5. $3 \geq (y - 1)^2 + 2x$
$y \geq -3x + 1$

6. $(x - 1)^2 + (y - 2)^2 < 9$
$4(y + 1)^2 + x^2 \leq 16$

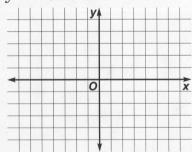

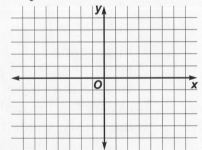

7. Sales Vincent's Pizzeria reduced prices for large specialty pizzas by $5 for 1 week in March. In the previous week, sales for large specialty pizzas totaled $400. During the sale week, the number of large pizzas sold increased by 20 and total sales amounted to $600. Write a system of second-degree equations to model this situation. Find the regular price and the sale price of large specialty pizzas.

Column 1 (10-1)

10-1

Practice

Introduction to Analytic Geometry

Find the distance between each pair of points with the given coordinates. Then find the midpoint of the segment that has endpoints at the given coordinates.

1. $(-2, 1), (3, 4)$
$\sqrt{34}; (0.5, 2.5)$

2. $(1, 1), (9, 7)$
$10; (5, 4)$

3. $(3, -4), (5, 2)$
$2\sqrt{10}; (4, -1)$

4. $(-1, 2), (5, 4)$
$2\sqrt{10}; (2, 3)$

5. $(-7, -4), (2, 8)$
$15; (-2.5, 2)$

6. $(-4, 10), (4, -5)$
$17; (0, 2.5)$

Determine whether the quadrilateral having vertices with the given coordinates is a parallelogram.

7. $(4, 4), (2, -2), (-5, -1), (-3, 5)$
yes

8. $(3, 5), (-1, 1), (-6, 2), (-3, 7)$
no

9. $(4, -1), (2, -5), (-3, -3), (-1, 1)$
yes

10. $(2, 6), (1, 2), (-4, 4), (-3, 9)$
no

11. *Hiking* Jenna and Maria are hiking to a campsite located at (2, 1) on a map grid, where each side of a square represents 2.5 miles. If they start their hike at $(-3, 1)$, how far must they hike to reach the campsite?
12.5 mi

Column 2 (10-2)

10-2

Practice

Circles

Write the standard form of the equation of each circle described. Then graph the equation.

1. center at (3, 3) tangent to the *x*-axis
$(x - 3)^2 + (y - 3)^2 = 9$

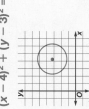

2. center at (2, −1), radius 4
$(x - 2)^2 + (y + 1)^2 = 16$

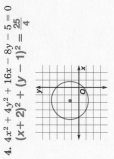

Write the standard form of each equation. Then graph the equation.

3. $x^2 + y^2 - 8x - 6y + 21 = 0$
$(x - 4)^2 + (y - 3)^2 = 4$

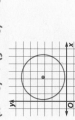

4. $4x^2 + 4y^2 + 16x - 8y - 5 = 0$
$(x + 2)^2 + (y - 1)^2 = \frac{25}{4}$

Write the standard form of the equation of the circle that passes through the points with the given coordinates. Then identify the center and radius.

5. $(-3, -2), (-2, -3), (-4, -3)$
$(x + 3)^2 + (y + 3)^2 = 1$;
$(-3, -3); 1$

6. $(0, -1), (2, -3), (4, -1)$
$(x - 2)^2 + (y + 1)^2 = 4$;
$(2, -1); 2$

7. *Geometry* A square inscribed in a circle and centered at the origin has points at (2, 2), (−2, 2), (2, −2) and (−2, −2). What is the equation of the circle that circumscribes the square?
$x^2 + y^2 = 8$

NAME _____ DATE _____ PERIOD _____

10-3 Practice

Ellipses

Write the equation of each ellipse in standard form. Then find the coordinates of its foci.

1.

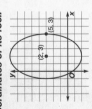

$$\frac{(y-3)^2}{25} + \frac{(x-2)^2}{9} = 1;$$
$$(2, -1), (2, 7)$$

2.

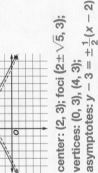

$$\frac{(x-4)^2}{36} + \frac{(y-2)^2}{16} = 1;$$
$$(4 - \sqrt{20}, 2), (4 + \sqrt{20}, 2)$$

For the equation of each ellipse, find the coordinates of the center, foci, and vertices. Then graph the equation.

3. $4x^2 + 9y^2 - 8x - 36y + 4 = 0$

center: (1, 2);
foci: $(1 \pm \sqrt{5}, 2)$
vertices:
$(-2, 2), (1, 4),$
$(4, 2), (1, 0)$

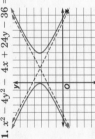

4. $25x^2 + 9y^2 - 50x - 90y + 25 = 0$

center: (1, 5);
foci: (1, 9),
(1, 1)
vertices:
(1, 10), (1, 0),
(4, 5), (-2, 5)

Write the equation of the ellipse that meets each set of conditions.

5. The center is at (1, 3), the major axis is parallel to the y-axis, and one vertex is at (1, 8), and $b = 3$.
$$\frac{(y-3)^2}{25} + \frac{(x-1)^2}{9} = 1$$

6. The foci are at (-2, 1) and (-2, -7), and $a = 5$.
$$\frac{(y+3)^2}{25} + \frac{(x+2)^2}{9} = 1$$

7. Construction A semi elliptical arch is used to design a headboard for a bed frame. The headboard will have a height of 2 feet at the center and a width of 5 feet at the base. Where should the craftsman place the foci in order to sketch the arch?
1.5 ft from the center

NAME _____ DATE _____ PERIOD _____

10-4 Practice

Hyperbolas

For each equation, find the coordinates of the center, foci, and vertices, and the equations of the asymptotes of its graph. Then graph the equation.

1. $x^2 - 4y^2 - 4x + 24y - 36 = 0$

center: (2, 3); foci $(2 \pm \sqrt{5}, 3)$;
vertices: (0, 3), (4, 3);
asymptotes: $y - 3 = \pm \frac{1}{2}(x - 2)$

2. $y^2 - 4x^2 + 8x = 20$

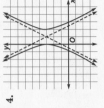

center: (1, 0); foci: $(1, \pm 2\sqrt{5})$;
vertices: $(1, \pm 4)$
asymptotes: $y = \pm 2(x - 1)$

Write the equation of each hyperbola.

3.

$$\frac{(x-1)^2}{4} - \frac{(y+2)^2}{9} = 1$$

4.

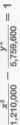

$$\frac{(x-1)^2}{1} - \frac{(y-3)^2}{4} = 1$$

5. Write an equation of the hyperbola for which the length of the transverse axis is 8 units, and the foci are at (6, 0) and (-4, 0).
$$\frac{(x-1)^2}{16} - \frac{y^2}{9} = 1$$

6. Environmental Noise Two neighbors who live one mile apart hear an explosion while they are talking on the telephone. One neighbor hears the explosion two seconds before the other. If sound travels at 1100 feet per second, determine the equation of the hyperbola on which the explosion was located.
$$\frac{x^2}{1,210,000} - \frac{y^2}{5,759,600} = 1$$

NAME _____ DATE _____ PERIOD _____

10-5 Practice

Parabolas

For the equation of each parabola, find the coordinates of the vertex and focus, and the equations of the directrix and axis of symmetry. Then graph the equation.

1. $x^2 - 2x - 8y + 17 = 0$

vertex: (1, 2); focus: (1, 4);
directrix: $y = 0$;
axis of symmetry: $x = 1$

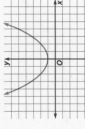

2. $y^2 + 6y + 9 = 12 - 12x$

vertex: (1, −3); focus: (−2, −3);
directrix: $x = 4$;
axis of symmetry: $y = -3$

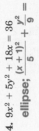

Write the equation of the parabola that meets each set of conditions. Then graph the equation.

3. The vertex is at (−2, 4) and the focus is at (−2, 3).

$(x + 2)^2 = -4(y - 4)$

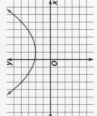

4. The focus is at (2, 1), and the equation of the directrix is $x = -2$.

$(y - 1)^2 = 8x$

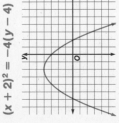

5. Satellite Dish Suppose the receiver in a parabolic dish antenna is 2 feet from the vertex and is located at the focus. Assume that the vertex is at the origin and that the dish is pointed upward. Find an equation that models a cross section of the dish.

$x^2 = 8y$

NAME _____ DATE _____ PERIOD _____

10-6 Practice

Rectangular and Parametric Forms of Conic Sections

Identify the conic section represented by each equation. Then write the equation in standard form and graph the equation.

1. $x^2 - 4y + 4 = 0$
parabola; $x^2 = 4(y - 1)$

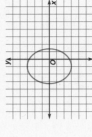

2. $x^2 + y^2 - 6x - 6y - 18 = 0$
circle;
$(x - 3)^2 + (y - 3)^2 = 36$

3. $4x^2 - y^2 - 8x + 6y = 9$
hyperbola; $\dfrac{(x - 1)^2}{1} - \dfrac{(y - 3)^2}{4} = 1$

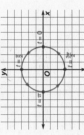

4. $9x^2 + 5y^2 + 18x = 36$
ellipse; $\dfrac{(x + 1)^2}{5} + \dfrac{y^2}{9} = 1$

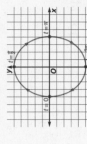

Find the rectangular equation of the curve whose parametric equations are given. Then graph the equation using arrows to indicate orientation.

5. $x = 3\cos t, y = 3\sin t, 0 \le t \le 2\pi$
$x^2 + y^2 = 9$

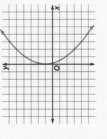

6. $x = -4\cos t, y = 5\sin t, 0 \le t \le 2\pi$
$\dfrac{x^2}{16} + \dfrac{y^2}{25} = 1$

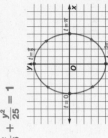

10-7 Practice

Transformations of Conics

Identify the graph of each equation. Write an equation of the translated or rotated graph in general form.

1. $2x^2 + 5y^2 = 9$ for $T_{(-2, 1)}$
ellipse
$2x^2 + 5y^2 + 8x - 10y + 4 = 0$

2. $2x^2 - 4x + 3 - y = 0$ for $T_{(1, -1)}$
parabola
$2x^2 - 8x - y + 8 = 0$

3. $xy = 1$, $\theta = \frac{\pi}{4}$
hyperbola
$-\frac{1}{2}x^2 + \frac{1}{2}y^2 - 1 = 0$

4. $x^2 - 4y = 0$, $\theta = 90°$
parabola
$y^2 + 4x = 0$

Identify the graph of each equation. Then find θ to the nearest degree.

5. $2x^2 + 2y^2 - 2x = 0$
circle
$45°$

6. $3x^2 + 8xy + 4y^2 - 7 = 0$
hyperbola
$-41°$

7. $16x^2 - 24xy + 9y^2 - 30x - 40y = 0$
parabola
$-37°$

8. $13x^2 - 8xy + 7y^2 - 45 = 0$
ellipse
$-27°$

9. **Communications** Suppose the orientation of a satellite dish that monitors radio waves is modeled by the equation $4x^2 + 2xy + 4y^2 + \sqrt{2}x - \sqrt{2}y = 0$. What is the angle of rotation of the satellite dish about the origin?
$45°$

10-8 Practice

Systems of Second-Degree Equations and Inequalities

Solve each system of equations algebraically. Round to the nearest tenth. Check the solutions by graphing each system.

1. $2x - y = 8$
$x^2 + y^2 = 9$
no real solutions

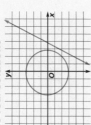

2. $x^2 - y^2 = 4$
$y = 1$
$(-2.2, 1)$ and $(2.2, 1)$

3. $xy = 4$
$x^2 = y^2 + 1$
$(2.1, 1.9)$ and $(-2.1, -1.9)$

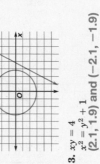

4. $x^2 + y^2 = 4$
$4x^2 + 9y^2 = 36$
$(0, -2)$ and $(0, 2)$

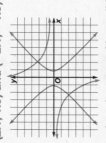

Graph each system of inequalities.

5. $3 \geq (y - 1)^2 + 2x$
$y \geq -3x + 1$

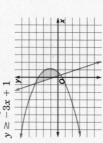

6. $(x - 1)^2 + (y - 2)^2 < 9$
$4(y + 1)^2 + x^2 \leq 16$

7. **Sales** Vincent's Pizzeria reduced prices for large specialty pizzas by \$5 for 1 week in March. In the previous week, sales for large specialty pizzas totaled \$400. During the sale week, the number of large pizzas sold increased by 20 and total sales amounted to \$600. Write a system of second-degree equations to model this situation. Find the regular price and the sale price of large specialty pizzas. $xy = 400$, $(x + 20)(y - 5) = 600$; regular price: \$20.00, sale price: \$15.00

11-1

Study Guide

Rational Exponents

Example 1   Simplify each expression.

a. $\left(\dfrac{c^5d^3}{c^3d^2}\right)^{\frac{1}{2}}$

$\left(\dfrac{c^5d^3}{c^3d^2}\right)^{\frac{1}{2}} = (c^2d)^{\frac{1}{2}}$ $\dfrac{a^m}{a^n} = a^{m-n}$

$\qquad\qquad = c^{\frac{2}{2}}d^{\frac{1}{2}}$ $(a^m)^n = a^{mn}$

$\qquad\qquad = |c|\sqrt{d}$

b. $\left(\dfrac{p^2}{q^3}\right)^{-3}$

$\left(\dfrac{p^2}{q^3}\right)^{-3} = \dfrac{p^{-6}}{q^{-9}}$ $\left(\dfrac{a}{b}\right)^m = \dfrac{a^m}{b^m}$

$\qquad\qquad = \dfrac{q^9}{p^6}$ $b^{-n} = \dfrac{1}{b^n}$

Example 2   Evaluate each expression.

a. $64^{\frac{2}{3}}$

$64^{\frac{2}{3}} = (4^3)^{\frac{2}{3}}$ $64 = 4^3$

$\qquad = 4^2$ or 16 $(a^m)^n = a^{mn}$

b. $\dfrac{27^{\frac{2}{3}}}{27^{\frac{1}{3}}}$

$\dfrac{27^{\frac{2}{3}}}{27^{\frac{1}{3}}} = 27^{\frac{2}{3}-\frac{1}{3}}$ $\dfrac{a^m}{a^n} = a^{m-n}$

$\qquad\quad = 27^{\frac{1}{3}}$ or 3

c. $\sqrt{35} \cdot \sqrt{10}$

$\sqrt{35} \cdot \sqrt{10} = 35^{\frac{1}{2}} \cdot 10^{\frac{1}{2}}$ $\sqrt[n]{b} = b^{\frac{1}{n}}$

$\qquad\qquad = (7 \cdot 5)^{\frac{1}{2}} \cdot (5 \cdot 2)^{\frac{1}{2}}$

$\qquad\qquad = 7^{\frac{1}{2}} \cdot 5^{\frac{1}{2}} \cdot 5^{\frac{1}{2}} \cdot 2^{\frac{1}{2}}$ $(ab)^m = a^mb^m$

$\qquad\qquad = 7^{\frac{1}{2}} \cdot 5 \cdot 2^{\frac{1}{2}}$ $a^ma^n = a^{m+n}$

$\qquad\qquad = 5 \cdot \sqrt{7} \cdot \sqrt{2}$

$\qquad\qquad = 5\sqrt{14}$ $\sqrt[n]{a} \cdot \sqrt[n]{b} = \sqrt[n]{ab}$

Example 3   Express $\sqrt[3]{8x^6y^{12}}$ using rational exponents.

$\sqrt[3]{8x^6y^{12}} = (8x^6y^{12})^{\frac{1}{3}}$ $b^{\frac{1}{n}} = \sqrt[n]{b}$

$\qquad\qquad = 8^{\frac{1}{3}}x^{\frac{6}{3}}y^{\frac{12}{3}}$ $(ab)^m = a^mb^m$

$\qquad\qquad = 2x^2y^4$

Example 4   Express $16x^{\frac{3}{4}}y^{\frac{1}{2}}$ using radicals.

$16x^{\frac{3}{4}}y^{\frac{1}{2}} = 16(x^3y^2)^{\frac{1}{4}}$ $(ab)^m = a^mb^m$

$\qquad\qquad = 16\sqrt[4]{x^3y^2}$

11-1

Practice

Rational Exponents

Evaluate each expression.

1. $\dfrac{8^{\frac{2}{3}}}{8^{\frac{1}{3}}}$

2. $\left(\dfrac{4}{5}\right)^{-2}$

3. $343^{\frac{2}{3}}$

4. $\sqrt[3]{8^3}$

5. $\sqrt{5} \cdot \sqrt{10}$

6. $9^{-\frac{1}{2}}$

Simplify each expression.

7. $(5n^3)^2 \cdot n^{-6}$

8. $\left(\dfrac{x^2}{4y^{-2}}\right)^{-\frac{1}{2}}$

9. $(64x^6)^{\frac{1}{3}}$

10. $(5x^6y^4)^{\frac{1}{2}}$

11. $\sqrt{x^2y^3} \cdot \sqrt{x^3y^4}$

12. $\left(\dfrac{p^{6a}}{p^{-3a}}\right)^{\frac{1}{3}}$

Express each using rational exponents.

13. $\sqrt{x^5y^6}$

14. $\sqrt[5]{27x^{10}y^5}$

15. $\sqrt{144x^6y^{10}}$

16. $21\sqrt[3]{c^7}$

17. $\sqrt{1024a^3}$

18. $\sqrt[4]{36a^8b^5}$

Express each using radicals.

19. $64^{\frac{1}{3}}$

20. $2^{\frac{1}{2}}a^{\frac{3}{2}}b^{\frac{5}{2}}$

21. $s^{\frac{2}{3}}t^{\frac{1}{3}}v^{\frac{2}{3}}$

22. $y^{\frac{3}{2}}$

23. $x^{\frac{2}{5}}y^{\frac{3}{5}}$

24. $(x^6y^3)^{\frac{1}{2}}z^{\frac{3}{2}}$

11-2

Study Guide

Exponential Functions

Functions of the form $y = b^x$, in which the base b is a positive real number and the exponent is a variable, are known as **exponential functions.** Many real-world situations can be modeled by exponential functions. The equation $N = N_0(1 + r)^t$, where N is the final amount, N_0 is the initial amount, r is the rate of growth or decay, and t is time, is used for modeling exponential growth. The compound interest equation is $A = P\left(1 + \frac{r}{n}\right)^{nt}$, where P is the principal or initial investment, A is the final amount of the investment, r is the annual interest rate, n is the number of times interest is compounded each year, and t is the number of years.

Example 1 **Graph $y < 2^{-x}$.**
First, graph $y = 2^{-x}$. This graph is a function, since there is a unique y-value for each x-value.

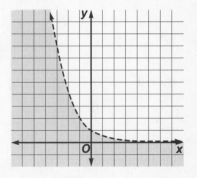

x	−3	−2	−1	0	1	2	3	4
2^{-x}	8	4	2	1	$\frac{1}{2}$	$\frac{1}{4}$	$\frac{1}{8}$	$\frac{1}{16}$

Since the points on this curve are not in the solution of the inequality, the graph of $y = 2^{-x}$ is shown as a dashed curve.

Then, use (0, 0) as a test point to determine which area to shade.
$y < 2^{-x}$
$0 < 2^0$
$0 < 1$
Since (0,0) satisfies the inequality, the region that contains (0,0) should be shaded.

Example 2 *Biology* **Suppose a researcher estimates that the initial population of a colony of cells is 100. If the cells reproduce at a rate of 25% per week, what is the expected population of the colony in six weeks?**
$N = N_0(1 + r)^t$
$N = 100(1 + 0.25)^6$ $N_0 = 100, r = 0.25, t = 6$
$N \approx 381.4697266$ *Use a calculator.*
There will be about 381 cells in the colony in 6 weeks.

Example 3 *Finance* **Determine the amount of money in a money market account that provides an annual rate of 6.3% compounded quarterly if \$1700 is invested and left in the account for eight years.**
$A = P\left(1 + \frac{r}{n}\right)^{nt}$
$A = 1700\left(1 + \frac{0.063}{4}\right)^{4 \cdot 8}$ *P = 1700, r = 0.063, n = 4, t = 8*
$A \approx 2803.028499$ *Use a calculator.*
After 8 years, the \$1700 investment will have a value of \$2803.03.

11-2

Practice

Exponential Functions

Graph each exponential function or inequality.

1. $y = 2^{x-1}$

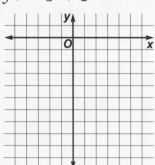

2. $y = 4^{-x+2}$

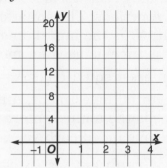

3. $y > -3^x + 1$

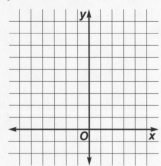

4. $y \geq 0.5^x$

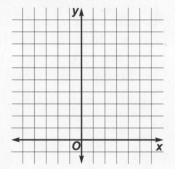

5. *Demographics* An area in North Carolina known as The Triangle is principally composed of the cities of Durham, Raleigh, and Chapel Hill. The Triangle had a population of 700,000 in 1990. The average yearly rate of growth is 5.9%. Find the projected population for 2010.

6. *Finance* Determine the amount of money in a savings account that provides an annual rate of 4% compounded monthly if the initial investment is $1000 and the money is left in the account for 5 years.

7. *Investments* How much money must be invested by Mr. Kaufman if he wants to have $20,000 in his account after 15 years? He can earn 5% compounded quarterly.

11-3

Study Guide

The Number *e*

The number *e* is a special irrational number with an approximate value of 2.718 to three decimal places. The formula for exponential growth or decay is $N = N_0e^{kt}$, where N is the final amount, N_0 is the initial amount, k is a constant, and t is time. The equation $A = Pe^{rt}$, where P is the initial amount, A is the final amount, r is the annual interest rate, and t is time in years, is used for calculating interest that is compounded continuously.

Example 1 **Demographics** **The population of Dubuque, Iowa, declined at a rate of 0.4% between 1997 1998. In 1998, the population was 87,806.**
a. Let *t* be the number of years since 1998 and write a function to model the population.
b. Suppose that the rate of decline remains steady at 0.4%. Find the projected population of Dubuque in 2010.

a. $y = ne^{kt}$
$y = 87,806e^{-0.004t}$ $n = 87,806; k = -0.004$

b. In 2010, it will have been $2010 - 1998$ or 12 years since the initial population figure. Thus, $t = 12$.

$y = 87,806e^{-0.004t}$
$y = 87,806e^{-0.004(12)}$ $t = 12$
$y \approx 83690.86531$ *Use a calculator.*

Given a population of 87,806 in 1998 and a steady rate of decline of 0.4%, the population of Dubuque, Iowa, will be approximately 83,691 in 2010.

Example 2 **Finance** **Compare the balance after 10 years of a $5000 investment earning 8.5% interest compounded continuously to the same investment compounded quarterly.**

In both cases, $P = 5000$, $r = 0.085$, and $t = 10$. When the interest is compounded quarterly, $n = 4$. Use a calculator to evaluate each expression.

Continuously

$A = Pe^{rt}$
$A = 5000e^{(0.085)(10)}$
$A = 11,698.23$

Quarterly

$A = P\left(1 + \dfrac{r}{n}\right)^{nt}$
$A = 5000\left(1 + \dfrac{0.085}{4}\right)^{4\cdot10}$
$A = 11,594.52$

You would earn $\$11,698.23 - \$11,594.52 = \$103.71$ more by choosing the account that compounds continuously.

11-3

Practice

The Number *e*

1. **Demographics** In 1995, the population of Kalamazoo, Michigan, was 79,089. This figure represented a 0.4% annual decline from 1990.

   a. Let t be the number of years since 1995 and write a function that models the population in Kalamazoo in 1995.

   b. Predict the population in 2010 and 2015. Assume a steady rate of decline.

2. **Biology** Suppose a certain type of bacteria reproduces according to the model $P(t) = 100e^{0.271t}$, where t is time in hours.

   a. At what rate does this type of bacteria reproduce?

   b. What was the initial number of bacteria?

   c. Find the number of bacteria at $P(5)$, $P(10)$, $P(24)$, and $P(72)$. Round to the nearest whole number.

3. **Finance** Suppose Karyn deposits $1500 in a savings account that earns 6.75% interest compounded continuously. She plans to withdraw the money in 6 years to make a $2500 down payment on a car. Will there be enough funds in Karyn's account in 6 years to meet her goal?

4. **Banking** Given the original principal, the annual interest rate, the amount of time for each investment, and the type of compounded interest, find the amount at the end of the investment.

   a. $P = \$1250$, $r = 8.5\%$, $t = 3$ years, semiannually

   b. $P = \$2575$, $r = 6.25\%$, $t = 5$ years 3 months, continuously

11-4

Study Guide

Logarithmic Functions

In the function $x = a^y$, y is called the **logarithm** of x. It is usually written as $y = \log_a x$ and is read "y equals the log, base a, of x." Knowing that if $a^u = a^v$ then $u = v$, you can evaluate a logarithmic expression to determine its logarithm.

Example 1 **Write $\log_7 49 = 2$ in exponential form.**

The base is 7 and the exponent is 2.
$7^2 = 49$

Example 2 **Write $2^5 = 32$ in logarithmic form.**

The base is 2, and the exponent or logarithm is 5.
$\log_2 32 = 5$

Example 3 **Evaluate the expression $\log_5 \frac{1}{25}$.**

Let $x = \log_5 \frac{1}{25}$.

$x = \log_5 \frac{1}{25}$

$5^x = \frac{1}{25}$ *Definition of logarithm.*

$5^x = (25)^{-1}$ $a^{-m} = \frac{1}{a^m}$

$5^x = (5^2)^{-1}$ $5^2 = 25$

$5^x = 5^{-2}$ $(a^m)^n = a^{mn}$

$x = -2$ *If $a^u = a^v$, then $u = v$.*

Example 4 **Solve each equation.**

a. $\log_6 (4x + 6) = \log_6 (8x - 2)$

$\log_6 (4x + 6) = \log_6 (8x - 2)$

$4x + 6 = 8x - 2$ *If $\log_b m = \log_b n$, then $m = n$.*

$-4x = -8$

$x = 2$

b. $\log_9 x + \log_9 (x - 2) = \log_9 3$

$\log_9 x + \log_9 (x - 2) = \log_9 3$

$\log_9 [x(x - 2)] = \log_9 3$ $\log_b mn = \log_b m + \log_b n$

$x^2 - 2x = 3$ *If $\log_b m = \log_b n$, then $m = n$.*

$x^2 - 2x - 3 = 0$

$(x - 3)(x + 1) = 0$ *Factor.*

$x - 3 = 0$ or $x + 1 = 0$ *Find the zeros.*

$x = 3$ or $x = -1$.

The log of a negative value does not exist, so the answer is $x = 3$.

11-4

Practice

Logarithmic Functions

Write each equation in exponential form.

1. $\log_3 81 = 4$

2. $\log_8 2 = \frac{1}{3}$

3. $\log_{10} \frac{1}{100} = -2$

Write each equation in logarithmic form.

4. $3^3 = 27$

5. $5^{-3} = \frac{1}{125}$

6. $\left(\frac{1}{4}\right)^{-4} = 256$

Evaluate each expression.

7. $\log_7 7^3$

8. $\log_{10} 0.001$

9. $\log_8 4096$

10. $\log_4 32$

11. $\log_3 1$

12. $\log_6 \frac{1}{216}$

Solve each equation.

13. $\log_x 64 = 3$

14. $\log_4 0.25 = x$

15. $\log_4 (2x - 1) = \log_4 16$

16. $\log_{10} \sqrt{10} = x$

17. $\log_7 56 - \log_7 x = \log_7 4$

18. $\log_5 (x + 4) + \log_5 x = \log_5 12$

19. *Chemistry* How long would it take 100,000 grams of radioactive iodine, which has a half-life of 60 days, to decay to 25,000 grams? Use the formula $N = N_0 \left(\frac{1}{2}\right)^t$, where N is the final amount of the substance, N_0 is the initial amount, and t represents the number of half-lives.

11-5

Study Guide

Common Logarithms

Logarithms with base 10 are called **common logarithms.**
The change of base formula, $\log_a n = \frac{\log_b n}{\log_b a}$, where a, b, and n
are positive numbers and neither a nor b is 1, allows you to
evaluate logarithms in other bases with a calculator.
Logarithms can be used to solve **exponential equations.**

Example 1   **Evaluate each expression.**

     a. log 8(3)^2

$$\begin{aligned}
\log 8(3)^2 &= \log 8 + 2 \log 3 &&\text{$\log ab = \log a + \log b$, $\log b^n = n \log b$}\\
&\approx 0.9031 + 2(0.4771) &&\text{Use a calculator.}\\
&\approx 0.9031 + 0.9542\\
&\approx 1.8573
\end{aligned}$$

     b. log $\frac{15^3}{7}$

$$\begin{aligned}
\log \frac{15^3}{7} &= 3 \log 15 - \log 7 &&\text{$\log \frac{a}{b} = \log a - \log b$, $\log a^m = m \log a$}\\
&\approx 3(1.1761) - 0.8451 &&\text{Use a calculator.}\\
&\approx 3.5283 - 0.8451\\
&\approx 2.6832
\end{aligned}$$

Example 2   **Find the value of $\log_8 2037$ using the change of
base formula.**

$$\begin{aligned}
\log_8 2037 &= \frac{\log_{10} 2037}{\log_{10} 8} &&\log_a n = \frac{\log_b n}{\log_b a}\\
&\approx \frac{3.3090}{0.9031} &&\text{Use a calculator.}\\
&\approx 3.6641
\end{aligned}$$

Example 3   **Solve $7^{2x} = 93$.**

$$\begin{aligned}
7^{2x} &= 93\\
\log 7^{2x} &= \log 93 &&\text{Take the logarithm of each side.}\\
2x \log 7 &= \log 93 &&\log_b m^p = p \cdot \log_b m\\
2x &= \frac{\log 93}{\log 7} &&\text{Divide each side by log 7.}\\
2x &\approx 2.3293 &&\text{Use a calculator.}\\
x &\approx 1.1646
\end{aligned}$$

11-5

Practice

Common Logarithms

**Given that log 3 = 0.4771, log 5 = 0.6990, and log 9 = 0.9542,
evaluate each logarithm.**

1. log 300,000

2. log 0.0005

3. log 9000

4. log 27

5. log 75

6. log 81

Evaluate each expression.

7. log 66.3

8. log $\frac{17^4}{5}$

9. log $7(4^3)$

Find the value of each logarithm using the change of base formula.

10. $\log_6 832$

11. $\log_{11} 47$

12. $\log_3 9$

Solve each equation or inequality.

13. $8^x = 10$

14. $2.4^x \leq 20$

15. $1.8^{x-5} = 19.8$

16. $3^{5x} = 85$

17. $4^{2x} > 25$

18. $3^{2x-2} = 2^x$

19. *Seismology* The intensity of a shock wave from an earthquake
is given by the formula $R = \log_{10} \frac{I}{I_0}$, where R is the magnitude, I is
a measure of wave energy, and $I_0 = 1$. Find the intensity per unit
of area for the following earthquakes.
a. Northridge, California, in 1994, $R = 6.7$

b. Hector Mine, California, in 1999, $R = 7.1$

11-6

Study Guide

Natural Logarithms

Logarithms with base e are called **natural logarithms** and are usually written **ln x.** Logarithms with a base other than e can be converted to natural logarithms using the change of base formula. The antilogarithm of a natural logarithm is written **antiln x.** You can use the properties of logarithms and antilogarithms to simplify and solve exponential and logarithmic equations or inequalities with natural logarithms.

Example 1 **Convert $\log_4 381$ to a natural logarithm and evaluate.**

$$\log_a n = \frac{\log_b n}{\log_b a}$$

$$\log_4 381 = \frac{\log_e 381}{\log_e 4} \qquad a = 4,\ b = e,\ n = 381$$

$$= \frac{\ln 381}{\ln 4} \qquad log_e\ x = ln\ x$$

$$\approx 4.2868 \qquad Use\ a\ calculator.$$

So, $\log_4 381$ is about 4.2868.

Example 2 **Solve $3.75 = -7.5 \ln x$.**

$$3.75 = -7.5 \ln x$$
$$-0.5 = \ln x \qquad Divide\ each\ side\ by\ -7.5$$
$$\text{antiln}\ (-0.5) = x \qquad Take\ the\ antilogarithm\ of\ each\ side.$$
$$0.6065 \approx x \qquad Use\ a\ calculator.$$

The solution is about 0.6065.

Example 3 **Solve each equation or inequality by using natural logarithms.**

a. $4^{3x} = 6^{x+1}$

$$4^{3x} = 6^{x+1}$$
$$\ln 4^{3x} = \ln 6^{x+1} \qquad Take\ the\ natural\ logarithm\ of\ each\ side.$$
$$3x \ln 4 = (x + 1) \ln 6 \qquad ln\ a^n = n\ ln\ a$$
$$3x(1.3863) = (x + 1)(1.7918) \qquad Use\ a\ calculator.$$
$$4.1589x = 1.7918x + 1.7918$$
$$2.3671x = 1.7918$$
$$x \approx 0.7570$$

b. $25 > e^{0.2t}$

$$25 > e^{0.2t}$$
$$\ln 25 > \ln e^{0.2t} \qquad Take\ the\ natural\ logarithm\ of\ each\ side.$$
$$\ln 25 > 0.2t \ln e \qquad ln\ a^n = n\ ln\ a$$
$$3.2189 > 0.2t \qquad Use\ a\ calculator.$$
$$16.0945 > t$$

Thus, $t < 16.0945$

Advanced Mathematical Concepts

11-6

Practice

Natural Logarithms

Evaluate each expression.

1. ln 71

2. ln 8.76

3. ln 0.532

4. antiln −0.256

5. antiln 4.62

6. antiln −1.62

Convert each logarithm to a natural logarithm and evaluate.

7. $\log_7 94$

8. $\log_5 256$

9. $\log_9 0.712$

Use natural logarithms to solve each equation or inequality.

10. $6^x = 42$

11. $7^x = 4^{x+3}$

12. $1249 = 175e^{-0.04t}$

13. $10^{x+1} > 3^x$

14. $12 < e^{0.048y}$

15. $8.4 < e^{t-2}$

16. *Banking*   Ms. Cubbatz invested a sum of money in a certificate
of deposit that earns 8% interest compounded continuously. The
formula for calculating interest that is compounded continuously
is $A = Pe^{rt}$. If Ms. Cubbatz made the investment on January 1,
1995, and the account was worth $12,000 on January 1, 1999,
what was the original amount in the account?

11-7

Study Guide

Modeling Real-World Data with Exponential and Logarithmic Functions

The **doubling time,** or amount of time t required for a quantity modeled by the exponential equation $N = N_0 e^{kt}$ to double, is given by $t = \frac{\ln 2}{k}$.

Example   *Finance*   **Tara's parents invested $5000 in an account that earns 11.5% compounded continuously. They would like to double their investment in 5 years to help finance Tara's college education.**

a. Will the initial investment of $5000 double within 5 years?

Find the doubling time for the investment. For continuously compounded interest, the constant k is the interest rate written as a decimal.

$t = \frac{\ln 2}{k}$

$\quad = \frac{\ln 2}{0.115}$ *The decimal for 11.5% is 0.115.*

$\quad \approx 6.03$ years *Use a calculator.*

Five years is not enough time for the initial investment to double.

b. What interest rate is required for an investment with continuously compounded interest to double in 5 years?

$t = \frac{\ln 2}{k}$

$5 = \frac{\ln 2}{k}$

$\frac{1}{5} = \frac{k}{\ln 2}$ *Take the reciprocal of each side.*

$\frac{\ln 2}{5} = k$ *Multiply each side by ln 2 to solve for k.*

$0.1386 \approx k$

An interest rate of 13.9% is required for an investment with continuously compounded interest to double in 5 years.

11-7

Practice

Modeling Real-World Data with Exponential and Logarithmic Functions

Find the amount of time required for an amount to double at the given rate if the interest is compounded continuously.

1. 4.75%

2. 6.25%

3. 5.125%

4. 7.1%

5. *City Planning* At a recent town council meeting, proponents of increased spending claimed that spending should be doubled because the population of the city would double over the next three years. Population statistics for the city indicate that population is growing at the rate of 16.5% per year. Is the claim that the population will double in three years correct? Explain.

6. *Conservation* A wildlife conservation group released 14 black bears into a protected area. Their goal is to double the population of black bears every 4 years for the next 12 years.

a. If they are to meet their goal at the end of the first four years, what should be the yearly rate of increase in population?

b. Suppose the group meets its goal. What will be the minimum number of black bears in the protected area in 12 years?

c. What type of model would best represent such data?

Answers (Lessons 11-1 and 11-2)

11-1 Practice

Rational Exponents

Evaluate each expression.

1. $8^{\frac{2}{3}}$ $\frac{1}{8^{\frac{1}{3}}}$ **2**

2. $\left(\frac{4}{5}\right)^{-2}$ $\frac{25}{16}$

3. $343^{\frac{2}{3}}$ **49**

4. $\sqrt[3]{8^3}$ **8**

5. $\sqrt{5} \cdot \sqrt{10}$ $5\sqrt{2}$

6. $9^{\frac{1}{2}}$ $\frac{1}{3}$

Simplify each expression.

7. $(5n^3)^2 \cdot n^{-6}$ **25**

8. $\left(\frac{x^2}{4y^{-2}}\right)^{-\frac{1}{2}}$ $2|x|^{-1}|y|^{-1}$ or $\frac{2}{|x||y|}$

9. $(64x^6)^{\frac{1}{3}}$ $4x^2$

10. $(5x^6y^4)^{\frac{1}{2}}$ $|x|^3 y^2 \sqrt{5}$

11. $\sqrt{x^2y^3} \cdot \sqrt{x^3y^4}$ $|x|^{\frac{5}{2}}|y|^{\frac{7}{2}}$ or $x^2|y|^3 \sqrt{xy}$

12. $\left(\frac{p^{6a}}{p^{-3a}}\right)^{\frac{1}{3}}$ p^{3a}

Express each using rational exponents.

13. $\sqrt{x^5y^6}$ $|x|^{\frac{5}{2}}|y|^3$

14. $\sqrt[5]{27x^{10}y^5}$ $27^{\frac{1}{5}}x^2y$

15. $\sqrt{144x^6y^{10}}$ $12|x|^3|y|^5$

16. $21\sqrt[3]{c^7}$ $21c^{\frac{7}{3}}$

17. $\sqrt{1024a^3}$ $32a^{\frac{3}{2}}$

18. $\sqrt[4]{36a^8b^5}$ $6^{\frac{1}{2}}a^2b^{\frac{5}{4}}$

Express each using radicals.

19. $64^{\frac{1}{3}}$ $\sqrt[3]{64}$ or 4

20. $2^{\frac{1}{2}}a^{\frac{3}{2}}b^{\frac{5}{2}}$ $\sqrt{2a^3b^5}$ or $ab^2\sqrt{2ab}$

21. $s^{\frac{2}{3}}t^{\frac{1}{2}}v^{\frac{3}{2}}$ $\sqrt[3]{s^2tv^2}$

22. $y^{\frac{3}{2}}$ $\sqrt{y^3}$ or $y\sqrt{y}$

23. $x^{\frac{2}{5}}y^5$ $\sqrt[5]{x^2y^3}$

24. $(x^6y^3)^{\frac{1}{2}}z^{\frac{3}{2}}$ $\sqrt{x^6y^3z^3}$ or $|x|^3yz\sqrt{yz}$

11-2 Practice

Exponential Functions

Graph each exponential function or inequality.

1. $y = 2^{x-1}$

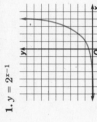

2. $y = 4^{-x+2}$

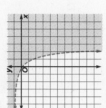

3. $y > -3^x + 1$

4. $y \geq 0.5^x$

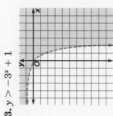

5. **Demographics** An area in North Carolina known as The Triangle is principally composed of the cities of Durham, Raleigh, and Chapel Hill. The Triangle had a population of 700,000 in 1990. The average yearly rate of growth is 5.9%. Find the projected population for 2010.   **about 2,203,014**

6. **Finance** Determine the amount of money in a savings account that provides an annual rate of 4% compounded monthly if the initial investment is $1000 and the money is left in the account for 5 years.   **about $1221.00**

7. **Investments** How much money must be invested by Mr. Kaufman if he wants to have $20,000 in his account after 15 years? He can earn 5% compounded quarterly.   **about $9491.35**

11-3

Practice

The Number e

1. Demographics In 1995, the population of Kalamazoo, Michigan, was 79,089. This figure represented a 0.4% annual decline from 1990.

a. Let t be the number of years since 1995 and write a function that models the population in Kalamazoo in 1995.
$y = 79,089e^{-0.004t}$

b. Predict the population in 2010 and 2015. Assume a steady rate of decline. **2010: 74,483; 2015: 73,008**

2. Biology Suppose a certain type of bacteria reproduces according to the model $P(t) = 100e^{0.271t}$, where t is time in hours.

a. At what rate does this type of bacteria reproduce?
27.1%

b. What was the initial number of bacteria?
100

c. Find the number of bacteria at $P(5)$, $P(10)$, $P(24)$, and $P(72)$. Round to the nearest whole number.
$P(5)$: **388**
$P(10)$: **1503**
$P(24)$: **66,781**
$P(72)$: **29,782,004,910**

3. Finance Suppose Karyn deposits $1500 in a savings account that earns 6.75% interest compounded continuously. She plans to withdraw the money in 6 years to make a $2500 down payment on a car. Will there be enough funds in Karyn's account in 6 years to meet her goal?
No. Karyn will have $2249 in her account in 6 years. She will be $251 short.

4. Banking Given the original principal, the annual interest rate, the amount of time for each investment, and the type of compounded interest, find the amount at the end of the investment.

a. $P = \$1250$, $r = 8.5\%$, $t = 3$ years, semiannually
$1604.60

b. $P = \$2575$, $r = 6.25\%$, $t = 5$ years 3 months, continuously
$3575.03

11-4

Practice

Logarithmic Functions

Write each equation in exponential form.

1. $\log_3 81 = 4$
$3^4 = 81$

2. $\log_8 2 = \frac{1}{3}$
$8^{\frac{1}{3}} = 2$

3. $\log_{10} \frac{1}{100} = -2$
$10^{-2} = \frac{1}{100}$

Write each equation in logarithmic form.

4. $3^3 = 27$
$\log_3 27 = 3$

5. $5^{-3} = \frac{1}{125}$
$\log_5 \frac{1}{125} = -3$

6. $\left(\frac{1}{4}\right)^{-4} = 256$
$\log_{\frac{1}{4}} 256 = -4$

Evaluate each expression.

7. $\log_7 7^3$
3

8. $\log_{10} 0.001$
−3

9. $\log_8 4096$
4

10. $\log_4 32$
$\frac{5}{2}$

11. $\log_3 1$
0

12. $\log_6 \frac{1}{216}$
−3

Solve each equation.

13. $\log_x 64 = 3$
4

14. $\log_4 0.25 = x$
−1

15. $\log_4 (2x - 1) = \log_4 16$
$\frac{17}{2}$

16. $\log_{10} \sqrt{10} = x$
$\frac{1}{2}$

17. $\log_7 56 - \log_7 x = \log_7 4$
14

18. $\log_5 (x + 4) + \log_5 x = \log_5 12$
2

19. Chemistry How long would it take 100,000 grams of radioactive iodine, which has a half-life of 60 days, to decay to 25,000 grams? Use the formula $N = N_0\left(\frac{1}{2}\right)^t$, where N is the final amount of the substance, N_0 is the initial amount, and t represents the number of half-lives. **120 days**

Answers (Lessons 11-5 and 11-6)

11-5 Practice

Common Logarithms

Given that log 3 = 0.4771, log 5 = 0.6990, and log 9 = 0.9542, evaluate each logarithm.

1. log 300,000
5.4771

2. log 0.0005
−3.3010

3. log 9000
3.9542

4. log 27
1.4313

5. log 75
1.8751

6. log 81
1.9084

Evaluate each expression.

7. log 66.3
1.8215

8. $\log \frac{17^4}{5}$
4.2228

9. $\log 7(4^3)$
2.6513

Find the value of each logarithm using the change of base formula.

10. $\log_6 832$
3.7526

11. $\log_{11} 47$
1.6056

12. $\log_3 9$
2

Solve each equation or inequality.

13. $8^x = 10$
1.1073

14. $2.4^x \le 20$
$x \le 3.4219$

15. $1.8^{x-5} = 19.8$
10.0795

16. $3^{5x} = 85$
0.8088

17. $4^{2x} > 25$
$x > 1.1610$

18. $3^{2x-2} = 2^x$
1.4608

19. Seismology The intensity of a shock wave from an earthquake is given by the formula $R = \log_{10} \frac{I}{I_0}$, where R is the magnitude, I is a measure of wave energy, and $I_0 = 1$. Find the intensity per unit of area for the following earthquakes.
a. Northridge, California, in 1994, $R = 6.7$
about 5,011,872
b. Hector Mine, California, in 1999, $R = 7.1$
about 12,589,254

11-6 Practice

Natural Logarithms

Evaluate each expression.

1. ln 71
4.2627

2. ln 8.76
2.1702

3. ln 0.532
−0.6311

4. antiln −0.256
0.7741

5. antiln 4.62
101.4940

6. antiln −1.62
0.1979

Convert each logarithm to a natural logarithm and evaluate.

7. $\log_7 94$
2.3348

8. $\log_5 256$
3.4454

9. $\log_9 0.712$
−0.1546

Use natural logarithms to solve each equation or inequality.

10. $6^x = 42$
2.0860

11. $7^x = 4^{x+3}$
7.4317

12. $1249 = 175e^{-0.04t}$
−49.1328

13. $10^{x+1} > 3^x$
$x > -1.9125$

14. $12 < e^{0.048y}$
$y > 51.7689$

15. $8.4 < e^{t-2}$
$t > 4.1282$

16. Banking Ms. Cubbatz invested a sum of money in a certificate of deposit that earns 8% interest compounded continuously. The formula for calculating interest that is compounded continuously is $A = Pe^{rt}$. If Ms. Cubbatz made the investment on January 1, 1995, and the account was worth $12,000 on January 1, 1999, what was the original amount in the account? **$8713.79**

11-7 Practice

Modeling Real-World Data with Exponential and Logarithmic Functions

Find the amount of time required for an amount to double at the given rate if the interest is compounded continuously.

1. 4.75%
14.59 years

2. 6.25%
11.09 years

3. 5.125%
13.52 years

4. 7.1%
9.76 years

5. *City Planning* At a recent town council meeting, proponents of increased spending claimed that spending should be doubled because the population of the city would double over the next three years. Population statistics for the city indicate that population is growing at the rate of 16.5% per year. Is the claim that the population will double in three years correct? Explain.
No. To double in size, the population of the city would have to be increasing at the rate of 23.1% per year. The population of the city will double in 4.2 years.

6. *Conservation* A wildlife conservation group released 14 black bears into a protected area. Their goal is to double the population of black bears every 4 years for the next 12 years.

a. If they are to meet their goal at the end of the first four years, what should be the yearly rate of increase in population?
17.3%

b. Suppose the group meets its goal. What will be the minimum number of black bears in the protected area in 12 years?
There will be at least 112 black bears in the protected area.

c. What type of model would best represent such data?
An exponential model would best represent these data.

12-1

Study Guide

Arithmetic Sequences and Series

A **sequence** is a function whose domain is the set of natural numbers. The **terms** of a sequence are the range elements of the function. The difference between successive terms of an **arithmetic sequence** is a constant called the **common difference**, denoted as d. An **arithmetic series** is the indicated sum of the terms of an arithmetic sequence.

Example 1 **a. Find the next four terms in the arithmetic sequence $-7, -5, -3, \ldots$.**
b. Find the 38th term of this sequence.

a. Find the common difference.
$$a_2 - a_1 = -5 - (-7) \text{ or } 2$$

The common difference is 2. Add 2 to the third term to get the fourth term, and so on.
$$a_4 = -3 + 2 \text{ or } -1 \qquad a_5 = -1 + 2 \text{ or } 1$$
$$a_6 = 1 + 2 \text{ or } 3 \qquad a_7 = 3 + 2 \text{ or } 5$$

The next four terms are $-1, 1, 3,$ and 5.

b. Use the formula for the nth term of an arithmetic sequence.
$$a_n = a_1 + (n-1)d$$
$$a_{38} = -7 + (38-1)2 \quad n = 38, a_1 = -7, d = 2$$
$$a_{38} = 67$$

Example 2 **Write an arithmetic sequence that has three arithmetic means between 3.2 and 4.4.**

The sequence will have the form 3.2, _?_, _?_, _?_, 4.4.

First, find the common difference.
$$a_n = a_1 + (n-1)d$$
$$4.4 = 3.2 + (5-1)d \quad n = 5, a_5 = 4.4, a_1 = 3.2$$
$$4.4 = 3.2 + 4d$$
$$d = 0.3$$

Then, determine the arithmetic means.

a_2	a_3	a_4
3.2 + 0.3 = 3.5	3.5 + 0.3 = 3.8	3.8 + 0.3 = 4.1

The sequence is 3.2, 3.5, 3.8, 4.1, 4.4.

Example 3 **Find the sum of the first 50 terms in the series $11 + 14 + 17 + \cdots + 158$.**

$$S_n = \frac{n}{2}(a_1 + a_n)$$
$$S_{50} = \frac{50}{2}(11 + 158) \quad n = 50, a_1 = 11, a_{50} = 158$$
$$= 4225$$

12-1

Practice

Arithmetic Sequences and Series

Find the next four terms in each arithmetic sequence.

1. $-1.1, 0.6, 2.3, \ldots$ **2.** $16, 13, 10, \ldots$ **3.** $p, p+2, p+4, \ldots$

For exercises 4–12, assume that each sequence or series is arithmetic.

4. Find the 24th term in the sequence for which $a_1 = -27$ and $d = 3$.

5. Find n for the sequence for which $a_n = 27$, $a_1 = -12$, and $d = 3$.

6. Find d for the sequence for which $a_1 = -12$ and $a_{23} = 32$.

7. What is the first term in the sequence for which $d = -3$ and $a_6 = 5$?

8. What is the first term in the sequence for which $d = -\frac{1}{3}$ and $a_7 = -3$?

9. Find the 6th term in the sequence $-3 + \sqrt{2}, 0, 3 - \sqrt{2}, \ldots$.

10. Find the 45th term in the sequence $-17, -11, -5, \ldots$.

11. Write a sequence that has three arithmetic means between 35 and 45.

12. Write a sequence that has two arithmetic means between -7 and 2.75.

13. Find the sum of the first 13 terms in the series $-5 + 1 + 7 + \cdots + 67$.

14. Find the sum of the first 62 terms in the series $-23 - 21.5 - 20 - \cdots$.

15. *Auditorium Design*   Wakefield Auditorium has 26 rows, and the first row has 22 seats. The number of seats in each row increases by 4 as you move toward the back of the auditorium. What is the seating capacity of this auditorium?

12-2

Study Guide

Geometric Sequences and Series

A **geometric sequence** is a sequence in which each term after the first, a_1, is the product of the preceding term and the **common ratio**, r. The terms between two nonconsecutive terms of a geometric sequence are called **geometric means**. The indicated sum of the terms of a geometric sequence is a **geometric series.**

Example 1   **Find the 7th term of the geometric sequence 157, −47.1, 14.13, ...**

First, find the common ratio.
$a_2 \div a_1 = -47.1 \div 157$ or -0.3
The common ratio is -0.3.

Then, use the formula for the nth term of a geometric sequence.
$a_n = a_1 r^{n-1}$
$a_7 = 157(-0.3)^6$ *$n = 7, a_1 = 157, r = -0.3$*
$a_7 = 0.114453$

The 7th term is 0.114453.

Example 2   **Write a sequence that has two geometric means between 6 and 162.**

The sequence will have the form 6, __?__, __?__, 162.

First, find the common ratio.
$a_n = a_1 r^{n-1}$
$162 = 6r^3$ *$a_4 = 162, a_1 = 6, n = 4$*
$27 = r^3$ *Divide each side by 6.*
$3 = r$ *Take the cube root of each side.*

Then, determine the geometric sequence.
$a_2 = 6 \cdot 3$ or 18 $a_3 = 18 \cdot 3$ or 54
The sequence is 6, 18, 54, 162.

Example 3   **Find the sum of the first twelve terms of the geometric series $12 - 12\sqrt{2} + 24 - 24\sqrt{2} + \cdots$.**

First, find the common ratio.
$a_2 \div a_1 = -12\sqrt{2} \div 12$ or $-\sqrt{2}$
The common ratio is $-\sqrt{2}$.

$S_n = \dfrac{a_1 - a_1 r^n}{1 - r}$

$S_{12} = \dfrac{12 - 12(-\sqrt{2})^{12}}{1 - (-\sqrt{2})}$ *$n = 12, a_1 = 12, r = -\sqrt{2}$*

$S_{12} = 756(1 - \sqrt{2})$ *Simplify.*

The sum of the first twelve terms of the series is $756(1 - \sqrt{2})$.

12-2

Practice

Geometric Sequences and Series

Determine the common ratio and find the next three terms of each geometric sequence.

1. $-1, 2, -4, \ldots$ **2.** $-4, -3, -\frac{9}{4}, \ldots$ **3.** $12, -18, 27, \ldots$

For exercises 4–9, assume that each sequence or series is geometric.

4. Find the fifth term of the sequence $20, 0.2, 0.002, \ldots$.

5. Find the ninth term of the sequence $\sqrt{3}, -3, 3\sqrt{3}, \ldots$.

6. If $r = 2$ and $a_4 = 28$, find the first term of the sequence.

7. Find the first three terms of the sequence for which $a_4 = 8.4$ and $r = 4$.

8. Find the first three terms of the sequence for which $a_6 = \frac{1}{32}$ and $r = \frac{1}{2}$.

9. Write a sequence that has two geometric means between 2 and 0.25.

10. Write a sequence that has three geometric means between -32 and -2.

11. Find the sum of the first eight terms of the series $\frac{3}{4} + \frac{9}{20} + \frac{27}{100} + \cdots$.

12. Find the sum of the first 10 terms of the series $-3 + 12 - 48 + \cdots$.

13. *Population Growth*   A city of 100,000 people is growing at a rate of 5.2% per year. Assuming this growth rate remains constant, estimate the population of the city 5 years from now.

12-3

Study Guide

Infinite Sequences and Series

An **infinite sequence** is one that has infinitely many terms. An **infinite series** is the indicated sum of the terms of an infinite sequence.

Example 1   Find $\lim\limits_{n\to\infty} \dfrac{4n^2 - n + 3}{n^2 + 1}$.

Divide each term in the numerator and the denominator by the highest power of n to produce an equivalent expression. In this case, n^2 is the highest power.

$$\lim \frac{4n^2 - n + 3}{n^2 + 1} = \lim \frac{\dfrac{4n^2}{n^2} - \dfrac{n}{n^2} + \dfrac{3}{n^2}}{\dfrac{n^2}{n^2} + \dfrac{1}{n^2}}$$

$$= \lim_{n\to\infty} \frac{4 - \dfrac{1}{n} + \dfrac{3}{n^2}}{1 + \dfrac{1}{n^2}} \qquad \textit{Simplify.}$$

$$= \frac{\lim\limits_{n\to\infty} 4 - \lim\limits_{n\to\infty} \dfrac{1}{n} + \lim\limits_{n\to\infty} 3 \cdot \lim\limits_{n\to\infty} \dfrac{1}{n^2}}{\lim\limits_{n\to\infty} 1 + \lim\limits_{n\to\infty} \dfrac{1}{n^2}} \qquad \textit{Apply limit theorems.}$$

$$= \frac{4 - 0 + 3 \cdot 0}{1 + 0} \text{ or } 4 \qquad \textit{$\lim\limits_{n\to\infty} 4 = 4$, $\lim\limits_{n\to\infty} \dfrac{1}{n} = 0$, $\lim\limits_{n\to\infty} 3 = 3$,}$$
$$\textit{$\lim\limits_{n\to\infty} \dfrac{1}{n^2} = 0$, $\lim\limits_{n\to\infty} 1 = 1$}$$

Thus, the limit is 4.

Example 2   Find the sum of the series $\dfrac{3}{2} - \dfrac{3}{8} + \dfrac{3}{32} - \cdots$.

In the series $a_1 = \dfrac{3}{2}$ and $r = -\dfrac{1}{4}$.

Since $|r| < 1$, $S = \dfrac{a_1}{1 - r}$.

$$S = \frac{a_1}{1 - r} = \frac{\dfrac{3}{2}}{1 - \left(-\dfrac{1}{4}\right)} \qquad a_1 = \frac{3}{2} \text{ and } r = -\frac{1}{4}$$

$$= \frac{12}{10} \text{ or } 1\frac{1}{5}$$

The sum of the series is $1\frac{1}{5}$.

12-3

Practice

Infinite Sequence and Series

Find each limit, or state that the limit does not exist and explain your reasoning.

1. $\lim\limits_{n\to\infty} \dfrac{n^2-1}{n^2+1}$

2. $\lim\limits_{n\to\infty} \dfrac{4n^2-5n}{3n^2+4}$

3. $\lim\limits_{n\to\infty} \dfrac{5n^2+1}{6n}$

4. $\lim\limits_{n\to\infty} \dfrac{(n-1)(3n+1)}{5n^2}$

5. $\lim\limits_{n\to\infty} \dfrac{3n-(-1)^n}{4n^2}$

6. $\lim\limits_{n\to\infty} \dfrac{n^3+1}{n^2}$

Write each repeating decimal as a fraction.

7. $0.\overline{75}$

8. $0.\overline{592}$

Find the sum of each infinite series, or state that the sum does not exist and explain your reasoning.

9. $\dfrac{2}{5} + \dfrac{6}{25} + \dfrac{18}{125} + \cdots$

10. $\dfrac{3}{4} + \dfrac{15}{8} + \dfrac{75}{16} + \cdots$

11. *Physics* A tennis ball is dropped from a height of 55 feet and bounces $\dfrac{3}{5}$ of the distance after each fall.

  a. Find the first seven terms of the infinite series representing the vertical distances traveled by the ball.

  b. What is the total vertical distance the ball travels before coming to rest?

12-4

Study Guide

Convergent and Divergent Series

If an infinite series has a sum, or limit, the series is **convergent.** If a series is not convergent, it is **divergent.** When a series is neither arithmetic nor geometric and all the terms are positive, you can use the **ratio test** or the **comparison test** to determine whether the series is convergent or divergent.

Ratio Test	Let a_n and a_{n+1} represent two consecutive terms of a series of positive terms. Suppose $\lim\limits_{n\to\infty} \frac{a_{n+1}}{a_n}$ exists and $r = \lim\limits_{n\to\infty} \frac{a_{n+1}}{a_n}$. The series is convergent if $r < 1$ and divergent if $r > 1$. If $r = 1$, the test provides no information.

Comparison Test	• A series of positive terms is convergent if, for $n > 1$, each term of the series is equal to or less than the value of the corresponding term of some convergent series of positive terms. • A series of positive terms is divergent if, for $n > 1$, each term of the series is equal to or greater than the value of the corresponding term of some divergent series of positive terms.

Example 1 Use the ratio test to determine whether the series $\frac{1 \cdot 2}{2^1} + \frac{2 \cdot 3}{2^2} + \frac{3 \cdot 4}{2^3} + \frac{4 \cdot 5}{2^4} + \cdots$ is convergent or divergent.

First, find the nth term. Then use the ratio test.

$$a_n = \frac{n(n+1)}{2^n} \qquad a_{n+1} = \frac{(n+1)(n+2)}{2^{n+1}}$$

$$r = \lim \frac{\dfrac{(n+1)(n+2)}{2^{n+1}}}{\dfrac{n(n+1)}{2^n}}$$

$$r = \lim \frac{(n+1)(n+2)}{2^{n+1}} \cdot \frac{2^n}{n(n+1)} \qquad \textit{Multiply by the reciprocal of the divisor.}$$

$$r = \lim \frac{n+2}{2n} \qquad \frac{2^n}{2^{n+1}} = \frac{1}{2}$$

$$r = \lim \frac{1 + \dfrac{2}{n}}{2} \qquad \textit{Divide by the highest power of } n \textit{ and apply limit theorems.}$$

$$r = \frac{1}{2} \qquad \textit{Since } r < 1, \textit{ the series is convergent.}$$

Example 2 Use the comparison test to determine whether the series $\frac{1}{4^2} + \frac{1}{7^2} + \frac{1}{10^2} + \frac{1}{13^2} + \cdots$ is convergent or divergent.

The general term of the series is $\frac{1}{(3n+1)^2}$. The general term of the convergent series $1 + \frac{1}{2^2} + \frac{1}{3^2} + \frac{1}{4^2} + \cdots$ is $\frac{1}{n^2}$. Since $\frac{1}{(3n+1)^2} < \frac{1}{n^2}$ for all $n \geq 1$, the series $\frac{1}{4^2} + \frac{1}{7^2} + \frac{1}{10^2} + \frac{1}{13^2} + \cdots$ is also convergent.

12-4

Practice

Convergent and Divergent Series

Use the ratio test to determine whether each series is convergent or divergent.

1. $\dfrac{1}{2} + \dfrac{2^2}{2^2} + \dfrac{3^2}{2^3} + \dfrac{4^2}{2^4} + \cdots$ **2.** $0.006 + 0.06 + 0.6 + \cdots$

3. $\dfrac{4}{1 \cdot 2 \cdot 3} + \dfrac{8}{1 \cdot 2 \cdot 3 \cdot 4} + \dfrac{16}{1 \cdot 2 \cdot 3 \cdot 4 \cdot 5} + \cdots$

4. $5 + \dfrac{5}{3^3} + \dfrac{5}{5^3} + \dfrac{5}{7^3} + \cdots$

Use the comparison test to determine whether each series is convergent or divergent.

5. $2 + \dfrac{2}{2^3} + \dfrac{2}{3^3} + \dfrac{2}{4^3} + \cdots$ **6.** $\dfrac{5}{2} + 1 + \dfrac{5}{8} + \dfrac{5}{11} + \cdots$

7. *Ecology*   A landfill is leaking a toxic chemical. Six months after the leak was detected, the chemical had spread 1250 meters from the landfill. After one year, the chemical had spread 500 meters more, and by the end of 18 months, it had reached an additional 200 meters.

   a. If this pattern continues, how far will the chemical spread from the landfill after 3 years?

   b. Will the chemical ever reach the grounds of a hospital located 2500 meters away from the landfill? Explain.

12-5

Study Guide

Sigma Notation and the *n*th Term

A series may be written using **sigma notation**.

$$\text{maximum value of } n \to \quad \overset{k}{\underset{n=1}{\sum}} a_n \leftarrow \text{expression for general term}$$
$$\text{starting value of } n \to \quad \underset{\uparrow}{}$$
$$\text{index of summation}$$

Example 1 **Write each expression in expanded form and then find the sum.**

a. $\displaystyle\sum_{n=1}^{5} (n + 2)$

First, write the expression in expanded form.

$$\sum_{n=1}^{5} (n + 2) = (1 + 2) + (2 + 2) + (3 + 2) + (4 + 2) + (5 + 2)$$

Then, find the sum by simplifying the expanded form. $3 + 4 + 5 + 6 + 7 = 25$

b. $\displaystyle\sum_{m=1}^{\infty} 2\left(\frac{1}{4}\right)^m$

$$\sum_{m=1}^{\infty} 2\left(\frac{1}{4}\right)^m = 2\left(\frac{1}{4}\right)^1 + 2\left(\frac{1}{4}\right)^2 + 2\left(\frac{1}{4}\right)^3 + \cdots$$
$$= \frac{1}{2} + \frac{1}{8} + \frac{1}{32} + \cdots$$

This is an infinite series. Use the formula $S = \dfrac{a_1}{1 - r}$.

$$S = \frac{\frac{1}{2}}{1 - \frac{1}{4}} \quad a_1 = \frac{1}{2}, r = \frac{1}{4}$$

$$S = \frac{2}{3}$$

Example 2 **Express the series $26 + 37 + 50 + 65 + \cdots + 170$ using sigma notation.**

Notice that each term is one more than a perfect square. Thus, the *n*th term of the series is $n^2 + 1$. Since $5^2 + 1 = 26$ and $13^2 + 1 = 170$, the index of summation goes from $n = 5$ to $n = 13$.

Therefore, $26 + 37 + 50 + 65 + \cdots + 170 = \displaystyle\sum_{n=5}^{13} (n^2 + 1)$.

12-5

Practice

Sigma Notation and the *n*th Term

Write each expression in expanded form and then find the sum.

1. $\displaystyle\sum_{n=3}^{5}(n^2 - 2^n)$

2. $\displaystyle\sum_{q=1}^{4}\frac{2}{q}$

3. $\displaystyle\sum_{t=1}^{5}t(t-1)$

4. $\displaystyle\sum_{t=0}^{3}(2t-3)$

5. $\displaystyle\sum_{c=2}^{5}(c-2)^2$

6. $\displaystyle\sum_{i=1}^{\infty}10\left(\frac{1}{2}\right)^i$

Express each series using sigma notation.

7. $3 + 6 + 9 + 12 + 15$

8. $6 + 24 + 120 + \cdots + 40{,}320$

9. $\dfrac{1}{1} + \dfrac{1}{4} + \dfrac{1}{9} + \cdots + \dfrac{1}{100}$

10. $24 + 19 + 14 + \cdots + (-1)$

11. *Savings* Kathryn started saving quarters in a jar. She began by putting two quarters in the jar the first day and then she increased the number of quarters she put in the jar by one additional quarter each successive day.

  a. Use sigma notation to represent the total number of quarters Kathryn had after 30 days.

  b. Find the sum represented in part **a.**

12-6

Study Guide

The Binomial Theorem

Two ways to expand a binomial are to use either **Pascal's triangle** or the **Binomial Theorem.** The Binomial Theorem states that if n is a positive integer, then the following is true.

$$(x + y)^n = x^n + nx^{n-1}y + \frac{n(n-1)}{1 \cdot 2}x^{n-2}y^2 + \frac{n(n-1)(n-2)}{1 \cdot 2 \cdot 3}x^{n-3}y^3 + \cdots + y^n$$

To find individual terms of an expansion, use this form of the Binomial Theorem:

$$(x + y)^n = \sum_{r=0}^{n} \frac{n!}{r!(n-r)!}x^{n-r}y^r.$$

Example 1 **Use Pascal's triangle to expand $(x + 2y)^5$.**

First, write the series without the coefficients. The expression should have $5 + 1$, or 6, terms, with the first term being x^5 and the last term being y^5. The exponents of x should decrease from 5 to 0 while the exponents of y should increase from 0 to 5. The sum of the exponents of each term should be 5.

$x^5 + x^4y + x^3y^2 + x^2y^3 + xy^4 + y^5$ $x^0 = 1$ and $y^0 = 1$

Replace each y with $2y$.

$x^5 + x^4(2y) + x^3(2y)^2 + x^2(2y)^3 + x(2y)^4 + (2y)^5$

Then, use the numbers in the sixth row of Pascal's triangle as the coefficients of the terms, and simplify each term.

$$\begin{array}{cccccc} 1 & 5 & 10 & 10 & 5 & 1 \\ \downarrow & \downarrow & \downarrow & \downarrow & \downarrow & \downarrow \end{array}$$

$(x + 2y)^5 = x^5 + 5x^4(2y) + 10x^3(2y)^2 + 10x^2(2y)^3 + 5x(2y)^4 + (2y)^5$

$\qquad = x^5 + 10x^4y + 40x^3y^2 + 80x^2y^3 + 80xy^4 + 32y^5$

Example 2 **Find the fourth term of $(5a + 2b)^6$.**

$$(5a + 2b)^6 = \sum_{r=0}^{6} \frac{6!}{r!(6-r)!}(5a)^{6-r}(2b)^r$$

To find the fourth term, evaluate the general term for $r = 3$. *Since r increases from 0 to n, r is one less than the number of the term.*

$\dfrac{6!}{r!(6-r)!}(5a)^{6-r}(2b)^r = \dfrac{6!}{3!(6-3)!}(5a)^{6-3}(2b)^3$

$\qquad\qquad\qquad = \dfrac{6 \cdot 5 \cdot 4 \cdot 3!}{3!3!}(5a)^3(2b)^3$

$\qquad\qquad\qquad = 20{,}000a^3b^3$

The fourth term of $(5a + 2b)^6$ is $20{,}000a^3b^3$.

     225   *Advanced Mathematical Concepts*

12-6

Practice

The Binomial Theorem

Use Pascal's triangle to expand each binomial.

1. $(r + 3)^5$

2. $(3a - b)^4$

Use the Binomial Theorem to expand each binomial.

3. $(x - 5)^4$

4. $(3x + 2y)^4$

5. $(a - \sqrt{2})^5$

6. $(2p - 3q)^6$

Find the designated term of each binomial expansion.

7. 4th term of $(2n - 3m)^4$

8. 5th term of $(4a + 2b)^8$

9. 6th term of $(3p + q)^9$

10. 3rd term of $(a - 2\sqrt{3})^6$

11. A varsity volleyball team needs nine members. Of these nine members, at least five must be seniors. How many of the possible groups of juniors and seniors have at least five seniors?

12-7

Study Guide

Special Sequences and Series

The value of e^x can be approximated by using the **exponential series**. The **trigonometric series** can be used to approximate values of the trigonometric functions. **Euler's formula** can be used to write the exponential form of a complex number and to find a complex number that is the natural logarithm of a negative number.

Example 1 **Use the first five terms of the trigonometric series to approximate the value of $\sin \frac{\pi}{6}$ to four decimal places.**

$\sin x \approx x - \frac{x^3}{3!} + \frac{x^5}{5!} - \frac{x^7}{7!} + \frac{x^9}{9!}$

Let $x = \frac{\pi}{6}$, or about 0.5236.

$\sin \frac{\pi}{6} \approx 0.5236 - \frac{(0.5236)^3}{3!} + \frac{(0.5236)^5}{5!} - \frac{(0.5236)^7}{7!} + \frac{(0.5236)^9}{9!}$

$\sin \frac{\pi}{6} \approx 0.5236 - 0.02392 + 0.00033 - 0.000002 + 0.000000008$

$\sin \frac{\pi}{6} \approx 0.5000$ *Compare this result to the actual value, 0.5.*

Example 2 **Write $4 - 4i$ in exponential form.**

Write the polar form of $4 - 4i$.
Recall that $a + bi = r(\cos \theta + i \sin \theta)$, where $r = \sqrt{a^2 + b^2}$ and $\theta = \text{Arctan} \frac{b}{a}$ when $a > 0$.

$r = \sqrt{4^2 + (-4)^2}$ or $4\sqrt{2}$, and $a = 4$ and $b = -4$

$\theta = \text{Arctan} \frac{-4}{4}$ or $-\frac{\pi}{4}$

$4 - 4i = 4\sqrt{2}\left[\cos\left(-\frac{\pi}{4}\right) + i \sin\left(-\frac{\pi}{4}\right)\right]$

$\qquad = 4\sqrt{2}e^{-i\frac{\pi}{4}}$

Thus, the exponential form of $4 - 4i$ is $4\sqrt{2}e^{-i\frac{\pi}{4}}$.

Example 3 **Evaluate $\ln(-12.4)$.**

$\ln(-12.4) = \ln(-1) + \ln(12.4)$
$\qquad\qquad \approx i\pi + 2.5177$ *Use a calculator to compute ln(12.4).*

Thus, $\ln(-12.4) \approx i\pi + 2.5177$. *The logarithm is a complex number.*

227

12-7

Practice

Special Sequences and Series

Find each value to four decimal places.

1. $\ln(-5)$ **2.** $\ln(-5.7)$ **3.** $\ln(-1000)$

Use the first five terms of the exponential series and a calculator to approximate each value to the nearest hundredth.

4. $e^{0.5}$ **5.** $e^{1.2}$

6. $e^{2.7}$ **7.** $e^{0.9}$

Use the first five terms of the trigonometric series to approximate the value of each function to four decimal places. Then, compare the approximation to the actual value.

8. $\sin \frac{5\pi}{6}$ **9.** $\cos \frac{3\pi}{4}$

Write each complex number in exponential form.

10. $13\left(\cos \frac{\pi}{3} + i \sin \frac{\pi}{3}\right)$ **11.** $5 + 5i$

12. $1 - \sqrt{3}i$ **13.** $-7 + 7\sqrt{3}i$

14. *Savings* Derika deposited \$500 in a savings account with a 4.5% interest rate compounded continuously. (*Hint:* The formula for continuously compounded interest is $A = Pe^{rt}$.)

    a. Approximate Derika's savings account balance after 12 years using the first four terms of the exponential series.

    b. How long will it take for Derika's deposit to double, provided she does not deposit any additional funds into her account?

12-8

Study Guide

Sequences and Iteration

Each output of composing a function with itself is called an *iterate*. To iterate a function $f(x)$, find the function value $f(x_0)$ of the initial value x_0. The second iterate is the value of the function performed on the output, and so on.

The function $f(z) = z^2 + c$, where c and z are complex numbers, is central to the study of **fractal geometry.** This type of geometry can be used to describe things such as coastlines, clouds, and mountain ranges.

Example 1   **Find the first four iterates of the function**
                $f(x) = 4x + 1$ if the initial value is -1.

$x_0 = -1$
$x_1 = 4(-1) + 1$ or -3
$x_2 = 4(-3) + 1$ or -11
$x_3 = 4(-11) + 1$ or -43
$x_4 = 4(-43) + 1$ or -171

The first four iterates are -3, -11, -43, and -171.

Example 2   **Find the first three iterates of the function**
                $f(z) = 3z - i$ if the initial value is $1 + 2i$.

$z_0 = 1 + 2i$
$z_1 = 3(1 + 2i) - i$ or $3 + 5i$
$z_2 = 3(3 + 5i) - i$ or $9 + 14i$
$z_3 = 3(9 + 14i) - i$ or $27 + 41i$

The first three iterates are $3 + 5i$, $9 + 14i$, and $27 + 41i$.

Example 3   **Find the first three iterates of the function**
                $f(z) = z^2 + c$, where $c = 2 - i$ and $z_0 = 1 + i$.

$z_1 = (1 + i)^2 + 2 - i$.
$\quad = 1 + i + i + i^2 + 2 - i$
$\quad = 1 + i + i + (-1) + 2 - i \quad\quad i^2 = -1$
$\quad = 2 + i$

$z_2 = (2 + i)^2 + 2 - i$
$\quad = 4 + 2i + 2i + i^2 + 2 - i$
$\quad = 4 + 2i + 2i + (-1) + 2 - i$
$\quad = 5 + 3i$

$z_3 = (5 + 3i)^2 + 2 - i$
$\quad = 25 + 15i + 15i + 9i^2 + 2 - i$
$\quad = 25 + 15i + 15i + 9(-1) + 2 - i$
$\quad = 18 + 29i$

The first three iterates are $2 + i$, $5 + 3i$, and $18 + 29i$.

12-8

Practice

Sequences and Iteration

Find the first four iterates of each function using the given initial value. If necessary, round your answers to the nearest hundredth.

1. $f(x) = x^2 + 4; x_0 = 1$

2. $f(x) = 3x + 5; x_0 = -1$

3. $f(x) = x^2 - 2; x_0 = -2$

4. $f(x) = x(2.5 - x); x_0 = 3$

Find the first three iterates of the function $f(z) = 2z - (3 + i)$ for each initial value.

5. $z_0 = i$

6. $z_0 = 3 - i$

7. $z_0 = 0.5 + i$

8. $z_0 = -2 - 5i$

Find the first three iterates of the function $f(z) = z^2 + c$ for each given value of c and each initial value.

9. $c = 1 - 2i; z_0 = 0$

10. $c = i; z_0 = i$

11. $c = 1 + i; z_0 = -1$

12. $c = 2 - 3i; z_0 = 1 + i$

13. *Banking*   Mai deposited $1000 in a savings account. The annual yield on the account is 5.2%. Find the balance of Mai's account after each of the first 3 years.

12-9

Study Guide

Mathematical Induction

A method of proof called **mathematical induction** can be used to prove certain conjectures and formulas. The following example demonstrates the steps used in proving a summation formula by mathematical induction.

Example   **Prove that the sum of the first n positive even integers is $n(n + 1)$.**

Here S_n is defined as $2 + 4 + 6 + \cdots + 2n = n(n + 1)$.

1. First, verify that S_n is valid for the first possible case, $n = 1$. Since the first positive even integer is 2 and $1(1 + 1) = 2$, the formula is valid for $n = 1$.

2. Then, assume that S_n is valid for $n = k$.

   $S_k \Rightarrow 2 + 4 + 6 + \cdots + 2k = k(k + 1)$.   *Replace n with k.*

   Next, prove that S_n is also valid for $n = k + 1$.

   $S_{k + 1} \Rightarrow 2 + 4 + 6 + \cdots + 2k + 2(k + 1)$

   $\qquad = k(k + 1) + 2(k + 1)$ *Add 2(k + 1) to both sides.*

   We can simplify the right side by adding $k(k + 1) + 2(k + 1)$.

   $S_{k + 1} \Rightarrow 2 + 4 + 6 + \cdots + 2k + 2(k + 1)$

   $\qquad = (k + 1)(k + 2)$ *(k + 1) is a common factor.*

   If $k + 1$ is substituted into the original formula ($n(n + 1)$), the same result is obtained.

   $(k + 1)[(k + 1) + 1]$ or $(k + 1)(k + 2)$

   Thus, if the formula is valid for $n = k$, it is also valid for $n = k + 1$. Since S_n is valid for $n = 1$, it is also valid for $n = 2$, $n = 3$, and so on. That is, the formula for the sum of the first n positive even integers holds.

12-9

Practice

Mathematical Induction

Use mathematical induction to prove that each proposition is valid for all positive integral values of n.

1. $\frac{1}{3} + \frac{2}{3} + \frac{3}{3} + \cdots + \frac{n}{3} = \frac{n(n+1)}{6}$

2. $5^n + 3$ is divisible by 4.

Answers (Lessons 12-1 and 12-2)

12-1 Practice

Arithmetic Sequences and Series

Find the next four terms in each arithmetic sequence.

1. $-1.1, 0.6, 2.3, \ldots$
   4.0, 5.7, 7.4, 9.1

2. $16, 13, 10, \ldots$
   7, 4, 1, -2

3. $p, p + 2, p + 4, \ldots$
   $p + 6, p + 8, p + 10, p + 12$

For exercises 4–12, assume that each sequence or series is arithmetic.

4. Find the 24th term in the sequence for which $a_1 = -27$ and $d = 3$.
   42

5. Find n for the sequence for which $a_n = 27$, $a_1 = -12$, and $d = 3$.
   14

6. Find d for the sequence for which $a_1 = -12$ and $a_{23} = 32$.
   2

7. What is the first term in the sequence for which $d = -3$ and $a_6 = 5$?
   20

8. What is the first term in the sequence for which $d = -\frac{1}{3}$ and $a_7 = -3$?
   -1

9. Find the 6th term in the sequence $-3 + \sqrt{2}, 0, 3 - \sqrt{2}, \ldots$.
   $12 - 4\sqrt{2}$

10. Find the 45th term in the sequence $-17, -11, -5, \ldots$.
    247

11. Write a sequence that has three arithmetic means between 35 and 45.
    35, 37.5, 40, 42.5, 45

12. Write a sequence that has two arithmetic means between -7 and 2.75.
    $-7, -3.75, -0.5, 2.75$

13. Find the sum of the first 13 terms in the series $-5 + 1 + 7 + \cdots + 67$.
    403

14. Find the sum of the first 62 terms in the series $-23 - 21.5 - 20 - \cdots$.
    1410.5

15. *Auditorium Design* Wakefield Auditorium has 26 rows, and the first row has 22 seats. The number of seats in each row increases by 4 as you move toward the back of the auditorium. What is the seating capacity of this auditorium?
    1872

12-2 Practice

Geometric Sequences and Series

Determine the common ratio and find the next three terms of each geometric sequence.

1. $-1, 2, -4, \ldots$
   $-2; 8, -16, 32$

2. $-4, -3, -\frac{9}{4}, \ldots$
   $\frac{3}{4}; -\frac{27}{16}, -\frac{81}{64}, -\frac{243}{256}$

3. $12, -18, 27, \ldots$
   $-\frac{3}{2}; -\frac{81}{2}, \frac{243}{4}, -\frac{729}{8}$

For exercises 4–9, assume that each sequence or series is geometric.

4. Find the fifth term of the sequence $20, 0.2, 0.002, \ldots$.
   0.0000002

5. Find the ninth term of the sequence $\sqrt{3}, -3, 3\sqrt{3}, \ldots$.
   $81\sqrt{3}$

6. If $r = 2$ and $a_4 = 28$, find the first term of the sequence.
   $\frac{7}{2}$

7. Find the first three terms of the sequence for which $a_4 = 8.4$ and $r = 4$.
   0.13125, 0.525, 2.1

8. Find the first three terms of the sequence for which $a_6 = \frac{1}{32}$ and $r = \frac{1}{2}$.
   $1, \frac{1}{2}, \frac{1}{4}$

9. Write a sequence that has two geometric means between 2 and 0.25.
   2, 1, 0.5, 0.25

10. Write a sequence that has three geometric means between -32 and -2.
    $-32, \pm 16, -8, \pm 4, -2$

11. Find the sum of the first eight terms of the series $\frac{3}{4} + \frac{9}{20} + \frac{27}{100} + \cdots$.
    about 1.84351

12. Find the sum of the first 10 terms of the series $-3 + 12 - 48 + \cdots$.
    629,145

13. *Population Growth* A city of 100,000 people is growing at a rate of 5.2% per year. Assuming this growth rate remains constant, estimate the population of the city 5 years from now.
    about 128,848

12-3

Practice

Infinite Sequence and Series

Find each limit, or state that the limit does not exist and explain your reasoning.

1. $\lim\limits_{n \to \infty} \dfrac{n^2 - 1}{n^2 + 1}$

    1

2. $\lim\limits_{n \to \infty} \dfrac{4n^2 - 5n}{3n^2 + 4}$

    $\dfrac{4}{3}$

3. $\lim\limits_{n \to \infty} \dfrac{5n^2 + 1}{6n}$

    does not exist; dividing by n^2,
    we find $\lim\limits_{n \to \infty} \dfrac{5 + \frac{1}{n^2}}{\frac{6}{n}}$, which

    simplifies to $\dfrac{5 + 0}{6 \cdot 0} = \dfrac{5}{0}$ as n
    approaches infinity. Since this
    fraction is undefined, the
    sequence has no limit.

4. $\lim\limits_{n \to \infty} \dfrac{(n - 1)(3n + 1)}{5n^2}$

    $\dfrac{3}{5}$

5. $\lim\limits_{n \to \infty} \dfrac{3n - (-1)^n}{4n^2}$

    0

6. $\lim\limits_{n \to \infty} \dfrac{n^3 + 1}{n^2}$

    does not exist; $\lim\limits_{n \to \infty} \dfrac{n^3 + 1}{n^2} =$
    $\lim\limits_{n \to \infty} \left(n + \dfrac{1}{n^2}\right)$. $\lim\limits_{n \to \infty} \dfrac{1}{n^2} = 0$, but as n
    approaches infinity, n becomes
    increasingly large, so the
    sequence has no limit.

Write each repeating decimal as a fraction.

7. $0.\overline{75}$

    $\dfrac{25}{33}$

8. $0.\overline{592}$

    $\dfrac{16}{27}$

Find the sum of each infinite series, or state that the sum does not exist and explain your reasoning.

9. $\dfrac{2}{5} + \dfrac{6}{25} + \dfrac{18}{125} + \cdots$

    1

10. $\dfrac{3}{4} + \dfrac{15}{8} + \dfrac{75}{16} + \cdots$

    does not exist; since $r = \dfrac{5}{2}$, $|r| > 1$ and
    the sequence increases without limit.

11. *Physics* A tennis ball is dropped from a height of 55 feet and bounces $\dfrac{3}{5}$ of the distance after each fall.

    a. Find the first seven terms of the infinite series representing the vertical distances traveled by the ball. **55, 33, 33, 19.8, 19.8, 11.88, 11.88**

    b. What is the total vertical distance the ball travels before coming to rest? **220 ft**

12-4

Practice

Convergent and Divergent Series

Use the ratio test to determine whether each series is convergent or divergent.

1. $\dfrac{1}{2} + \dfrac{2^2}{2^2} + \dfrac{3^2}{2^3} + \dfrac{4^2}{2^4} + \cdots$

    convergent

2. $0.006 + 0.06 + 0.6 + \cdots$

    divergent

3. $\dfrac{4}{1 \cdot 2 \cdot 3} + \dfrac{8}{1 \cdot 2 \cdot 3 \cdot 4} + \dfrac{16}{1 \cdot 2 \cdot 3 \cdot 4 \cdot 5} + \cdots$

    convergent

4. $5 + \dfrac{5}{3^3} + \dfrac{5}{5^3} + \dfrac{5}{7^3} + \cdots$

    divergent

Use the comparison test to determine whether each series is convergent or divergent.

5. $2 + \dfrac{2}{2^3} + \dfrac{2}{3^3} + \dfrac{2}{4^3} + \cdots$

    convergent

6. $\dfrac{5}{2} + 1 + \dfrac{5}{8} + \dfrac{5}{11} + \cdots$

    divergent

7. *Ecology* A landfill is leaking a toxic chemical. Six months after the leak was detected, the chemical had spread 1250 meters from the landfill. After one year, the chemical had spread 500 meters more, and by the end of 18 months, it had reached an additional 200 meters.

    a. If this pattern continues, how far will the chemical spread from the landfill after 3 years? **about 2075 m**

    b. Will the chemical ever reach the grounds of a hospital located 2500 meters away from the landfill? Explain.
    No, the sum of the infinite series modeling this situation is about 2083. Thus the chemical will spread no more than about 2083 meters.

12-5 Practice

Sigma Notation and the nth Term

Write each expression in expanded form and then find the sum.

1. $\displaystyle\sum_{n=3}^{5}(n^2 - 2^n)$

$(3^2 - 2^3) + (4^2 - 2^4) + (5^2 - 2^5); -6$

2. $\displaystyle\sum_{q=1}^{4}\frac{2}{q}$

$\frac{2}{1} + \frac{2}{2} + \frac{2}{3} + \frac{2}{4}; \frac{25}{6}$

3. $\displaystyle\sum_{t=1}^{5} t(t-1)$

$1(1-1) + 2(2-1) + 3(3-1) + 4(4-1) + 5(5-1); 40$

4. $\displaystyle\sum_{t=0}^{3}(2t-3)$

$[2(0)-3] + [2(1)-3] + [2(2)-3] + [2(3)-3]; 0$

5. $\displaystyle\sum_{c=2}^{5}(c-2)^2$

$(2-2)^2 + (3-2)^2 + (4-2)^2 + (5-2)^2; 14$

6. $\displaystyle\sum_{i=1}^{\infty}10\left(\frac{1}{2}\right)^i$

$10\left(\frac{1}{2}\right) + 10\left(\frac{1}{2}\right)^2 + 10\left(\frac{1}{2}\right)^3 + \cdots + 10\left(\frac{1}{2}\right)^\infty; 10$

Express each series using sigma notation.

7. $3 + 6 + 9 + 12 + 15$

$\displaystyle\sum_{n=1}^{5} 3n$

8. $6 + 24 + 120 + \cdots + 40,320$

$\displaystyle\sum_{n=3}^{8} n!$

9. $\frac{1}{1} + \frac{1}{4} + \frac{1}{9} + \cdots + \frac{1}{100}$

$\displaystyle\sum_{n=1}^{10}\frac{1}{n^2}$

10. $24 + 19 + 14 + \cdots + (-1)$

$\displaystyle\sum_{n=0}^{5}(24 - 5n)$

11. **Savings** Kathryn started saving quarters in a jar. She began by putting two quarters in the jar the first day and then she increased the number of quarters she put in the jar by one additional quarter each successive day.

a. Use sigma notation to represent the total number of quarters Kathryn had after 30 days. $\displaystyle\sum_{n=1}^{30}(n+1)$

b. Find the sum represented in part a. 495 quarters

12-6 Practice

The Binomial Theorem

Use Pascal's triangle to expand each binomial.

1. $(r+3)^5$

$r^5 + 15r^4 + 90r^3 + 270r^2 + 405r + 243$

2. $(3a - b)^4$

$81a^4 - 108a^3b + 54a^2b^2 - 12ab^3 + b^4$

Use the Binomial Theorem to expand each binomial.

3. $(x-5)^4$

$x^4 - 20x^3 + 150x^2 - 500x + 625$

4. $(3x + 2y)^4$

$81x^4 + 216x^3y + 216x^2y^2 + 96xy^3 + 16y^4$

5. $(a - \sqrt{2})^5$

$a^5 - 5\sqrt{2}a^4 + 20a^3 - 20\sqrt{2}a^2 + 20a - 4\sqrt{2}$

6. $(2p - 3q)^6$

$64p^6 - 576p^5q + 2160p^4q^2 - 4320p^3q^3 + 4860p^2q^4 - 2916pq^5 + 729q^6$

Find the designated term of each binomial expansion.

7. 4th term of $(2n - 3m)^4$

$-216nm^3$

8. 5th term of $(4a + 2b)^8$

$286,720a^4b^4$

9. 6th term of $(3p + q)^9$

$10,206p^4q^5$

10. 3rd term of $(a - 2\sqrt{3})^6$

$180a^4$

11. A varsity volleyball team needs nine members. Of these nine members, at least five must be seniors. How many of the possible groups of juniors and seniors have at least five seniors? 256

Answers (Lessons 12-7 and 12-8)

12-7 Practice

Special Sequences and Series

Find each value to four decimal places.

1. $\ln(-5)$
$i\pi + 1.6094$

2. $\ln(-5.7)$
$i\pi + 1.7405$

3. $\ln(-1000)$
$i\pi + 6.9078$

Use the first five terms of the exponential series and a calculator to approximate each value to the nearest hundredth.

4. $e^{0.5}$
1.65

5. $e^{1.2}$
3.29

6. $e^{2.7}$
12.84

7. $e^{0.9}$
2.45

Use the first five terms of the trigonometric series to approximate the value of each function to four decimal places. Then, compare the approximation to the actual value.

8. $\sin \frac{5\pi}{6}$
0.5009; 0.5

9. $\cos \frac{3\pi}{4}$
$-0.7057; -0.7071$

Write each complex number in exponential form.

10. $13\left(\cos \frac{\pi}{3} + i \sin \frac{\pi}{3}\right)$
$13e^{i\frac{\pi}{3}}$

11. $5 + 5i$
$5\sqrt{2}e^{i\frac{\pi}{4}}$

12. $1 - \sqrt{3}i$
$2e^{i\frac{5\pi}{3}}$

13. $-7 + 7\sqrt{3}i$
$14e^{i\frac{2\pi}{3}}$

14. **Savings** Derika deposited $500 in a savings account with a 4.5% interest rate compounded continuously. (*Hint:* The formula for continuously compounded interest is $A = Pe^{rt}$.)

a. Approximate Derika's savings account balance after 12 years using the first four terms of the exponential series.
approximately $856.02

b. How long will it take for Derika's deposit to double, provided she does not deposit any additional funds into her account?
about 15.4 years

12-8 Practice

Sequences and Iteration

Find the first four iterates of each function using the given initial value. If necessary, round your answers to the nearest hundredth.

1. $f(x) = x^2 + 4; x_0 = 1$
5, 29, 845, 714,029

2. $f(x) = 3x + 5; x_0 = -1$
2, 11, 38, 119

3. $f(x) = x^2 - 2; x_0 = -2$
2, 2, 2, 2

4. $f(x) = x(2.5 - x); x_0 = 3$
$-1.5, -6, -51, -2728.5$

Find the first three iterates of the function $f(z) = 2z - (3 + i)$ for each initial value.

5. $z_0 = i$
$-3 + i$
$-9 + i$
$-21 + i$

6. $z_0 = 3 - i$
$3 - 3i$
$3 - 7i$
$3 - 15i$

7. $z_0 = 0.5 + i$
$-2 + i$
$-7 + i$
$-17 + i$

8. $z_0 = -2 - 5i$
$-7 - 11i$
$-17 - 23i$
$-37 - 47i$

Find the first three iterates of the function $f(z) = z^2 + c$ for each given value of c and each initial value.

9. $c = 1 - 2i; z_0 = 0$
$1 - 2i$
$-2 - 6i$
$-31 + 22i$

10. $c = i; z_0 = i$
$-1 + i$
$-i$
$-1 + i$

11. $c = 1 + i; z_0 = -1$
$2 + i$
$4 + 5i$
$-8 + 41i$

12. $c = 2 - 3i; z_0 = 1 + i$
$2 - i$
$5 - 7i$
$-22 - 73i$

13. **Banking** Mai deposited $1000 in a savings account. The annual yield on the account is 5.2%. Find the balance of Mai's account after each of the first 3 years.
$1052.00, $1106.70, $1164.25

12-9 Practice

Mathematical Induction

Use mathematical induction to prove that each proposition is valid for all positive integral values of n.

1. $\frac{1}{3} + \frac{2}{3} + \frac{3}{3} + \cdots + \frac{n}{3} = \frac{n(n+1)}{6}$

Step 1: Verify that the formula is valid for $n = 1$. Since $\frac{1}{3}$ is the first term in the sentence and $\frac{1(1+1)}{6} = \frac{1}{3}$, the formula is valid for $n = 1$.

Step 2: Assume that the formula is valid for $n = k$ and then prove that it is also valid for $n = k + 1$.

$S_k \Rightarrow \frac{1}{3} + \frac{2}{3} + \frac{3}{3} + \cdots + \frac{k}{3} = \frac{k(k+1)}{6}$

$S_{k+1} \Rightarrow \frac{1}{3} + \frac{2}{3} + \frac{3}{3} + \cdots + \frac{k}{3} + \frac{k+1}{3} = \frac{k(k+1)}{6} + \frac{k+1}{3}$

$= \frac{k(k+1) + 2(k+1)}{6}$

$= \frac{(k+1)(k+2)}{6}$

Apply the original formula for $n = k + 1$.

$\frac{k+1(k+1+1)}{6}$ or $\frac{(k+1)(k+2)}{6}$

Thus, if the formula is valid for $n = k$, it is also valid for $n = k + 1$. Since the formula is valid for $n = 1$, it is also valid for $n = 2, n = 3$, and so on. That is, the formula is valid for all positive integral values of n.

2. $5^n + 3$ is divisible by 4.

Step 1: Verify that S_n is valid for $n = 1$.

$S_1 \Rightarrow 5^1 + 3 = 8$. Since 8 is divisible by 4, S_n is valid for $n = 1$.

Step 2: Assume that S_n is valid for $n = k$ and then prove that it is valid for $n = k + 1$.

$S_k \Rightarrow 5^k + 3 = 4r$ for some integer r

$S_{k+1} \Rightarrow 5^{k+1} + 3 = 4t$ for some integer t

$5^k + 3 = 4r$

$5(5^k + 3) = 5(4r)$

$5^{k+1} + 15 = 20r$

$5^{k+1} + 3 = 20r - 12$

$5^{k+1} + 3 = 4(5r - 3)$

Let $t = 5r - 3$, an integer. Then $5^{k+1} + 3 = 4t$.

Thus, if S_k is valid, then S_{k+1} is also valid. Since S_n is valid for $n = 1$, it is also valid for $n = 2, n = 3$, and so on. Hence, $5^n + 3$ is divisible by 4 for all positive integral values of n.

13-1

Study Guide

Permutations and Combinations

Use the **Basic Counting Principle** to determine different possibilities for the arrangement of objects. The arrangement of objects in a certain order is called a **permutation**. A **combination** is an arrangement in which order is *not* a consideration.

Example 1 **Eight students on a student council are assigned 8 seats around a U-shaped table.**

　　　a. **How many different ways can the students be assigned seats at the table?**

　　　Since order is important, this situation is a permutation. The eight students are taken all at once, so the situation can be represented as $P(8, 8)$.

$$P(8, 8) = 8! \qquad\qquad P(n, n) = n!$$
$$= 8 \cdot 7 \cdot 6 \cdot 5 \cdot 4 \cdot 3 \cdot 2 \cdot 1 \text{ or } 40,320$$

　　　There are 40,320 ways the students can be seated.

　　　b. **How many ways can a president and a vice-president be elected from the eight students?**

　　　This is a permutation of 8 students being chosen 2 at a time.

$$P(8, 2) = \frac{8!}{(8-2)!} \qquad P(n, r) = \frac{n!}{(n-r)!}$$
$$= \frac{8 \cdot 7 \cdot 6!}{6!} \text{ or } 56$$

　　　There are 56 ways a president and vice-president can be chosen.

Example 2 **The Outdoor Environmental Club consists of 20 members, of which 9 are male and 11 are female. Seven members will be selected to form an event-planning committee. How many committees of 4 females and 3 males can be formed?**

Order is not important. There are three questions to consider.

How many ways can 3 males be chosen from 9?
How many ways can 4 females be chosen from 11?
How many ways can 3 males and 4 females be chosen together?

The answer is the product of the combinations $C(9, 3)$ and $C(11, 4)$.

$$C(9, 3) \cdot C(11, 4) = \frac{9!}{(9-3)!3!} \cdot \frac{11!}{(11-4)!4!} \qquad C(n, r) = \frac{n!}{(n-r)!r!}$$
$$= \frac{9!}{6!3!} \cdot \frac{11!}{7!4!}$$
$$= 84 \cdot 330 \text{ or } 27,720$$

There are 27,720 possible committees.

13-1

Practice

Permutations and Combinations

1. A golf manufacturer makes irons with 7 different shaft lengths, 3 different grips, and 2 different club head materials. How many different combinations are offered?

2. A briefcase lock has 3 rotating cylinders, each containing 10 digits. How many numerical codes are possible?

3. How many 7-digit telephone numbers can be formed if the first digit cannot be 0 or 1?

Find each value.

4. $P(10, 7)$

5. $P(7, 7)$

6. $P(6, 3)$

7. $C(7, 2)$

8. $C(10, 4)$

9. $C(12, 4) \cdot C(8, 3)$

10. How many ways can the 4 call letters of a radio station be arranged if the first letter must be W or K and no letters can be repeated?

11. There are 5 different routes that a commuter can take from her home to her office. How many ways can she make a roundtrip if she uses different routes for coming and going?

12. How many committees of 5 students can be selected from a class of 25?

13. A box contains 12 black and 8 green marbles. How many ways can 3 black and 2 green marbles be chosen?

14. *Basketball* How many ways can a coach select a starting team of one center, two forwards, and two guards if the basketball team consists of three centers, five forwards, and three guards?

13-2

Study Guide

Permutations with Repetitions and Circular Permutations

For permutations involving repetitions, the number of permutations of n objects of which p are alike and q are alike is $\frac{n!}{p!q!}$. When n objects are arranged in a circle, there are $\frac{n!}{n}$, or $(n-1)!$, permutations of the objects around the circle. If n objects are arranged relative to a fixed point, then there are $n!$ permutations.

Example 1 **How many 10-letter patterns can be formed from the letters of the word *basketball*?**

The ten letters can be arranged in $P(10, 10)$, or $10!$, ways. However, some of these 3,628,800 ways have the same appearance because some of the letters appear more than once.

$\frac{10!}{2!2!2!}$ *There are 2 a's, 2 b's, and 2 l's in basketball.*

$\frac{10!}{2!2!2!} = \frac{10 \cdot 9 \cdot 8 \cdot 7 \cdot 6 \cdot 5 \cdot 4 \cdot 3 \cdot 2 \cdot 1}{2 \cdot 1 \cdot 2 \cdot 1 \cdot 2 \cdot 1}$

$= 453,600$

There are 453,600 ten-letter patterns that can be formed from the letters of the word *basketball*.

Example 2 **Six people are seated at a round table to play a game of cards.**
a. Is the seating arrangement around the table a linear or circular permutation? Explain.
b. How many possible seating arrangements are there?

a. The arrangement of people is a circular permutation since the people form a circle around the table.

b. There are 6 people, so the number of arrangements can be described by $(6-1)!$.

$(6-1)! = 5!$
$= 5 \cdot 4 \cdot 3 \cdot 2 \cdot 1$ or 120

There are 120 possible seating arrangements.

13-2

Practice

Permutations with Repetitions and Circular Permutations

How many different ways can the letters of each word be arranged?

1. *members*

2. *annually*

3. *Missouri*

4. *concert*

5. How many different 5-digit street addresses can have the digits 4, 7, 3, 4, and 8?

6. Three hardcover books and 5 paperbacks are placed on a shelf. How many ways can the books be arranged if all the hardcover books must be together and all the paperbacks must be together?

Determine whether each arrangement of objects is a linear or circular permutation. Then determine the number of arrangements for each situation.

7. 9 keys on a key ring with no chain

8. 5 charms on a bracelet with no clasp

9. 6 people seated at a round table with one person seated next to a door

10. 12 different symbols around the face of a watch

11. **Entertainment**   Jasper is playing a word game and has the following letters in his tray: QUOUNNTAGGRA. How many 12-letter arrangements could Jasper make to check if a single word could be formed from all the letters?

13-3

Study Guide

Probability and Odds

The **probability** of an event is the ratio of the number of ways an event can happen to the total number of ways an event can and cannot happen.

Example   **A bag contains 3 black, 5 green, and 4 yellow marbles.**

a. What is the probability that a marble selected at random will be green?

The probability of selecting a green marble is written P(green). There are 5 ways to select a green marble from the bag and $3 + 4$, or 7, ways not to select a green marble. So, success $(s) = 5$ and failure $(f) = 7$. Use the probability formula.

$$P(\text{green}) = \frac{5}{5+7} \text{ or } \frac{5}{12} \qquad P(s) = \frac{s}{s+f}$$

The probability of selecting a green marble is $\frac{5}{12}$.

b. What is the probability that a marble selected at random will *not* be yellow?

There are 8 ways not to select a yellow marble and 4 ways to select a yellow marble.

$$P(\text{not yellow}) = \frac{8}{4+8} \text{ or } \frac{2}{3} \qquad P(f) = \frac{f}{s+f}$$

The probability of not selecting a yellow marble is $\frac{2}{3}$.

c. What is the probability that 2 marbles selected at random will both be black?

Use counting methods to determine the probability. There are $C(3, 2)$ ways to select 2 black marbles out of 3, and $C(12, 2)$ ways to select 2 marbles out of 12.

$$P(\text{2 black marbles}) = \frac{C(3, 2)}{C(12, 2)}$$

$$= \frac{\frac{3!}{1!2!}}{\frac{12!}{10!2!}} \text{ or } \frac{1}{22}$$

The probability of selecting 2 black marbles is $\frac{1}{22}$.

13-3 Practice

Probability and Odds

**A kitchen drawer contains 7 forks, 4 spoons, and 5 knives.
Three are selected at random. Find each probability.**

1. P(3 forks)

2. P(2 forks, 1 knife)

3. P(3 spoons)

4. P(1 fork, 1 knife, 1 spoon)

**A laundry bag contains 5 red, 9 blue, and 6 white socks.
Two socks are selected at random. Find each probability.**

5. P(2 red)

6. P(2 blue)

7. P(1 red, 1 blue)

8. P(1 red, 1 white)

**Sharon has 8 mystery books and 9 science-fiction books. Four are
selected at random. Find each probability.**

9. P(4 mystery books)

10. P(4 science-fiction books)

11. P(2 mysteries, 2 science-fiction)

12. P(3 mysteries, 1 science-fiction)

**From a standard deck of 52 cards, 5 cards are drawn. What are
the odds of each event occurring?**

13. 5 aces

14. 5 face cards

15. **Meteorology**   A local weather forecast states that the chance of sunny
weather on Wednesday is 70%. What are the odds that it will be sunny
on Wednesday?

13-4

Study Guide

Probabilities of Compound Events

Example 1 **Using a standard deck of playing cards, find the probability of drawing a king, replacing it, then drawing a second king.**

Since the first card is returned to the deck, the outcome of the second draw is not affected by the first. The events are independent. The probability is the product of each individual probability.

$P(A \text{ and } B) = P(A) \cdot P(B)$ *Let A represent the first draw and B the second draw.*

$P(A) = P(B) = \frac{4}{52} = \frac{1}{13}$ $\dfrac{4 \text{ kings}}{52 \text{ cards in a standard deck}}$

$P(A \text{ and } B) = \frac{1}{13} \cdot \frac{1}{13} \cdot = \frac{1}{169}$

The probability of selecting a king, replacing it, and then selecting another king is $\frac{1}{169}$.

Example 2 **What is the probability of selecting a yellow or a blue marble from a box of 5 green, 3 yellow, and 2 blue marbles?**

A yellow marble and a blue marble cannot be selected at the same time. Thus, the events are mutually exclusive. Find the sum of the individual probabilities.

$P(\text{yellow or blue}) = P(\text{yellow}) + P(\text{blue})$

$\qquad\qquad = \frac{3}{10} + \frac{2}{10}$ $P(yellow) = \frac{3}{10};\ P(blue) = \frac{2}{10}$

$\qquad\qquad = \frac{5}{10} \text{ or } \frac{1}{2}$

Example 3 **What is the probability that a card drawn from a standard deck is either a face card or black?**

The card drawn could be both a face card and black, so the events are mutually inclusive.

$P(\text{face card}) = \frac{12}{52}$

$P(\text{black}) = \frac{26}{52}$

$P(\text{face card and black}) = \frac{6}{52}$

$P(\text{face card or black}) = \frac{12}{52} + \frac{26}{52} - \frac{6}{52} = \frac{32}{52} \text{ or } \frac{8}{13}$

13-4

Practice

Probabilities of Compound Events

Determine if each event is independent or dependent. Then determine the probability.

1. the probability of drawing a black card from a standard deck of cards, replacing it, then drawing another black card

2. the probability of selecting 1 jazz, 1 country, and 1 rap CD in any order from 3 jazz, 2 country, and 5 rap CDs, replacing the CDs each time

3. the probability that two cards drawn from a deck are both aces

Determine if each event is mutually exclusive or mutually inclusive. Then determine each probability.

4. the probability of rolling a 3 or a 6 on one toss of a number cube

5. the probability of selecting a queen or a red card from a standard deck of cards

6. the probability of selecting at least three white crayons when four crayons are selected from a box containing 7 white crayons and 5 blue crayons

7. **Team Sports** Conrad tried out for both the volleyball team and the football team. The probability of his being selected for the volleyball team is $\frac{4}{5}$, while the probability of his being selected for the football team is $\frac{3}{4}$. The probability of his being selected for both teams is $\frac{7}{10}$. What is the probability that Conrad will be selected for either the volleyball team or the football team?

13-5

Study Guide

Conditional Probabilities

The **conditional probability** of event A, given event B, is defined as $P(A \mid B) = \frac{P(A \text{ and } B)}{P(B)}$ where $P(B) \neq 0$. In some situations, event A is a subset of event B. In these situations, $P(A \mid B) = \frac{P(A)}{P(B)}$.

Example   **A box contains 3 red pencils and 4 yellow pencils. Three pencils are selected at random. What is the probability that exactly two red pencils are selected if the second pencil is red?**

Sample spaces and reduced sample spaces can be used to help determine the outcomes that satisfy a given condition.

The sample space is $S = \{RRR, RRY, RYR, RYY,$ $YRR, YRY, YYR, YYY\}$ and includes all of the possible outcomes of selecting 3 pencils out of a box of 3 red and 4 yellow pencils.

Event B represents the condition that the second pencil is red.
$B = \{RRR, RRY, YRR, YRY\}$

$P(B) = \frac{4}{8}$ or $\frac{1}{2}$

Event A represents the condition that exactly two of the pencils are red.

$A = \{RRY, RYR, YRR\}$

$P(A) = \frac{3}{8}$

$(A \text{ and } B)$ is the intersection of A and B.
$(A \text{ and } B) = \{RRY, YRR\}$.

So, $P(A \text{ and } B) = \frac{2}{8}$ or $\frac{1}{4}$.

$P(A \mid B) = \frac{P(A \text{ and } B)}{P(B)}$

$\qquad = \frac{\frac{1}{4}}{\frac{1}{2}}$ or $\frac{1}{2}$

The probability that exactly two pencils are red given that the second pencil is red is $\frac{1}{2}$.

13-5

Practice

Conditional Probabilities

Find each probability.

1. Two number cubes are tossed. Find the probability that the numbers showing on the cubes match, given that their sum is greater than 7.

2. A four-digit number is formed from the digits 1, 2, 3, and 4. Find the probability that the number ends in the digits 41, given that the number is odd.

3. Three coins are tossed. Find the probability that exactly two coins show tails, given that the third coin shows tails.

A card is chosen from a standard deck of cards. Find each probability, given that the card is red.

4. P(diamond)

5. P(six of hearts)

6. P(queen or 10)

7. P(face card)

A survey taken at Stirers High School shows that 48% of the respondents like soccer, 66% like basketball, and 38% like hockey. Also, 30% like soccer and basketball, 22% like basketball and hockey, and 28% like soccer and hockey. Finally, 12% like all three sports.

8. If Meg likes basketball, what is the probability that she also likes soccer?

9. If Jaime likes soccer, what is the probability that he also likes hockey and basketball?

10. If Ashley likes basketball, what is the probability that she also likes hockey?

11. If Brett likes soccer, what is the probability that he also likes basketball?

13-6

Study Guide

The Binomial Theorem and Probability

Problems that meet the conditions of a **binomial experiment** can be solved using the binomial expansion. Use the Binomial Theorem to find the probability when the number of trials makes working with the binomial expansion unrealistic.

Example 1 **The probability that Misha will win a word game is $\frac{3}{4}$. If Misha plays the game 5 times, what is the probability that he will win exactly 3 games?**

There are 5 games and each game has only two possible outcomes, win W or lose L. These events are independent and the probability is $\frac{3}{4}$ for each game. So this is a binomial experiment.

When $(W + L)^5$ is expanded, the term W^3L^2 represents 3 wins and 2 losses. The coefficient of W^3L^2 is $C(5, 3)$, or 10.

$$P(\text{exactly 3 wins}) = 10\left(\frac{3}{4}\right)^3\left(\frac{1}{4}\right)^2 \quad W = \frac{3}{4}, L = \frac{1}{4}$$

$$= 10\left(\frac{27}{64}\right)\left(\frac{1}{16}\right)$$

$$= \frac{270}{1024}$$

$$= \frac{135}{512} \text{ or about } 26.4\%$$

Example 2 **The probability that a computer salesperson will make a sale when approaching a customer is $\frac{1}{2}$. If the salesperson approaches 12 customers, what is the probability that 8 sales will be made?**

Let S be the probability of a sale.
Let N be the probability of not making a sale.

$$(S + N)^{12} = \sum_{r=0}^{12} \frac{12!}{r!(12 - r)!} P_S^{12-r} P_N^{r}$$

Making 8 sales means that 4 sales will not be made. So the probability can be found using the term where $r = 4$.

$$\frac{12!}{4!(12 - 4)!}S^8N^4 = 495S^8N^4$$

$$= 495\left(\frac{1}{2}\right)^8\left(\frac{1}{2}\right)^4 \quad S = \frac{1}{2}, N = \frac{1}{2}$$

$$= \frac{495}{4096} \text{ or } 0.120849609$$

The probability of making exactly 8 sales is about 12.1%.

13-6

Practice

The Binomial Theorem and Probability

Find each probability if six coins are tossed.

1. P(3 heads and 3 tails)

2. P(at least 4 heads)

3. P(2 heads or 3 tails)

4. P(all heads or all tails)

The probability of Chris's making a free throw is $\frac{2}{3}$. Find each probability if she shoots five times.

5. P(all missed)

6. P(all made)

7. P(exactly 4 made)

8. P(at least 3 made)

When Maria and Len play a certain board game, the probability that Maria will win the game is $\frac{3}{4}$. Find each probability if they play five games.

9. P(Len wins only 1 game)

10. P(Maria wins exactly 2 games)

11. P(Len wins at least 2 games)

12. P(Maria wins at least 3 games)

13. *Gardening*   Assume that 60% of marigold seeds that are sown directly in the ground produce plants. If Tomaso plants 10 seeds, what is the probability that 7 plants will be produced?

13-1

Practice

Permutations and Combinations

1. A golf manufacturer makes irons with 7 different shaft lengths, 3 different grips, and 2 different club head materials. How many different combinations are offered? **42**

2. A briefcase lock has 3 rotating cylinders, each containing 10 digits. How many numerical codes are possible? **1000**

3. How many 7-digit telephone numbers can be formed if the first digit cannot be 0 or 1? **8,000,000**

Find each value.

4. $P(10, 7)$
604,800

5. $P(7, 7)$
5040

6. $P(6, 3)$
120

7. $C(7, 2)$
21

8. $C(10, 4)$
210

9. $C(12, 4) \cdot C(8, 3)$
27,720

10. How many ways can the 4 call letters of a radio station be arranged if the first letter must be W or K and no letters can be repeated? **27,600**

11. There are 5 different routes that a commuter can take from her home to her office. How many ways can she make a roundtrip if she uses different routes for coming and going? **20**

12. How many committees of 5 students can be selected from a class of 25? **53,130**

13. A box contains 12 black and 8 green marbles. How many ways can 3 black and 2 green marbles be chosen? **6160**

14. *Basketball* How many ways can a coach select a starting team of one center, two forwards, and two guards if the basketball team consists of three centers, five forwards, and three guards? **90**

13-2

Practice

Permutations with Repetitions and Circular Permutations

How many different ways can the letters of each word be arranged?

1. *members*
1260

2. *annually*
5040

3. *Missouri*
10,080

4. *concert*
2520

5. How many different 5-digit street addresses can have the digits 4, 7, 3, 4, and 8?
60

6. Three hardcover books and 5 paperbacks are placed on a shelf. How many ways can the books be arranged if all the hardcover books must be together and all the paperbacks must be together?
56

Determine whether each arrangement of objects is a linear or circular permutation. Then determine the number of arrangements for each situation.

7. 9 keys on a key ring with no chain **circular; 40,320**

8. 5 charms on a bracelet with no clasp **circular; 24**

9. 6 people seated at a round table with one person seated next to a door **linear; 720**

10. 12 different symbols around the face of a watch **circular; 39,916,800**

11. *Entertainment* Jasper is playing a word game and has the following letters in his tray: QUOUNNTAGGRA. How many 12-letter arrangements could Jasper make to check if a single word could be formed from all the letters?
29,937,600

Answers (Lessons 13-3 and 13-4)

13-3 Practice

Probability and Odds

A kitchen drawer contains 7 forks, 4 spoons, and 5 knives. Three are selected at random. Find each probability.

1. P(3 forks)
$\frac{1}{16}$

2. P(2 forks, 1 knife)
$\frac{3}{16}$

3. P(3 spoons)
$\frac{1}{140}$

4. P(1 fork, 1 knife, 1 spoon)
$\frac{1}{4}$

A laundry bag contains 5 red, 9 blue, and 6 white socks. Two socks are selected at random. Find each probability.

5. P(2 red)
$\frac{1}{19}$

6. P(2 blue)
$\frac{18}{95}$

7. P(1 red, 1 blue)
$\frac{9}{38}$

8. P(1 red, 1 white)
$\frac{3}{19}$

Sharon has 8 mystery books and 9 science-fiction books. Four are selected at random. Find each probability.

9. P(4 mystery books)
$\frac{1}{34}$

10. P(4 science-fiction books)
$\frac{9}{170}$

11. P(2 mysteries, 2 science-fiction)
$\frac{36}{85}$

12. P(3 mysteries, 1 science-fiction)
$\frac{18}{85}$

From a standard deck of 52 cards, 5 cards are drawn. What are the odds of each event occurring?

13. 5 aces
0

14. 5 face cards
$\frac{33}{108,257}$

15. *Meteorology* A local weather forecast states that the chance of sunny weather on Wednesday is 70%. What are the odds that it will be sunny on Wednesday? $\frac{7}{3}$ or 7 to 3

13-4 Practice

Probabilities of Compound Events

Determine if each event is independent or dependent. Then determine the probability.

1. the probability of drawing a black card from a standard deck of cards, replacing it, then drawing another black card
independent; $\frac{1}{4}$

2. the probability of selecting 1 jazz, 1 country, and 1 rap CD in any order from 3 jazz, 2 country, and 5 rap CDs, replacing the CDs each time
independent; $\frac{3}{100}$

3. the probability that two cards drawn from a deck are both aces
dependent; $\frac{1}{221}$

Determine if each event is mutually exclusive or mutually inclusive. Then determine each probability.

4. the probability of rolling a 3 or a 6 on one toss of a number cube
mutually exclusive; $\frac{1}{3}$

5. the probability of selecting a queen or a red card from a standard deck of cards
mutually inclusive; $\frac{7}{13}$

6. the probability of selecting at least three white crayons when four crayons are selected from a box containing 7 white crayons and 5 blue crayons
mutually exclusive; $\frac{14}{33}$

7. *Team Sports* Conrad tried out for both the volleyball team and the football team. The probability of his being selected for the volleyball team is $\frac{4}{5}$, while the probability of his being selected for the football team is $\frac{3}{4}$. The probability of his being selected for both teams is $\frac{7}{10}$. What is the probability that Conrad will be selected for either the volleyball team or the football team? $\frac{17}{20}$

NAME _____ DATE _____ PERIOD _____

13-5 Practice

Conditional Probabilities

Find each probability.

1. Two number cubes are tossed. Find the probability that the numbers showing on the cubes match, given that their sum is greater than 7. $\frac{1}{5}$

2. A four-digit number is formed from the digits 1, 2, 3, and 4. Find the probability that the number ends in the digits 41, given that the number is odd. $\frac{1}{6}$

3. Three coins are tossed. Find the probability that exactly two coins show tails, given that the third coin shows tails. $\frac{1}{2}$

A card is chosen from a standard deck of cards. Find each probability, given that the card is red.

4. P(diamond) $\frac{1}{2}$

5. P(six of hearts) $\frac{1}{26}$

6. P(queen or 10) $\frac{2}{13}$

7. P(face card) $\frac{3}{13}$

A survey taken at Stirers High School shows that 48% of the respondents like soccer, 66% like basketball, and 38% like hockey. Also, 30% like soccer and basketball, 22% like basketball and hockey, and 28% like soccer and hockey. Finally, 12% like all three sports.

8. If Meg likes basketball, what is the probability that she also likes soccer? $\frac{5}{11}$

9. If Jaime likes soccer, what is the probability that he also likes hockey and basketball? $\frac{1}{4}$

10. If Ashley likes basketball, what is the probability that she also likes hockey? $\frac{1}{3}$

11. If Brett likes soccer, what is the probability that he also likes basketball? $\frac{5}{8}$

NAME _____ DATE _____ PERIOD _____

13-6 Practice

The Binomial Theorem and Probability

Find each probability if six coins are tossed.

1. P(3 heads and 3 tails) $\frac{5}{16}$

2. P(at least 4 heads) $\frac{11}{32}$

3. P(2 heads or 3 tails) $\frac{35}{64}$

4. P(all heads or all tails) $\frac{1}{32}$

The probability of Chris's making a free throw is $\frac{2}{3}$. Find each probability if she shoots five times.

5. P(all missed) $\frac{1}{243}$

6. P(all made) $\frac{32}{243}$

7. P(exactly 4 made) $\frac{80}{243}$

8. P(at least 3 made) $\frac{64}{81}$

When Maria and Len play a certain board game, the probability that Maria will win the game is $\frac{3}{4}$. Find each probability if they play five games.

9. P(Len wins only 1 game) $\frac{405}{1024}$

10. P(Maria wins exactly 2 games) $\frac{45}{512}$

11. P(Len wins at least 2 games) $\frac{47}{128}$

12. P(Maria wins at least 3 games) $\frac{459}{512}$

13. *Gardening* Assume that 60% of marigold seeds that are sown directly in the ground produce plants. If Tomaso plants 10 seeds, what is the probability that 7 plants will be produced? **about 21.5%**

14-1

Study Guide

The Frequency Distribution

A **frequency distribution** is a convenient system for organizing large amounts of data. A number of classes are determined, and all values in a class are tallied and grouped together. The most common way of displaying frequency distributions is by using a type of bar graph called a **histogram**.

Example   **The number of passengers who boarded planes at 36 airports in the United States in one year are shown below.**

30,526	30,372	26,623	22,722	16,287	15,246	14,807	14,117	14,054
13,547	12,916	12,616	11,906	11,622	11,489	10,828	10,653	10,008
9703	9594	9463	9348	9125	8572	7300	6772	6549
6126	5907	5712	5287	4848	4832	4820	4750	4684

Source: U.S. Department of Transportation

a. Find the range of the data.
The range of the data is $30,526 - 4684$ or 25,842.

b. Determine an appropriate class interval.
An appropriate class interval is 4500 passengers, beginning with 4500 and ending with 31,500. There will be six classes.

c. Name the class limits and the class marks.
The class limits are the upper and lower values in each interval, or 4500, 9000, 13,500, 18,000, 22,500, 27,000, and 31,500. The class marks are the averages of the class limits of each interval, or 6750, 11,250, 15,750, 20,250, 24,750, and 29,250.

d. Construct a frequency distribution of the data.
Use tallies to determine the number of passengers in each interval.

Number of Passengers	Tallies	Frequency
4500-9000	ⅢⅢ Ⅲ	13
9000-13,500	ⅢⅢ Ⅲ	13
13,500-18,000	Ⅲ Ⅰ	6
18,000-22,500		0
22,500-27,000	‖	2
27,000-31,500	‖	2

e. Draw a histogram of the data.
Label the horizontal axis with the class limits. The vertical axis should be labeled from 0 to a value that will allow for the greatest frequency. Draw the bars side by side so that the height of each bar corresponds to its interval's frequency.

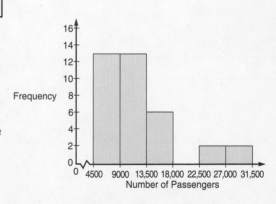

14-1

Practice

The Frequency Distribution

Determine which class intervals would be appropriate for the data below. Explain your answers.

1. 25, 32, 18, 99, 43, 16, 29, 35, 36, 34, 21, 33, 26, 26, 17, 40, 22, 38, 16, 19

   a. 1
   b. 10
   c. 2

2. 111, 115, 130, 200, 234, 98, 115, 72 305, 145, 87, 63, 245, 285, 256, 302

   a. 25
   b. 10
   c. 30

3. *Meteorology*   The average wind speeds recorded at various weather stations in the United States are listed below.

Station	Speed (mph)	Station	Speed (mph)	Station	Speed (mph)
Albuquerque	8.9	Anchorage	7.1	Atlanta	9.1
Baltimore	9.1	Boston	12.5	Chicago	10.4
Dallas-Ft. Worth	10.8	Honolulu	11.3	Indianapolis	9.6
Kansas City	10.7	Las Vegas	9.3	Little Rock	7.8
Los Angeles	6.2	Memphis	8.8	Miami	9.2
Minneapolis– St. Paul	10.5	New Orleans	8.1	New York City	9.4
Philadelphia	9.5	Phoenix	6.2	Seattle	9.0

Source: *National Climatic Data Center*

a. Find the range of the data.

b. Determine an appropriate class interval.

c. What are the class limits and the class marks?

d. Construct a frequency distribution of the data.

e. Draw a histogram of the data.

14-2

Study Guide

Measures of Central Tendency

The **mean** is found by adding the values in a set of data and dividing the sum by the number of values in that set. In other words, if a set of data has n values given by X_i such that i is an integer and $1 \le i \le n$, then the arithmetic mean $\overline{X}$ can be found as follows.

$$\overline{X} = \frac{1}{n}\sum_{i=1}^{n} X_i$$

The **median** of a set of data is the middle value. If there are two middle values, the median is the mean of the two middle values. The **mode** of a set of data is the most frequent value. Some sets have multiple modes, and others have no mode.

Example 1 **Find the mean of the set {13, 18, 21, 14, 16, 19, 25, 17}.**

$$\overline{X} = \frac{\text{sum of the values in the set of data}}{\text{number of values in the set}}$$

$$\overline{X} = \frac{13 + 18 + 21 + 14 + 16 + 19 + 25 + 17}{8}$$

$$\overline{X} = \frac{143}{8} \text{ or } 17.875$$

The mean of the set of data is 17.875.

Example 2 **The table at the right shows the number of households without a telephone in 1990.**

a. Find the mean of the data.
Since there are 11 states listed in the table, $n = 11$.

$$\frac{1}{11}\sum_{i=1}^{11} X_i = \frac{1}{11}(131{,}600 + 313{,}100 + 270{,}200 +$$
$$195{,}700 + 36{,}500 + 140{,}900 +$$
$$40{,}400 + 25{,}100 + 67{,}500 +$$
$$106{,}400 + 70{,}800)$$

The mean is about 127,109.

State	Number of Households
Alaska	131,600
California	313,100
Florida	270,200
Georgia	195,700
Iowa	36,500
Kentucky	140,900
Minnesota	40,400
Nevada	25,100
New Mexico	67,500
Oklahoma	106,400
West Virginia	70,800

Source: U.S. Census Bureau

b. Find the median of the data.
To find the median, order the data. Since all the numbers are multiples of 100, you can order the set by hundreds.

251 365 404 675 708 1064 1316 1409 1957 2702 3131

Since there are an odd number of values, the median is the middle value, or 106,400.

c. Find the mode of the data.
Since all elements in the set of data have the same frequency, there is no mode.

14-2

Practice

Measures of Central Tendency

Find the mean, median, and mode of each set of data.

1. {15, 42, 26, 39, 93, 42}

2. {32, 12, 61, 94, 73, 62, 94, 35, 44, 52}

3. {152, 697, 202, 312, 109, 134, 116}

4. {18, 6, 22, 33, 19, 34, 14, 54, 12, 22, 19}

5. A shoe store employee sets up a display by placing shoeboxes in 10 stacks. The numbers of boxes in each stack are 5, 7, 9, 11, 13, 10, 9, 8, 7, and 5.

    a. What is the mean of the number of boxes in a stack?

    b. Find the median of the number of boxes in a stack.

    c. If one box is removed from each stack, how will the mean and median be affected?

Find the mean, median, and mode of the data represented by each stem-and-leaf plot.

6.

Stem	Leaf
2	2 4 4 7
3	1 3 4
4	5 6 8
5	9

2/2 = 220

7.

Stem	Leaf
9	0 1 1 3
10	1 3 5 6
11	3 4 6 8

9/0 = 90

8.

Stem	Leaf
1	1 2 9
2	3 3 5
3	2
4	0
5	4 5 6 8 9

1/1 = 1.1

9. *Medicine* A frequency distribution for the number of patients treated at 50 U.S. cancer centers in one year is given at the right.

    a. Use the frequency chart to find the mean of the number of patients treated by a cancer center.

    b. What is the median class of the frequency distribution?

Patients	Number of Cancer Centers
500–1000	26
1000–1500	14
1500–2000	6
2000–2500	0
2500–3000	2
3000–3500	0
3500–4000	2

Source: *U.S. News Online*

14-3

Study Guide

Measures of Variability

If a set of data has been arranged in order and the median is found, the set of data is divided into two groups. If the median of each group is found, the data is divided into four groups. Each of these groups is called a **quartile,** and the quartile points Q_1, Q_2, and Q_3 denote the breaks for each quartile. The **interquartile range** is the difference between the first quartile point and the third quartile point.

Month	Temperature (°F)
Jan.	58.0
Feb.	57.9
March	61.6
April	62.5
May	68.7
June	67.4
July	69.3
Aug.	72.9
Sept.	75.5
Oct.	68.7
Nov.	64.0
Dec.	57.4

Source: National Climatic Data Center

Example 1 The table shows the average monthly temperatures for San Diego in 1997.

   a. Find the interquartile range of the temperatures and state what it represents.

   First, order the data from least to greatest and identify Q_1, Q_2, and Q_3.

   57.4 57.9 58.0 61.6 62.5 64.0
   67.4 68.7 68.7 69.3 72.9 75.5

   For this set of data, the quartile points Q_1, Q_2, and Q_3 are not members of the set. Instead, Q_2 is the mean of the middle values of the set. Thus, $Q_1 = 59.8$, $Q_2 = 65.7$, and $Q_3 = 69.0$. The interquartile range is $69.0 - 59.8$, or 9.2. This means that half the average monthly temperatures are within 9.2°F of each other.

   b. Find the semi-interquartile range of the temperatures.

   The semi-interquartile range is $\frac{9.2}{2}$, or 4.6.

Example 2 **Find the mean deviation of the temperatures in Example 1.**

   There are 12 temperatures listed, and the mean is $\frac{1}{12}\sum_{i=1}^{12} X_i$, or 65.325.

$$MD = \frac{1}{12}\sum_{i=1}^{12} |X_i - 65.325| \qquad MD = \frac{1}{n}\sum_{i=1}^{n} |X_i - \overline{X}|$$

$$MD = \frac{1}{12}(|75.5 - 65.325| + |72.9 - 65.325| + \cdots + |57.4 - 65.325|)$$

$$MD = \frac{1}{12}(|10.175| + |7.575| + \cdots + |-7.925|) \text{ or about } 5.092$$

   The mean deviation of the temperatures is about 5.092. This means that the temperatures are an average of about 5.092°F above or below the mean temperature of 65.325°F.

14-3

Practice

Measures of Variability

Find the interquartile range and the semi-interquartile range of each set of data. Then draw a box-and-whisker plot.

1. 43, 26, 92, 11, 8, 49, 52, 126, 86, 42, 63, 78, 91, 79, 86

2. 1.6, 9.8, 4.5, 6.2, 8.7, 5.6, 3.9, 6.8, 9.7, 1.1, 4.7, 3.8, 7.5, 2.8, 0.1

Find the mean deviation and the standard deviation of each set of data.

3. 146, 289, 121, 146, 212, 98, 86, 153, 128, 136, 181, 142

4. 1592, 1486, 1479, 1682, 1720, 1104, 1486, 1895, 1890, 2687, 2450

5. *Sociology*   The frequency distribution at the right shows the average life expectancy for males and females in 15 European Union countries in 1994.

a. Find the mean of the female life expectancy.

b. Find the mean of the male life expectancy.

c. What is the standard deviation of the female life expectancy?

d. What is the standard deviation of the male life expectancy?

Life Expectancy (years)	Frequency	
	Male	Female
71.5−73.0	3	0
73.0−74.5	9	0
74.5−76.0	2	0
76.0−77.5	1	0
77.5−79.0	0	3
79.0−80.5	0	8
80.5−82.0	0	4

Source: Department of Health and Children, Ireland

14-4

Study Guide

The Normal Distribution

A **normal distribution** is a frequency distribution that often occurs when there is a large number of values in a set of data. The graph of a normal distribution is a symmetric, bell-shaped curve known as a **normal curve.** The tables below give the fractional parts of a normally distributed set of data for selected areas about the mean. The letter t represents the number of standard deviations from the mean, that is, $\bar{X} \pm t\sigma$. P represents the fractional part that lies in the interval $\bar{X} \pm t\sigma$.

t	P		t	P		t	P		t	P		t	P		t	P
0.0	0.000		0.6	0.451		1.2	0.770		1.7	0.911		2.2	0.972		2.7	0.993
0.1	0.080		0.7	0.516		1.3	0.807		1.8	0.929		2.3	0.979		2.8	0.995
0.2	0.159		0.8	0.576		1.4	0.838		1.9	0.943		2.4	0.984		2.9	0.996
0.3	0.236		0.9	0.632		1.5	0.866		1.96	0.950		2.5	0.988		3.0	0.997
0.4	0.311		1.0	0.683		1.6	0.891		2.0	0.955		2.58	0.990		3.5	0.9995
0.5	0.383		1.1	0.729		1.65	0.900		2.1	0.964		2.6	0.991		4.0	0.9999

Example 1 **Air passengers traveling through Atlanta have an average layover of 82 minutes with a standard deviation of 7.5 minutes. Sketch a normal curve that represents the frequency of layover times.**

First, find the values defined by the standard deviation in a normal distribution.

$\bar{X} - 1\sigma = 82 - 1(7.5)$ or 74.5 $\bar{X} + 1\sigma = 82 + 1(7.5)$ or 89.5
$\bar{X} - 2\sigma = 82 - 2(7.5)$ or 67 $\bar{X} + 2\sigma = 82 + 2(7.5)$ or 97
$\bar{X} - 3\sigma = 82 - 3(7.5)$ or 59.5 $\bar{X} + 3\sigma = 82 + 3(7.5)$ or 104.5

Then, sketch the general shape of a normal curve. Replace the horizontal scale with the values you have calculated.

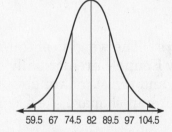

59.5 67 74.5 82 89.5 97 104.5

Example 2 **Find the upper and lower limits of an interval about the mean within which 15% of the values of a set of normally distributed data can be found if $\bar{X} = 725$ and $\sigma = 4$.**

Use the tables above to find the value of t that most closely approximates $P = 0.15$. For $t = 0.2$, $P = 0.159$. Choose $t = 0.2$.

Now find the limits. $\bar{X} \pm t\sigma = 725 \pm 0.2(4)$ $\bar{X} = 725$, $t = 0.2$, $\sigma = 4$
$= 724.2$ and 725.8

The interval in which 15% of the data lies is 724.2–725.8.

14-4

Practice

The Normal Distribution

A set of 1000 values has a normal distribution. The mean of the data is 120, and the standard deviation is 20.

1. How many values are within one standard deviation of the mean?

2. What percent of the data is between 110 and 130?

3. What percent of the data is between 90 and 110?

4. Find the interval about the mean that includes 90% of the data.

5. Find the interval about the mean that includes 77% of the data.

6. Find the limit below which 90% of the data lie.

7. *Dog Breeding*   The weights of full-grown German shepherds at the City View Kennels are normally distributed. The mean weight is 86 pounds, and the standard deviation is 3 pounds. Skipper, a full-grown German shepard, weighs 79 pounds.

   a. What percent of the full-grown German shepherds at City View Kennels weigh more than Skipper?

   b. What percent of the full-grown German shepherds at City View Kennels weigh less than Skipper?

14-5

Study Guide

Sample Sets of Data

In statistics, the word **population** refers to an entire set of items or individuals in a group. Rarely will 100% of a population be accessible as a source of data. Therefore, researchers usually select a **random sample** of the population to represent the entire population. Because discrepancies are common in random samples, researchers often take many samples and assume that the sample mean is near its true population mean. The standard deviation of the distribution of the sample means is known as the **standard error of the mean.**

Standard Error of the Mean	If a sample of data has N values and σ is the standard deviation, the standard error of the mean $\sigma_{\bar{x}}$ is $$\sigma_{\bar{x}} = \frac{\sigma}{\sqrt{N}}.$$

Example 1 **A sample of data has 4500 values and a standard deviation of 12. What is the standard error of the mean?**

For the sample, $N = 4500$. Find $\sigma_{\bar{x}}$.

$\sigma_{\bar{x}} = \frac{\sigma}{\sqrt{N}} = \frac{12}{\sqrt{4500}}$, or about 0.179

The standard error of the mean for the set of data is approximately 0.179.

Example 2 **The daily calorie consumption of people in the United States is normally distributed. A team of nutritionists takes a sample of 250 people and records their daily calorie consumption. From this sample, the average daily calorie consumption is 2150 with a standard deviation of 60 calories per day. Determine the interval about the sample mean that has a 1% level of confidence.**

A 1% level of confidence means that there is less than a 1% chance that the true mean differs from the sample mean by a certain amount. A 1% level of condifence is given when $P = 99\%$. When $P = 0.99$, $t = 2.58$.

Find $\sigma_{\bar{x}}$. $\sigma_{\bar{x}} = \frac{60}{\sqrt{250}}$ or about 3.795

Find the range. $\overline{X} = 2150 \pm 2.58(3.795)$
                              $\overline{X} = 2140.2089$ and 2159.7911

Thus, the probability is 99% that the true mean is within the interval of 2140.2089 calories per day to 2159.7911 calories per day.

14-5

Practice

Sample Sets of Data

Find the standard error of the mean for each sample. Then find the interval about the sample mean that has a 1% level of confidence and the interval about the sample mean that has a 5% level of confidence.

1. $\sigma = 50, N = 100, \overline{X} = 250$

2. $\sigma = 4, N = 64, \overline{X} = 100$

3. $\sigma = 2.6, N = 250, \overline{X} = 50$

4. $\sigma = 4.3, N = 375, \overline{X} = 110$

The table below shows a frequency distribution of the time in minutes required for students to wash a car during a car wash fundraiser. The distribution is a random sample of 250 cars. Use the table for Exercises 5-10.

Number of Minutes	5	6	7	8	9	10
Frequency	2	4	5	1	8	5

5. What is the mean of the data in the frequency distribution?

6. Find the standard deviation of the data.

7. Find the standard error of the mean.

8. Find the interval about the sample mean such that the probability is 0.90 that the true mean lies within the interval.

9. Find the interval about the sample mean such that the probability is 0.95 that the true mean lies within the interval.

10. Determine the interval about the sample mean that has a 1% level of confidence.

NAME _____ DATE _____ PERIOD _____

14-1 Practice

The Frequency Distribution

Determine which class intervals would be appropriate for the data below. Explain your answers.

1. 25, 32, 18, 99, 43, 16, 29, 35, 36, 34, 21, 33, 26, 26, 17, 40, 22, 38, 16, 19
a. 1 **no; too many classes**
b. 10 **yes; 8 classes**
c. 2 **no; too many classes**

2. 111, 115, 130, 200, 234, 98, 115, 72, 305, 145, 87, 63, 245, 285, 256, 302
a. 25 **yes; 10 classes**
b. 10 **no; too many classes**
c. 30 **yes; 9 classes**

3. *Meteorology* The average wind speeds recorded at various weather stations in the United States are listed below.

Station	Speed (mph)	Station	Speed (mph)	Station	Speed (mph)
Albuquerque	8.9	Anchorage	9.1	Atlanta	7.1
Baltimore	9.1	Boston	10.4	Chicago	12.5
Dallas-Ft. Worth	10.8	Honolulu	9.6	Indianapolis	11.3
Kansas City	10.7	Las Vegas	9.3	Little Rock	7.8
Los Angeles	6.2	Memphis	8.8	Miami	9.2
Minneapolis– St. Paul	10.5	New Orleans	8.1	New York City	9.4
Philadelphia	9.5	Phoenix	6.2	Seattle	9.0

Source: National Climatic Data Center

a. Find the range of the data. **6.3**

b. Determine an appropriate class interval. **Sample answer: 1**

c. What are the class limits and the class marks?
**Sample answer: 6.0, 7.0, 8.0, 9.0, 10.0, 11.0, 12.0, 13.0;
6.5, 7.5, 8.5, 9.5, 10.5, 11.5, 12.5**

d. Construct a frequency distribution of the data.

Wind Speed (mph)	Tallies	Frequency
6.0–7.0	||	2
7.0–8.0	||	3
8.0–9.0	|||	3
9.0–10.0	|||| |||	8
10.0–11.0	|||||	4
11.0–12.0			1
12.0–13.0			1

e. Draw a histogram of the data.

Wind Speeds at U.S. Weather Stations
Frequency vs. Wind Speed (mph): 6 7 8 9 10 11 12 13

© Glencoe/McGraw-Hill

Advanced Mathematical Concepts

NAME _____ DATE _____ PERIOD _____

14-2 Practice

Measures of Central Tendency

Find the mean, median, and mode of each set of data.

1. {15, 42, 26, 39, 93, 42}
42.83; 40.5; 42

2. {32, 12, 61, 94, 73, 62, 94, 35, 44, 52}
55.9; 56.5; 94

3. {152, 697, 202, 312, 109, 134, 116}
246; 152; no mode

4. {18, 6, 22, 33, 19, 34, 14, 54, 12, 22, 19}
23; 19; 22 and 19

5. A shoe store employee sets up a display by placing shoeboxes in 10 stacks. The numbers of boxes in each stack are 5, 7, 9, 11, 13, 10, 9, 8, 7, and 5.
a. What is the mean of the number of boxes in a stack? **8.4**
b. Find the median of the number of boxes in a stack. **8.5**
c. If one box is removed from each stack, how will the mean and median be affected? **Each will decrease by 1 box.**

Find the mean, median, and mode of the data represented by each stem-and-leaf plot.

6.

Stem	Leaf
2	2 4 4 7
3	1 3 4
4	5 6 8
5	9

$2/2 = 220$
about 357.3; 330; 240

7.

Stem	Leaf
9	0 1 1 3
10	1 3 5 6
11	3 4 6 8

$9/0 = 90$
about 103.42; 104; 91

8.

Stem	Leaf
1	1 2 9
2	3 3 5
3	2
4	0
5	4 5 6 8 9

$1/1 = 1.1$
about 3.59; 3.2; 2.3

9. *Medicine* A frequency distribution for the number of patients treated at 50 U.S. cancer centers in one year is given at the right.
a. Use the frequency chart to find the mean of the number of patients treated by a cancer center. **1210**
b. What is the median class of the frequency distribution? **500–1000**

Patients	Number of Cancer Centers
500–1000	26
1000–1500	14
1500–2000	6
2000–2500	0
2500–3000	2
3000–3500	0
3500–4000	2

Source: U.S. News Online

Advanced Mathematical Concepts

Practice — 14-3

NAME _____ DATE _____ PERIOD _____

Measures of Variability

Find the interquartile range and the semi-interquartile range of each set of data. Then draw a box-and-whisker plot.

1. 43, 26, 92, 11, 8, 49, 52, 126, 86, 42, 63, 78, 91, 79, 86   **44, 22**

2. 1.6, 9.8, 4.5, 6.2, 8.7, 5.6, 3.9, 6.8, 9.7, 1.1, 4.7, 3.8, 7.5, 2.8, 0.1   **4.7, 2.35**

Find the mean deviation and the standard deviation of each set of data.

3. 146, 289, 121, 146, 212, 98, 86, 153, 128, 136, 181, 142   **37.1, 51.99**

4. 1592, 1486, 1479, 1682, 1720, 1104, 1486, 1895, 1890, 2687, 2450   **334.84, 433.25**

5. **Sociology**   The frequency distribution at the right shows the average life expectancy for males and females in 15 European Union countries in 1994.

Life Expectancy (years)	Frequency	
	Male	Female
71.5–73.0	3	0
73.0–74.5	9	0
74.5–76.0	2	0
76.0–77.5	1	0
77.5–79.0	0	3
79.0–80.5	0	8
80.5–82.0	0	4

Source: Department of Health and Children, Ireland

a. Find the mean of the female life expectancy.   **79.85**

b. Find the mean of the male life expectancy.   **73.85**

c. What is the standard deviation of the female life expectancy?   **about 1.02**

d. What is the standard deviation of the male life expectancy?   **about 1.16**

Practice — 14-4

NAME _____ DATE _____ PERIOD _____

The Normal Distribution

A set of 1000 values has a normal distribution. The mean of the data is 120, and the standard deviation is 20.

1. How many values are within one standard deviation of the mean?   **683**

2. What percent of the data is between 110 and 130?   **38.3%**

3. What percent of the data is between 90 and 110?   **24.15%**

4. Find the interval about the mean that includes 90% of the data.   **87–153**

5. Find the interval about the mean that includes 77% of the data.   **96–144**

6. Find the limit below which 90% of the data lie.   **146**

7. **Dog Breeding**   The weights of full-grown German shepherds at the City View Kennels are normally distributed. The mean weight is 86 pounds, and the standard deviation is 3 pounds. Skipper, a full-grown German shepard, weighs 79 pounds.

a. What percent of the full-grown German shepherds at City View Kennels weigh more than Skipper?   **98.95%**

b. What percent of the full-grown German shepherds at City View Kennels weigh less than Skipper?   **1.05%**

Advanced Mathematical Concepts

14-5 Practice

Sample Sets of Data

Find the standard error of the mean for each sample. Then find the interval about the sample mean that has a 1% level of confidence and the interval about the sample mean that has a 5% level of confidence.

1. $\sigma = 50, N = 100, \overline{X} = 250$
5; 237.1–262.9; 240.2–259.8

2. $\sigma = 4, N = 64, \overline{X} = 100$
0.5; 98.71–101.29;
99.02–100.98

3. $\sigma = 2.6, N = 250, \overline{X} = 50$
0.16; 49.57–50.43;
49.68–50.32

4. $\sigma = 4.3, N = 375, \overline{X} = 110$
0.22; 109.42–110.57;
109.56–110.44

The table below shows a frequency distribution of the time in minutes required for students to wash a car during a car wash fundraiser. The distribution is a random sample of 250 cars. Use the table for Exercises 5–10.

Number of Minutes	5	6	7	8	9	10
Frequency	2	4	5	1	8	5

5. What is the mean of the data in the frequency distribution? 7.96

6. Find the standard deviation of the data. 1.64

7. Find the standard error of the mean. 0.327

8. Find the interval about the sample mean such that the probability is 0.90 that the true mean lies within the interval. 7.42045–8.49955 min

9. Find the interval about the sample mean such that the probability is 0.95 that the true mean lies within the interval. 7.31908–8.60092 min

10. Determine the interval about the sample mean that has a 1% level of confidence. 7.11634–8.80366 min

264 *Advanced Mathematical Concepts*

15-1

Study Guide

Limits

If the function $f(x)$ is continuous at a, then $\lim_{x \to a} f(x) = f(a)$. Continuous functions include polynomials as well as the functions $\sin x$, $\cos x$, and a^x. Also, $\log_a x$ is continuous if $x > 0$. To evaluate the **limit** when a function is not continuous at the x-value in question, apply algebraic methods to decompose the function into a simpler one. If the function cannot be simplified, compute values of the function using x-values that get closer and closer to a from either side.

Example 1   **Evaluate each limit.**

     a. $\lim_{x \to 1} (x^4 - 2x^2 + x + 3)$

         Since $f(x) = x^4 - 2x^2 + x + 3$ is a polynomial function, it is continuous at every number. So the limit as x approaches 1 is the same as the value of $f(x)$ at $x = 1$.

$$\lim_{x \to 1} (x^4 - 2x^2 + x + 3) = 1^4 - 2 \cdot 1^2 + 1 + 3 \quad \textit{Replace x with 1.}$$
$$= 1 - 2 + 1 + 3$$
$$= 3$$

         The limit of $x^4 - 2x^2 + x + 3$ as x approaches 1 is 3.

     b. $\lim_{x \to \pi} \frac{1 - \cos x}{x}$

         Since the denominator of $\frac{1 - \cos x}{x}$ is not 0 at $x = \pi$, the function is continuous at $x = \pi$.

$$\lim_{x \to \pi} \frac{1 - \cos x}{x} = \frac{1 - \cos \pi}{\pi} \quad \textit{Replace x with } \pi.$$
$$= \frac{1 - (-1)}{\pi} \text{ or } \frac{2}{\pi} \quad \cos \pi = -1$$

         The limit of $\frac{1 - \cos x}{x}$ as x approaches π is $\frac{2}{\pi}$.

Example 2   **Evaluate** $\lim_{x \to 4} \frac{x^2 - 9x + 20}{x - 4}$.

$$\lim_{x \to 4} \frac{x^2 - 9x + 20}{x - 4} = \lim_{x \to 4} \frac{(x - 5)(x - 4)}{(x - 4)} \quad \textit{Factor.}$$
$$= \lim_{x \to 4} (x - 5)$$
$$= 4 - 5 \quad \textit{Replace x with 4.}$$
$$= -1$$

15-1

Practice

Limits

Evaluate each limit.

1. $\lim\limits_{x \to 3} (x^2 + 3x - 8)$

2. $\lim\limits_{x \to -2} (2x + 7)$

3. $\lim\limits_{x \to -6} \dfrac{x^2 - 36}{x + 6}$

4. $\lim\limits_{x \to 2} \dfrac{x^2 - 5x + 6}{x - 2}$

5. $\lim\limits_{x \to 2} \dfrac{x - 2}{x^2 - 4}$

6. $\lim\limits_{x \to 3} \dfrac{x^2 - 9}{x^3 - 27}$

7. $\lim\limits_{x \to 0} \dfrac{(3 + x)^2 - 9}{x}$

8. $\lim\limits_{x \to 4} \sqrt{x^2 - 2x + 1}$

9. $\lim\limits_{x \to -3} \dfrac{2x^3 + 6x^2 - x - 3}{x + 3}$

10. $\lim\limits_{x \to 1} \dfrac{x^2 - x}{2x^2 + 5x - 7}$

11. $\lim\limits_{x \to 0} \dfrac{\sin 2x}{x}$

12. $\lim\limits_{x \to 0} \dfrac{1 - \cos x}{x}$

13. *Biology*   The number of cells in a culture doubles every 5 hours. The initial hourly growth rate is represented by $\lim\limits_{t \to 0} \dfrac{2^{\left(\frac{t}{5}\right)} - 1}{t}$, where t is the time in hours. Use a calculator to approximate the value of this limit to the nearest hundredth. What is the initial hourly growth rate? Write your answer as a percent.

15-2

Study Guide

Derivatives and Antiderivatives

The derivative of a function $f(x)$ is another function, $f'(x)$, that gives the slope of the tangent line to $y = f(x)$ at any point. The following are some of the rules used to find the derivatives of polynomials.

Constant Rule:	The derivative of a constant function is zero. If $f(x) = c$, then $f'(x) = 0$.
Power Rule:	If $f(x) = x^n$, where n is a rational number, then $f'(x) = nx^{n-1}$.
Constant Multiple of a Power Rule:	If $f(x) = cx^n$, where c is a constant and n is a rational number, then $f'(x) = cnx^{n-1}$.

Finding the **antiderivative** $F(x)$ of a function $f(x)$ is the inverse of finding the derivative. The following are some of the rules used to find the antiderivative of a function.

Constant Multiple of a Power Rule:	If $f(x) = kx^n$, where n is a rational number other than -1 and k is a constant, the antiderivative is $F(x) = k \cdot \frac{1}{n+1}x^{n+1} + C$.
Sum and Difference Rule:	If the antiderivatives of $f(x)$ and $g(x)$ are $F(x)$ and $G(x)$, respectively, then the antiderivative of $f(x) \pm g(x)$ is $F(x) \pm G(x)$.

Example 1   **Find the derivative of each function.**

     a. $f(x) = x^5$

$$f'(x) = 5x^{5-1} \quad \textit{Power Rule}$$
$$= 5x^4$$

     b. $f(x) = 3x + 2$

$$f(x) = 3x + 2$$
$$= 3x^1 + 2 \qquad \textit{Rewrite x as a power.}$$
$$f'(x) = 3 \cdot 1x^{1-1} + 0 \qquad \textit{Constant Multiple of a Power Rule,}$$
$$\textit{Constant Rule, and Sum Rule}$$
$$= 3x^0$$
$$= 3 \qquad\qquad x^0 = 1$$

Example 2   **Find the antiderivative of $f(x) = 6x^2 - 10x + 4$.**

$$f(x) = 6x^2 - 10x + 4 \qquad \textit{Rewrite the function so}$$
$$= 6x^2 - 10x^1 + 4x^0 \qquad \textit{that each term has a power of x.}$$

Use the Constant Multiple of a Power and Sum and Difference Rules.

$$F(x) = 6 \cdot \frac{1}{2+1}x^{2+1} + C_1 - \left(10 \cdot \frac{1}{1+1}x^{1+1} + C_2\right) + 4 \cdot \frac{1}{0+1}x^{0+1} + C_3$$
$$= \frac{6}{3}x^3 - \frac{10}{2}x^2 + \frac{4}{1}x^1 + C \qquad \textit{Let } C = C_1 - C_2 + C_3.$$
$$= 2x^3 - 5x^2 + 4x + C$$

15-2

Practice

Derivatives and Antiderivatives

Use the derivative rules to find the derivative of each function.

1. $f(x) = 2x^2 - 3x$

2. $f(x) = 6x^3 - 2x + 5$

3. $f(x) = (2x + 7)(3x - 8)$

4. $f(x) = (x^2 + 1)(3x - 2)$

5. $f(x) = (x^2 + 5x)^2$

6. $f(x) = x^2(x^3 + 3x^2)$

Find the antiderivative of each function.

7. $f(x) = x^8$

8. $f(x) = 4x^3$

9. $f(x) = 2x + 3$

10. $f(x) = x(x^2 - 3)$

11. $f(x) = (2x + 1)(3x - 2)$

12. $f(x) = 8x^2 + 2x - 3$

13. **Physics**   Acceleration is the rate at which the velocity of a moving object changes. The velocity in meters per second of a particle moving along a straight line is given by the function $v(t) = 3t^2 - 6t + 5$, where t is the time in seconds. Find the acceleration of the particle in meters per second squared after 5 seconds. (*Hint:* Acceleration is the derivative of velocity.)

15-3

Study Guide

Area Under a Curve

Example
Use limits to find the area of the region between the graph of $y = x^2$ and the x-axis from $x = 0$ to $x = 5$. That is, find $\int_0^5 x^2\, dx$.

Since $\int_a^b f(x)\, dx = \lim_{n\to\infty} \sum_{i=1}^{n} f(x_i)\Delta x$, we must first find Δx and x_i.

$\Delta x = \dfrac{5-0}{n}$ or $\dfrac{5}{n}$ $\qquad \Delta x = \dfrac{b-a}{n}$

$x_i = 0 + i \cdot \dfrac{5}{n}$ or $\dfrac{5i}{n}$ $\quad x_i = a + i\Delta x$

Now calculate the integral that gives the area.

$\int_0^5 x^2\, dx = \lim_{n\to\infty} \sum_{i=1}^{n} (x_i)^2 \Delta x \qquad\qquad f(x_i) = x_i^2$

$\qquad\qquad = \lim_{n\to\infty} \sum_{i=1}^{n} \left(\dfrac{5i}{n}\right)^2 \cdot \dfrac{5}{n} \qquad\quad x_i = \dfrac{5i}{n},\ \Delta x = \dfrac{5}{n}$

$\qquad\qquad = \lim_{n\to\infty} \sum_{i=1}^{n} \dfrac{125i^2}{n^3} \qquad\qquad\quad Multiply.$

$\qquad\qquad = \lim_{n\to\infty} \left(\dfrac{125 \cdot 1^2}{n^3} + \dfrac{125 \cdot 2^2}{n^3} + \cdots + \dfrac{125 \cdot n^2}{n^3}\right)$

$\qquad\qquad = \lim_{n\to\infty} \dfrac{125}{n^3} \cdot (1^2 + 2^2 + \cdots + n^2) \quad Factor.$

$\qquad\qquad = \lim_{n\to\infty} \dfrac{125}{n^3} \cdot \dfrac{n(n+1)(2n+1)}{6} \qquad 1^2 + 2^2 + \cdots + n^2 = \dfrac{n(n+1)(2n+1)}{6}$

$\qquad\qquad = \lim_{n\to\infty} \dfrac{250n^2 + 375n + 125}{6n^2} \qquad Multiply.$

$\qquad\qquad = \lim_{n\to\infty} \dfrac{1}{6}\left(250 + \dfrac{375}{n} + \dfrac{125}{n^2}\right) \qquad Factor\ and\ divide\ by\ n^2.$

$\qquad\qquad = \left(\lim_{n\to\infty} \dfrac{1}{6}\right)\left[\lim_{n\to\infty} 250 + \left(\lim_{n\to\infty} 375\right)\left(\lim_{n\to\infty} \dfrac{1}{n}\right) + \left(\lim_{n\to\infty} 125\right)\left(\lim_{n\to\infty} \dfrac{1}{n^2}\right)\right]$

$\qquad\qquad\qquad\qquad\qquad\qquad\qquad\qquad\qquad Limit\ theorems$

$\qquad\qquad = \dfrac{1}{6}[250 + (375)(0) + (125)(0)] \quad \lim_{n\to\infty} \dfrac{1}{n} = 0,\ \lim_{n\to\infty} \dfrac{1}{n^2} = 0$

$\qquad\qquad = \dfrac{1}{6} \cdot 250$

$\qquad\qquad = \dfrac{250}{6}$ or $\dfrac{125}{3}$

The area of the region is $\dfrac{125}{3}$ square units.

15-3

Practice

Area Under a Curve

Use limits to find the area between each curve and the x-axis for the given interval.

1. $y = x^3$ from $x = 0$ to $x = 2$ **2.** $y = x^2$ from $x = 1$ to $x = 6$

Use limits to evaluate each integral.

3. $\int_1^5 x^3$

4. $\int_1^3 x^4$

5. *Architecture and Design*   A designer is making a stained-glass window for a new building. The shape of the window can be modeled by the parabola $y = 5 - 0.05x^2$. What is the area of the window?

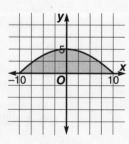

15-4

Study Guide

The Fundamental Theorem of Calculus

The **Fundamental Theorem of Calculus** states that if $F(x)$ is the antiderivative of the continuous function $f(x)$, then $\int_a^b f(x)\,dx = F(b) - F(a)$.

The statement may also be written $\int_a^b f(x)\,dx = F(x)\Big|_a^b$.

The antiderivative rules for **indefinite integrals,** denoted $\int f(x)\,dx$, are as follows.

Power Rule:	$\int x^n\,dx = \dfrac{1}{n+1}x^{n+1} + C$, where n is a rational number and $n \neq -1$.
Constant Multiple of a Power Rule:	$\int kx^n\,dx = k \cdot \dfrac{1}{n+1}x^{n+1} + C$, where k is a constant, n is a rational number, and $n \neq -1$.
Sum and Difference Rule:	$\int (f(x) \pm g(x))\,dx = \int f(x)\,dx \pm \int g(x)\,dx$

Example 1 Evaluate $\int_2^5 x^2\,dx.$

The antiderivative of $f(x) = x^2$ is $F(x) = \frac{1}{3}x^3 + C$

$$\int_2^5 x^2\,dx = \frac{1}{3}x^3 + C\Big|_2^5 \qquad \textit{Fundamental Theorem of Calculus}$$

$$= \left(\frac{1}{3} \cdot 5^3 + C\right) - \left(\frac{1}{3} \cdot 2^3 + C\right) \quad \textit{Let } x = 5 \textit{ and } 2 \textit{ and subtract.}$$

$$= \frac{117}{3} \text{ or } 39$$

Notice that the constant term C is eliminated when evaluating a definite integral using the Fundamental Theorem of Calculus.

Example 2 Evaluate the indefinite integral $\int (3x^2 + 4x - 1)\,dx.$

$$\int (3x^2 + 4x - 1)\,dx = \int (3x^2 + 4x^1 - x^0)\,dx \qquad x = x^1,\ 1 = x^0$$

$$= 3 \cdot \frac{1}{2+1}x^{2+1} + 4 \cdot \frac{1}{1+1}x^{1+1} - \left(\frac{1}{0+1}x^{0+1}\right) + C$$

$$\textit{Use antiderivative rules.}$$

$$= \frac{3}{3}x^3 + \frac{4}{2}x^2 - \frac{1}{1}x^1 + C$$

$$= x^3 + 2x^2 - x + C \qquad \textit{Simplify.}$$

15-4

Practice

The Fundamental Theorem of Calculus

Evaluate each indefinite integral.

1. $\int 8\, dx$

2. $\int (2x^3 + 6x)\, dx$

3. $\int (-6x^5 - 2x^2 + 5x)\, dx$

4. $\int (9x^2 + 12x - 9)\, dx$

Evaluate each definite integral.

5. $\int_{2}^{5} 2x\, dx$

6. $\int_{-5}^{-1} (-4x^3 - 3x^2)\, dx$

7. $\int_{-2}^{1} (1 - x)(x + 3)\, dx$

8. $\int_{-1}^{2} (x + 1)^3\, dx$

Find the area between each curve and the x-axis for the given interval.

9. $y = x^2 + 4x + 5$ from $x = 1$ to $x = 4$

10. $y = x + 1$ from $x = -1$ to $x = 2$

11. $y = x^3 + 1$ from $x = -1$ to $x = 3$

12. $y = x^2 + 1$ from $x = 0$ to $x = 3$

13. **Physics**   The work in foot-pounds required to compress a certain spring a distance of ℓ feet from its natural length is given by $W = \int_{0}^{\ell} 2x\, dx$. How much work is required to compress the spring 6 inches from its natural length?

Answers (Lessons 15-1 and 15-2)

15-1 Practice — Limits

Evaluate each limit.

1. $\lim\limits_{x\to3}(x^2+3x-8)$
   10

2. $\lim\limits_{x\to-2}(2x+7)$
   3

3. $\lim\limits_{x\to-6}\dfrac{x^2-36}{x+6}$
   −12

4. $\lim\limits_{x\to2}\dfrac{x^2-5x+6}{x-2}$
   −1

5. $\lim\limits_{x\to2}\dfrac{x-2}{x^2-4}$
   $\dfrac{1}{4}$

6. $\lim\limits_{x\to3}\dfrac{x^2-9}{x^3-27}$
   $\dfrac{2}{9}$

7. $\lim\limits_{x\to0}\dfrac{(3+x)^2-9}{x}$
   6

8. $\lim\limits_{x\to4}\sqrt{x^2-2x+1}$
   3

9. $\lim\limits_{x\to-3}\dfrac{2x^3+6x^2-x-3}{x+3}$
   17

10. $\lim\limits_{x\to1}\dfrac{x^2-x}{2x^2+5x-7}$
    $\dfrac{1}{9}$

11. $\lim\limits_{x\to0}\dfrac{\sin 2x}{x}$
    2

12. $\lim\limits_{x\to0}\dfrac{1-\cos x}{x}$
    0

13. **Biology** The number of cells in a culture doubles every 5 hours. The initial hourly growth rate is represented by $\lim\limits_{t\to0}\dfrac{2^{\left(\frac{t}{5}\right)}-1}{t}$, where t is the time in hours. Use a calculator to approximate the value of this limit to the nearest hundredth. What is the initial hourly growth rate? Write your answer as a percent. **14%**

15-2 Practice — Derivatives and Antiderivatives

Use the derivative rules to find the derivative of each function.

1. $f(x)=2x^2-3x$
   $f'(x)=4x-3$

2. $f(x)=6x^3-2x+5$
   $f'(x)=18x^2-2$

3. $f(x)=(2x+7)(3x-8)$
   $f'(x)=12x+5$

4. $f(x)=(x^2+1)(3x-2)$
   $f'(x)=9x^2-4x+3$

5. $f(x)=(x^2+5x)^2$
   $f'(x)=4x^3+30x^2+50x$

6. $f(x)=x^2(x^3+3x^2)$
   $f'(x)=5x^4+12x^3$

Find the antiderivative of each function.

7. $f(x)=x^8$
   $F(x)=\dfrac{1}{9}x^9+C$

8. $f(x)=4x^3$
   $F(x)=x^4+C$

9. $f(x)=2x+3$
   $F(x)=x^2+3x+C$

10. $f(x)=x(x^2-3)$
    $F(x)=\dfrac{1}{4}x^4-\dfrac{3}{2}x^2+C$

11. $f(x)=(2x+1)(3x-2)$
    $F(x)=2x^3-\dfrac{1}{2}x^2-2x+C$

12. $f(x)=8x^2+2x-3$
    $F(x)=\dfrac{8}{3}x^3+x^2-3x+C$

13. **Physics** Acceleration is the rate at which the velocity of a moving object changes. The velocity in meters per second of a particle moving along a straight line is given by the function $v(t)=3t^2-6t+5$, where t is the time in seconds. Find the acceleration of the particle in meters per second squared after 5 seconds. (*Hint:* Acceleration is the derivative of velocity.) **24 m/s²**

NAME _____ DATE _____ PERIOD _____

15-3

Practice

Area Under a Curve

Use limits to find the area between each curve and the x-axis for the given interval.

1. $y = x^3$ from $x = 0$ to $x = 2$

4 units²

2. $y = x^2$ from $x = 1$ to $x = 6$

$\dfrac{215}{3}$ **units²**

Use limits to evaluate each integral.

3. $\displaystyle\int_1^5 x^3$

156

4. $\displaystyle\int_1^3 x^4$

$\dfrac{242}{5}$

5. Architecture and Design A designer is making a stained-glass window for a new building. The shape of the window can be modeled by the parabola $y = 5 - 0.05x^2$. What is the area of the window? **about 66.67 units²**

NAME _____ DATE _____ PERIOD _____

15-4

Practice

The Fundamental Theorem of Calculus

Evaluate each indefinite integral.

1. $\displaystyle\int 8\,dx$

$8x + C$

2. $\displaystyle\int (2x^3 + 6x)\,dx$

$\dfrac{1}{2}x^4 + 3x^2 + C$

3. $\displaystyle\int (-6x^5 - 2x^2 + 5x)\,dx$

$-x^6 - \dfrac{2}{3}x^3 + \dfrac{5}{2}x^2 + C$

4. $\displaystyle\int (9x^2 + 12x - 9)\,dx$

$3x^3 + 6x^2 - 9x + C$

Evaluate each definite integral.

5. $\displaystyle\int_2^5 2x\,dx$

21

6. $\displaystyle\int_{-5}^{-1} (-4x^3 - 3x^2)\,dx$

500

7. $\displaystyle\int_{-2}^1 (1 - x)(x + 3)\,dx$

9

8. $\displaystyle\int_{-1}^2 (x + 1)^3\,dx$

$\dfrac{81}{4}$

Find the area between each curve and the x-axis for the given interval.

9. $y = x^2 + 4x + 5$ from $x = 1$ to $x = 4$

66 units²

10. $y = x + 1$ from $x = -1$ to $x = 2$

$\dfrac{9}{2}$ **units²**

11. $y = x^3 + 1$ from $x = -1$ to $x = 3$

24 units²

12. $y = x^2 + 1$ from $x = 0$ to $x = 3$

12 units²

13. Physics The work in foot-pounds required to compress a certain spring a distance of ℓ feet from its natural length is given by $W = \displaystyle\int_0^\ell 2x\,dx$. How much work is required to compress the spring 6 inches from its natural length? **0.25 ft-lb**